Running
Your
Remodeling Business

by
Harry Hardenbrook & Harold Hammerman

Craftsman Book Company
6058 Corte del Cedro, Carlsbad, CA 92009

Acknowledgements

The authors wish to express their appreciation to the following individuals and companies for furnishing materials used in the preparation of this book.

American Building Contractors Association, El Monte, CA

Armstrong World Industries, Inc., Lancaster, PA

Robert Drew, Dick Belson, Drew Builders, Palatine, IL

Dun & Bradstreet, Inc., New York, NY

Armand Fontaine

IBM, Rye Brook, NY

Kohler Company, Kohler, WI

Ken MacCowan, Multi-Tronics Inc., Arlington, IL

Ira Messing

Mr. Build, Windsor, CT

Dave Poirier, Motor City Home Improvement, Flint, MI

Rolscreen Company, Pella, IA

C. Rutherford, Jr., C. Rutherford & Son, Flint, MI

Barry Simon, Builder's Association of Metropolitan Flint, Flint, MI

Frank Spatz, Robert Spatz, Ashland Corporation, Des Plaines, IL

Joel Streich, Joel Streich Home Builder, Flint, MI

Charles Trim, Charles Trim Construction Company, Los Angeles, CA

Thomas Tuuri, Tuuri, Inc., Burton, MI

United States Chamber of Commerce, Washington, DC

Library of Congress Cataloging-in-Publication Data
Hardenbrook, Harry.
   Running your remodeling business / by Harry Hardenbrook & Harold Hammerman
      p.   cm.
   Includes index.
   ISBN 0-934041-37-7
   1. Construction industry — Management. 2. Dwellings — Remodeling.
3. Contractors. I. Hammerman, Harold. II. Title.
HD9715.A2H345 1988
690'.8'0286068--dc19

88-39937
CIP

Contents
Running Your Remodeling Business

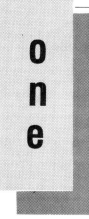

Starting Out:
Keep it Simple

Remodeling is big business today. It's the most active, profitable and growing part of the residential construction industry. Increases in the cost of homes and the aging of the home stock in this country make it likely that the professional remodeling industry will continue to grow for many years. That's going to create a lot of opportunities for remodeling contractors with the skills and know-how needed to make a good living in this thriving industry.

If you've been in the construction industry for a few years and haven't done any remodeling work, consider some of the advantages that remodelers enjoy.

First, the markups tend to be higher than in other types of construction. Many remodeling contractors earn profit margins that would turn other builders green with envy.

Second, remodeling is less prone to the boom and bust cycle that affects most construction. For most builders, work dries up when lenders don't have funds to lend or when high loan rates discourage prospective borrowers. But remodeling tends to go on, even when other projects are postponed. That's because the money for many remodeling projects comes out of the owner's pocket rather than from a lender. In fact, high interest rates will persuade many homeowners to add floor space to their home or remodel rather than buy a new home.

Third, remodeling contractors can handle a heavy workload without making a heavy investment in tools and equipment. Many remodelers do more than a million dollars worth of repair and remodeling work a year with little more than some pickup trucks and hand tools. Try doing that much work with so little equipment in nearly any other type of construction.

Fourth, the remodeling industry is thriving, growing much faster than construction as a whole. By the late 1990s, remodeling contractors are expected to be handling between $2.5 and $5 billion *more* business each year than they were handling ten years earlier. That much extra business opens up opportunities for thousands of contractors and tradesmen who are willing to master the skills required to succeed.

But please don't misunderstand. Remodeling contracting is no gravy train. Ask any remodeler. This is a very competitive business. There are probably a dozen or more remodeling contractors in your area who are every bit as eager and aggressive as you are. All are after their share of the work. Not all will be successful, of course. Some will grow and prosper; others will be out of the business in a year or two.

In addition to being competitive, the remodeling business is always changing. What was in vogue or worked well last year or five years ago may not work at all today. Remodeling contractors who don't change as the business changes probably have the smallest chance of getting their share of the prosperity that other remodelers will enjoy.

By now you should understand that it takes hard work, know-how and more than a little luck to make a good living as a remodeling specialist. But if you're willing to work hard and make your own luck, keep reading. We'll provide all the know-how you need, the practical "how-to" of remodeling contracting. Between this page and the end of the last chapter of this book, we've distilled nearly everything we've learned from years of experience in the remodeling business. Whether you're an experienced remodeling "pro" or a novice just learning the ropes, we think the information you find here will be well worth the time and trouble it takes to read these pages. We hope you'll agree.

The Industry Needs Professionalism

Before we get down to business, we want to make a pitch for professionalism. We're the first to admit that the remodeling industry has been plagued by fast buck artists and blue suede shoe hucksters in the past. That image gives all professional remodelers a bad name and makes it harder for each of us to earn an honest dollar. Resolve now that you're a responsible remodeling specialist building a reputation for craftsmanship and fair dealing. You do only first quality work and expect to earn a reasonable profit, like any other skilled professional. That's the surest way to build a successful career in the remodeling industry.

We're not going to claim that craftsmanship isn't important. It is. But every good craftsman isn't automatically a good candidate to become a professional remodeler. Many remodeling businesses were started by an owner who was a skilled tradesman. His (or her) skills as a carpenter, mason, painter or plasterer got the business started and kept it going. But, being a skilled craftsman is one thing. Running a successful remodeling business is another.

Today, good business skills are needed to build a successful remodeling company. Every remodeling contractor is running a complex business. And it's often business skills that make the difference between success and failure; between earning a profit and losing money; between getting the job and losing it to the competition.

We're not saying that there's no place for skilled craftsmen or single-trade contractors. There will always be a place for tradesmen who are selling little more than their time. But someone who handles only carpentry or only painting or only plumbing isn't really in the remodeling business.

Modern remodeling specialists have to offer a full line of services to their clients. And here's why. In our opinion, the best profits come from coordinating the skills of many trades to create a home environment that meets the owners' needs and expectations. You're not just installing a new sink or some new flooring or adding a room, you're making a dream come true. You're offering an investment in comfort and convenience, creating a modern kitchen or sophisticated bathroom or spacious playroom that will be a source of pride and enjoyment for many years. Work like that deserves a premium which should reward you with more profit than most craftsmen can earn. It's for the full-service remodeling contractor that this book is written.

Modern remodeling specialists need the resources, skills, and managerial ability to design and build a wide variety of remodeling projects, ranging from a simple outdoor deck to a complex kitchen job involving the skills of many trades. There may be a time when you'll be working in one section of town on a simple dining alcove like the one shown in Figure 1-1. And at the same time, in another section of town, you might be building an addition as complex as the one in Figure 1-2.

Both of these projects were done on small post-WWII bungalows. The dining alcove required knocking out an existing wall and creating an extension to an existing room. Eating and storage space was added to what was once a cramped and inefficient kitchen. The addition in Figure 1-2 involved removing the entire back of the house to create room for a new kitchen, wet bar, dining alcove (left of the wet bar), and a skylighted all-purpose living area. Notice how the windows and skylights appear to bring the outdoors in.

If you want to bid on and build projects like these, being a competent tradesman is simply not enough. To handle work like this requires specialized business skills in addition to expert craftsmanship.

New Construction vs. Remodeling

If you're a home builder accustomed to dealing with many trades, you may assume that the transition to remodeling contractor should be relatively easy. Right? Not so!

Remodeling is unique, very different from building new houses. It's a common mistake for experienced new home builders to ignore these important differences. Here's what most remodeling contractors cite as the major differences between their projects and new construction:

- They work with the owner still living in the home.

- Remodeling requires a different type of financing.

Courtesy: Pella / Rolscreen Co.
Simple room addition
Figure 1-1

Courtesy: Armstrong World Industries, Inc.
Complex room addition
Figure 1-2

- They work on a personal basis for an individual who may expect work to be completed faster than it can be done.

- The profit margins are different.

- To do the job right, you have to blend the new with the old.

Look at Figure 1-3. This sunroom, placed on the end of the house, captures sunshine throughout the day. The roof as well as the walls are glass for added light and spaciousness. The brick foundation *blends* into and *ties* the sunroom to the rest of this traditional home. Notice also how it doesn't detract from the existing roofline.

This is a case of successfully blending the old with the new. When more room is needed, it's often a mistake to do extensive interior work to gain space. That just wastes your client's budget. If space is available on the lot, a room addition is a much better choice. It also disrupts the owner's household much less while the work is in progress.

The design of every addition should blend into the existing building both inside and out. Professional remodelers avoid that "add-on" look which creates a jarring element that detracts from the harmony of the home. Not only does this sunroom provide additional room and an area of seclusion, it *looks* like it has always been there. And, it was done with minimal disruption to the main living areas.

Why Experience Counts

According to experienced remodeling contractors, new contractors are most likely to make this simple, but costly, mistake: missing something when they do an estimate. It takes a lot of experience and know-how to guess what's behind a wall. As one old hand in the business emphasizes, "You have to look at the wall, then look at the other side of it. Put together what you see now, and how it compares to what you've seen before. Then with a little luck, chances are your estimate for what you're going to do to that wall will be pretty much on target."

It also takes experience to schedule jobs and to run your crews efficiently. You need a schedule for every work day. You need to know where you're going, when you need to be there, and how you can fit one job in with another. If you don't run your crews efficiently, it's going to cost you money.

Another difference in the remodeling business is competition from cut-throat low price bidders and inexperienced contractors. It's a problem you hear about again and again.

One contractor, who's been operating in one of the most economically depressed cities in the country, explains it this way. "Our biggest single problem, and the one most experienced contractors have to fight, is trying to compete with remodelers who don't know what they're doing. You want to go out as a legitimate contractor and sell a quality job at a good price (for both the homeowner and the contractor) and have good tradesmen working with you. Then you find you're up against a lot of guys bidding for work who really don't know what they're talking about. They underbid the job, and all of a sudden you're in a market where you can't make a dollar. That's our biggest problem."

Courtesy: Pella / Rolscreen Co.

New additions must blend with the old
Figure 1-3

The guys who underbid experienced contractors hurt everyone involved. In one instance, two contractors, both with over ten years experience, bid on a small room addition. Their bids were $18,000 and $18,500 respectively. A third contractor, with only two years' experience, bid $8,400. He was an excellent carpenter who had decided to strike out on his own, working out of his truck. He got the bid. But he overextended himself and had to borrow money to complete the job. Today he's back working as a carpenter.

When we told this story to another contractor, he commented, "We run into that all of the time. I have competitors out there I just can't believe. They're happy to go out and make $1,000 on a job, which means they're lucky to make wages. They think it's profit, but it isn't. I have overhead to cover. I like to work hard, I'll even work seven days a week. But, when I work seven days a week, I want something in the till for me. I know I have to cut some of my overhead, but I have to keep my prices up, too. I have to make a profit . . . There's no sense in working if you don't make a profit. No money, no business!"

Here's the point. It's O.K. to keep your overhead low, working out of your truck and keeping unnecessary expenses to a minimum. But you won't go far if your bids are designed to undercut the competition by 50 percent. If you're content to work for wages, then work at an hourly rate like any tradesman. But if you want to be a contractor, you need to include a healthy profit margin in every bid. Working for wages can provide a comfortable living. But it won't generate enough capital to meet the cash requirements of a growing, successful remodeling business.

Remodeling Requires Special Talent

The remodeling industry today needs thousands of talented people with skills that aren't being taught in any school or vocational training program. These remodeling specialists will come from both within the industry and from the trades and professions closely associated with the industry. Here are some of the specialized skills that are needed:

Designers must be taught to design practical remodeling plans that blend the old and new into a harmonious whole that yields maximum value at minimum cost.

Estimators must learn to predict costs even when they're dealing with non-standard conditions and the unknowns that are common when remodeling an older home. Unlike new construction, the cost of the last job may have no bearing on the current job. Every job has its own peculiarities and each must be priced accordingly.

Look at the two room additions shown in Figures 1-3 and 1-4. Figure 1-3 shows a project where much of the construction was done with prefabricated glass panels that were assembled on site. Estimating costs on this job required pricing specialized labor and materials. The room in Figure 1-4 was a more traditional job, needing considerably more carpentry for framing and completion. An estimator could probably price the carpentry for this job by the square foot or thousand board feet of lumber.

Sales personnel are needed who know construction and the capabilities of the company they work for. They need to develop a sensitivity to what the owner needs, wants, and is

Large scale remodeling project
Figure 1-4

willing to pay for. They need to understand that they're professionals who represent the entire industry to the buying public, and conduct themselves accordingly.

Production supervisors must learn the special techniques that are needed to supervise remodeling work: scheduling, quality control and customer relations.

Lenders must be educated to the special advantages of loans made for remodeling projects. In most cases, home improvements are an enhancement to the value a home. But they also show an additional commitment by the owner. That extra commitment is worth special consideration.
    Progressive lenders must learn to work closely with remodeling contractors so qualified owners can find convenient sources of cash with a minimum of wasted effort and uncertainty.

Building inspectors and other city officials must be made aware of the special advantages and differences in remodeling. Everyone in the community benefits when homes are improved. Codes and building officials should encourage remodeling, not thwart it with burdensome restrictions designed primarily to regulate the building of new homes.

And last, *you,* the remodeling contractor or the business owner, must realize that to be a professional, you have to wear many hats and have many skills. You'll have to identify which tasks you can master and which have to be left to other professionals and counselors you hire as needed.

Too many remodeling contractors today feel that sales is the key to making big money in their business. Obviously, sales are important. But sales alone won't keep you afloat. For one thing, no one makes a sale until someone develops a lead. And the best leads are the result of recommendations offered by satisfied customers. You won't get those without good tradesmen and supervisors. In a remodeling business, every skill is like a spoke on a wheel. Selling is only one of many. Failure anywhere along the line can lead to disaster.

The Need for Public Recognition

One of the problems facing remodeling contractors is a misconception about the role of the remodeling contractor in the building industry. You'll hear the term *remodeling contractor* used to identify any builder who works on an existing home. Let's eliminate some of the confusion by defining three terms: *remodeling contractor, home improvement dealer,* and *renovator.* These are not just different names for the same thing. Here's how we define the differences between the three.

Remodeling Contractor: This is the type of contractor who takes on jobs that involve several trades. He's really a general contractor. The type of work he does generally requires a plan or design. As a rule, he's on the job longer than the other two. Payment for his services is generally spread out over the job, sometimes continuing several months after the job has been completed. To be effective, he has to have a knowledge of many trades.

Home Improvement Dealer: Most often, this is a single-trade dealer such as tiling, siding, roofing or painting. No plan or design is required for this work. Single trades are generally in and out within a week. And full payment is usually made upon completion, unless it's a particularly big job.

Renovator: The term *renovate* means replacing something that no longer functions or has been damaged to the point of not being usable. Renovators are usually involved in rehabilitating old and unoccupied buildings, or buildings damaged by fires or natural catastrophes such as tornadoes. Renovation usually involves repair of an entire building or a major portion of it. Plans may or may not be required, and payment terms vary with the type of job.

Establishing Yourself As a Contractor

If you're just starting out in business, there are a number of basic items you'll have to consider. Let's start with a simple one. Where are you going to do business?

Setting Up an Office

You'll need an office. It can be literally any size. However, it's best to have at least two rooms, even if the rooms are small. Use one room for your office and record storage and the other as a meeting and plans room. You'll need a designated place to meet with your customers and subcontractors. And if you have a staff, even if it's only one person, work can continue in one room while you're holding a meeting in the other room.

Your office can be almost anywhere in your service area. Many new remodeling contractors have an office in their home. There's nothing wrong with that. But keep in mind that there will be people coming and going, so your office should be easily accessible. It should also reflect favorably on your business. A desk in the corner of the basement just past the washing machine obviously won't do.

Your office, no matter its size, will need at least a pocket calculator, typewriter, adding machine with paper tape, file cabinet, desk, and enough chairs and tables to meet your immediate needs. You should also have a separate telephone and someone to answer it when you're not there. If you don't have someone who can answer the phone in your absence, either hire an answering service or buy an answering machine.

You're probably going to need a storage area for back files and materials. Even if you don't plan to stockpile materials, every job has something left over that can be put to good use in the future. Set aside some space for these items. You can probably turn a profit on them at a later date.

Don't feel that you need a large office or expensive furnishings to get started. Anything more than the minimum will just inflate your overhead. As your business grows, your overhead will grow almost automatically. And since overhead must be included in every job, keeping your overhead expense under control will make your bids more competitive.

Hiring Your Staff

As soon as projects start coming in, you'll probably need help. In addition to answering the phone, you'll need someone who can keep the books, type, maintain files, and prepare quotations and contracts.

You can use a family member at first, as long as that person is capable of doing the work. But don't let the tail wag the dog. As a professional, you need professional quality help. If you don't have a family member who can provide the service you need, it's better to hire someone who can.

Before you hire outside help, determine just how much time is actually needed. Chances are, it will be less than a 40-hour week. More people are looking for part-time work than full-time work. You should have no shortage of applicants even if you need help for only a few hours a day. Consider skilled older people who want to work only part-time or college students who can work full-time only during the busy summer months.

Before hiring anyone, define carefully what you require, estimate how long it will take to do the work, and the skills required. Then select the best part-timer able to meet your needs.

Generally, as a beginning remodeling contractor, you'll be your own salesman, estimator, and job supervisor. Budget your time accordingly. Make out a daily schedule and stick to it as much as possible. Remember — and this phrase will be repeated again and again — every job being worked must be checked at least once a day.

Bank Accounts and Contracts

Keep a separate bank account for your business. It's the only practical way to separate business expenses from your personal expenses. That's essential for tax purposes. Each job you handle should be recorded in a separate ledger book.

You should have a written contract for every job you do. All oral agreements, regardless of where or how they are made, should also be confirmed in writing. That way, you'll have written evidence to back you up if there's a dispute. Set up a file folder for every job. Into that folder goes all correspondence, estimates, receipts, bills and notes on that job. We prefer to keep records in chronological order in the file folder. An Acco fastener can be used to secure papers so they aren't as likely to fall out of the folder.

Change orders are a source of many disputes. Make sure they're in writing, even if no extra cost is involved in the change. Always have the owner sign it. If he refuses, tell him it's a standard part of your business practice and you can't be held liable unless he does. Our experience is that remodeling contractors don't get paid for changes in the plan unless the change is very clear, in writing and signed by both parties.

Insurance Is Mandatory

One of the biggest problems for many remodeling contractors is insurance. And in the remodeling business *you have to have it.* Our advice is to avoid using an insurance *agent.* An agent represents only one company. Instead, find a good *insurance broker.* The time spent will be worth it. Brokers represent many insurance companies, so they can shop around for the best deals for you and your business. An insurance broker can help reduce your cost of coverage.

Be aware that anyone hurt on one of your jobs will probably sue you to recover for their injury, even if they had no right to be in the area where they were hurt. Remember that most of your projects will be private homes. You have little control over who comes on the premises and what they do there. That's why adequate insurance coverage is so important. Your jobs will be accessible to children, relatives, friends of the owner, curious neighbors, and anyone passing by. Everyone wants to see what's new on the block. Protect yourself the only way you can. Get adequate liability coverage.

Most construction contracts require specific amounts for public liability and property damage coverage. Some jobs call for "excess limits" which can be covered by attaching an "umbrella" to an existing policy. The costs for the umbrella policy should be included in your job specifications. The cost of this insurance doesn't come out of your profit. It should be included in your cost estimate. So be sure the cost of all required insurance, including special insurance, is included in each bid you submit.

Most construction contracts require that you provide insurance coverage to protect the owner's interest during the period of construction. Be sure this coverage is included in your policy. If not, you'll have to specifically request it for every job. Some insurance companies charge extra for this.

If you have any employees, all states require that you carry workers' compensation insurance. You will also have to insure all moving vehicles. As your business grows, you'll need other types of insurance as well. That's another reason why it's important to find a good insurance broker. In fact, the three best friends you can have as a businessman are a good insurance broker, a good banker, and a good lawyer.

Most insurance policies require a minimum down payment, with additional premiums paid during the year. At the end of each policy year, the insurance company will audit your payroll records to determine the exact premium that was earned for the year. You'll get an invoice or a credit for any difference between what you've paid and the actual cost of coverage. No remodeling contractor, regardless of the type of work he does, should be without insurance.

The cost of a comprehensive contractor's liability insurance policy will vary with your loss history and the area where you do business. For most contractors, liability insurance will be between 2 and 3 percent of payroll. Workers' compensation insurance will usually be 6 to 8 percent of payroll, depending on the trade and your loss history. Auto and truck insurance, equipment floaters, and fidelity bonds will be additional costs.

How much can you expect to pay for taxes and insurance? Of course, it varies from state to state and from year to year. But most remodeling contractors have to pay about $25 in payroll taxes and insurance for each $100 of payroll. Here's a more detailed breakdown:

State unemployment tax ....4.0% of payroll
Social security ....7.5% of payroll
Federal unemployment insurance..............0.8% of payroll
Workers' compensation insurance ....8.0% of payroll
Contractors' liability insurance ....3.0% of payroll

Total these figures and you'll discover that your tax and insurance burden will be nearly 25 percent of payroll. For every $100 you pay employees, you have to pay the government and your insurance company an additional $25.

Is there any legal way to avoid making these tax and insurance payments? None. Don't even think about it. Sure, we've all known remodelers who had no insurance coverage and paid employees in cash to avoid withholding taxes and reporting wages. A little one-man operation can get away with that for a while — until someone has an accident on the job or until the tax auditor comes around. But it won't last long. And we've never heard of a little under-the-table business like that growing into a big, prosperous, legitimate remodeling company.

Our advice is to get legal and stay legal. Have the insurance the law requires and pay your taxes on time. You'll sleep better at night. The Yellow Pages of your phone book list at least several payroll services that can help you prepare the company payroll and make tax deposits when due. The cost of having your payroll prepared by experts is surprisingly small.

Write-Offs, Overhead and Markups

As long as you work out of your home, some part of the cost of maintaining your home is a business expense. Check with your tax advisor to determine exactly how to handle this deduction.

If you're operating a car or truck for your business, have an advertising program, carry liability and compensation insurance, have either a full-time office employee or a part-time bookkeeper, your business already has at least a 10 percent overhead. Ten cents of every dollar you take in is needed to cover overhead.

Overhead is easy to forget about when you're estimating a job. Many new remodelers make this mistake. They consider all overhead a fixed cost, the cost of doing business. If they can take just this one extra job without increasing their overhead, why add anything to the estimate to cover overhead? That's wishful thinking. Fixed costs *are* overhead, the biggest overhead item. Fixed overhead expense has to be included in every estimate.

There are also variable overhead costs that have to be included. Variable overhead changes as work volume increases or decreases. You should recognize variable expenses and include them in every estimate as a cost of doing business.

Overhead costs aren't phony expenses. They're just as real as labor and material costs for any job. Ignore them at your peril. The list that follows breaks overhead expense down into three categories.

I. Fixed Overhead:
    1) Rent
    2) Office utilities
    3) Office supplies
    4) Office upkeep and repairs
    5) Basic insurance
    6) Telephones
    7) Accounting and clerical help, if on payroll
    8) Advertising and sales expense
    9) General vehicle expense (not job-related)
    10) Taxes, state and local license fees

II. Variable Overhead:
    1) Workers' compensation insurance
    2) Public liability and property damage insurance
    3) Automobile expenses related to projects

III. Job-Site Overhead:
    1) Job-site telephone
    2) Job-site toilet
    3) Job-site temporary utilities
    4) Extra limits on insurance
    5) Special insurance (fire, vandalism, etc.)
    6) Plan fees and building permits
    7) Additional sets of plans
    8) Bond premiums

The best guide to your own variable overhead cost will be cost records from completed jobs. Most experienced remodeling contractors have developed a formula for figuring variable overhead expense. They usually start by identifying actual variable overhead costs for a typical job. On similar jobs you can expect variable overhead expense to be about the same. The pitfall here is that costs change with time. Be alert for new overhead costs that appear in some jobs. In some cases a special allowance will be needed on top of the usual overhead estimate.

Fixed overhead must also be added to each job. In most cases, contractors figure fixed overhead as a percentage of gross receipts. For example, if you expect to have fixed overhead expense of $100,000 and a gross volume of $1,000,000 for the year, fixed overhead will be 10 percent of receipts. Every bid you quote has to include 10 percent for fixed overhead. The larger the business, the higher the fixed overhead is likely to be. In larger remodeling companies fixed overhead may be as high as 25 percent of gross.

While you're adding overhead expense to your estimate, don't forget to add in something for a sales commission, even if you, the business owner, are making the sale. Part of the markup on the job should be a sales commission payable to yourself.

The total markup, including profit, will vary widely. Some contractors figure their markup by multiplying job costs by up to 100 percent. Markups of 60 to 80 percent aren't uncommon and a 100 percent markup can be justified in some situations. So, if your labor and material cost is $30,000, the bid price including markup can range from $48,000 (at 60 percent) to $54,000 (at 80 percent markup) depending on the location, overhead and other variables.

To someone who has been working in new construction, these figures will probably seem high. But the formulas that work in new construction don't apply in remodeling work. A 25 or 30 percent markup over cost just isn't enough.

Selecting a Market

If you live in a small town, say one with a populated area that's only ten miles in diameter, the entire city can be your market area. Avoid taking any jobs outside this area. With all jobs in easy commuting distance, you can visit every job site every day. If the jobs are spread out too thin, you'll spend all your time in the car commuting between jobs and the office. Equally important, your crews, your subcontractors, and your material suppliers will also have to spend too much time on the road.

You need time in the office every day as well — time for planning, making decisions, ordering materials or having meetings. Travel time costs you money. It can affect both your bid and your profit. Whether travel time is yours or your crew's, it's time *you* have to pay for.

There are two other marketing rules you should be aware of. One is to control your volume. Don't try to handle too much work at one time. The other is to be cautious when accepting business in low-income communities.

Too much work spreads your resources too thin. It's the direct cause of failure for many remodeling contractors. Overextension will leave you with too little cash, too little equipment, too few skilled tradesmen, too little supervision and too many unhappy clients. Building a remodeling business is like learning to ski. Take it easy at first. Save the more challenging stuff until you've perfected the basics.

The problem in low income areas is that it's easy to sell more than your clients can afford. It's irresponsible to sell a homeowner anything they obviously don't need or can't pay for.

Develop a Business Plan

Both new and established remodeling companies need a business plan, a set of goals to be met. Review and revise this plan occasionally. And draw up a new plan for every calendar or fiscal year.

With a new business, certain assumptions have to be made before you can prepare a plan. Let's look at an example. Assume that you want to set up a general remodeling business in a city of approximately 500,000 people. You intend to specialize in room additions, kitchens and baths. The *average* contract amount will be about $15,000 to $20,000. If you have five full-time employees and complete fifty projects a year, your annual sales will be between $700,000 and $1 million.

Based on those assumptions, how much cash do you need on hand to start and run the business for the first year? Most bankers and experienced contractors would say you need working capital equal to at least 10 percent of your first year's sales. So if you're anticipating $700,000 in sales, you need at least $70,000 to get started.

The next step is to estimate expenses so you can prepare a projected profit and loss statement. Let's look briefly at what's included in each expense category that's likely to appear on a P&L statement.

Hard Job Cost

The largest expense category on your jobs will be the hard costs: building materials, hourly pay for tradesmen, and the charges of subcontractors. Hard costs have to be paid for with your cash, usually shortly after the expense is incurred.

Hard costs vary with the size and complexity of the job. For budget purposes, plan on hard costs being 60 percent of the total contract price. Therefore, with a projected gross sales of $700,000, hard job costs can total $420,000.

Overhead Expenses

The largest overhead cost will be payroll for your staff. If you, as the owner, divide your time between managing and sales, you'll be responsible for about half of the sales that are made, or $350,000.

The staff— As your business grows, your staff will grow. The first two jobs to be filled will be a superintendent to supervise the work and a secretary-receptionist-office manager. You'll also need a bookkeeper on a part-time basis.

As volume increases, you'll add one salesperson and two full-time building tradesmen. They're not part of overhead expense, however. Sales will be made on commission, and wages for tradesmen are included in hard job cost. All other work may be done by subcontractors.

The initial budget for staff expenses may include the following:

Owner/Manager/Salesperson (draw) $30,000
Superintendent (salary, full time)...30,000
Secretary (salary, full time) 12,000
Bookkeeper (salary, part-time)...5,000

$77,000
FICA taxes (8.2 percent) 6,214

$83,214

Advertising and promotion— The next major overhead expense is advertising and promotion. The more you can afford to advertise, the more leads you'll generate. Advertising may take as much as 5 percent of gross revenue. With sales projected at $700,000,
your promotional budget could be $35,000. This probably includes ads in the Yellow
Pages and an attractive brochure or flyer prepared by a professional graphic artist.

Your promotion budget should also include regular ads in a local newspaper. If more
money is available, consider drive-time radio and spot advertising on local TV news programs to reach a large audience and reinforce the newspaper space ads. A typical advertising budget might include the following:

Yellow Pages display ad..$3,400
Newspaper display and classified 8,000
Local radio and TV spots 14,000
Printed brochure/flyers..9,600

Total promotion cost $35,000

Other overhead costs— Other ordinary business expenses which you include in the
overhead costs are:

Office rental $3,600
Utilities (gas/electric)..1,200
Auto/truck operation 7,000
Telephone 1,800
Insurance (liability and workers' comp) 5,000
Accounting services 2,000
Legal fees..1,000
Office supplies 1,500
Dues and subscriptions 1,500
Other miscellaneous expenses 2,000

Other business expenses total $26,600

When these are added to staff and promotional costs, the total overhead expenses are
$144,814, or 20.6 percent of your estimated gross.

Earnings Statement

For the Year Ending December 31, 19_____

Revenue:

Income from Remodeling Projects $700,000

Expenses:

Hard job costs $420,000

Overhead, Including salaries $144,814

Sales commissions $37,500

        Total expenses $602,314

        Net earnings $97,686

Sample earnings statement
Figure 1-5

Commission Costs

As mentioned previously, you (the owner) will probably be responsible for at least 50 percent of the sales made. A salesperson, working on a commission basis, will make the remaining 50 percent. At the level of advertising proposed in the business plan, you should develop 40 qualified leads per month.

Each salesperson should follow up on 20 of these leads. Assuming that each of you can sell slightly more than 10 percent of the leads generated, that would result in about 25 projects each per year. At an average of $15,000 per job, the commissioned salesman should generate $375,000 of business annually. Using a commission rate of 10 percent, payout for sales will be $37,500.

Actually, these assumptions for sales are conservative. A below-average salesman should sell 10 percent of the prospects he calls on. The average salesman will sell about 15 percent, and a good salesperson will close 20 percent of the time. The better the salesman, the higher the commissions you have to pay out, of course. But that super salesman is also generating a higher dollar amount of business.

The Earnings Statement

The costs just described will help when planning your own expenses and income. When the figures are combined, the result will be an Earnings Statement as shown in Figure 1-5. Pre-tax profits are 13.9 percent of gross revenues. This is a reasonable expectation for a remodeling business, and a goal worth working toward.

Failure vs. Success

A successful remodeling company can be *very* profitable. But not all remodeling companies are successful. The failure rate for construction businesses is the second highest of all types of business in the country.

Dun & Bradstreet's Annual Report issued early in the 1980s noted that failures in the construction and service industries reached more than 70 percent between 1979 and 1980. New home builders had the highest failure rate since the disastrous year of 1967.

Failures were more common in some parts of the country than in others. Failures increased slightly in New England and Middle Atlantic states, but were much higher in East, South, Central, South Atlantic, Mountain and Pacific states. These areas and figures were based on all types of businesses and not just construction, but it's safe to assume that construction took its share of lumps in these areas.

Of the businesses that failed, 53.6 percent were in their first five years of operation. The primary cause of failure was defined as *managerial ineptness.* This was cited as the major cause of bankruptcy in nine of ten businesses that failed. There was no mention of undercapitalization, which at one time was one of the largest causes of small business failure in the first five years.

More recently, the climate for construction business has begun to improve. The 1985-1986 reports show that the number of construction business failures in the first five years of operation had decreased to 43.6 percent. That's not great, but it's a far cry from the 70 percent of a few years ago.

The reports, indicating a trend toward recovery from the recession which began in 1980, underscores how shifts in the economy can have disastrous effects on the inexperienced or inept entrepreneur. Though the sagging economy affected all types of businesses, business failures were particularly severe in the construction and retail industries. Heavy operating expenses, high interest rates and difficulties in collecting receivables helped compound the problem.

The Dun & Bradstreet report makes it clear that the owner/operator of a remodeling business needs good management skills to run a successful remodeling business.

Fortunately, good management courses are available in nearly every community. Beginning and advanced courses in accounting, sales, advertising and management are offered by many schools and colleges throughout the country. Seminars for builders and remodelers are put on regularly by many organizations. Chambers of Commerce and Associations of Commerce and Industry offer many programs designed to help independent business people operate more efficiently and more profitably. Identify the areas where you're weak and find the courses that will help you most. This book will cover most of the information you need to know. But don't be reluctant to supplement our explanations with information from other sources.

There are pitfalls and headaches in any business, especially one as complicated as remodeling. Mistakes are inevitable. But the only error your client can complain about is the one you didn't correct. Your ultimate product is not remodeled bathrooms or converted basements or modern, highly efficient kitchens. It's happy customers. Experienced contractors have found, despite the hurdles and problems they face, that there's only one way to stay friendly with customers at the end of the job. That is to have a full and complete understanding with them at the beginning of the job.

Figure 1-6 shows the results of a survey of 163 multi-trade large, medium and small remodeling contractors. We'll refer to this figure several times in the following chapters.

Results of a Survey of 163 (Multi-Trade) Remodeling Contractors

Size of the area serviced:

Over 750,000 population	63
300,000-750,000 population	48
Under 350,000 population	52
	163

Do they consider their business:

Large volume	37
Medium volume	64
Small volume	62

What are their principal sources of leads:
(except referrals)

	Larger Contractors	Medium Contractors	Small Contractors
Newpaper advertising	18	24	10
TV	2	1	
Phone soliciting	8	8	2
House-to-house soliciting	1	4	4
Telephone directory	2	22	32
TV Guide magazine	2	2	
Direct mail	1	1	2
Radio	1		
Dodge Reports	1	1	
Job signs			4
Home shows	1	1	
None			8 (All from referral)

Leads from referrals

	Percentages
Large volume	50%
Medium volume	30%
Small volume	60%

What is the average percent of leads sold—to the number of leads called

Large volume	15%
Medium volume	18%
Small volume	30%

Do they take all kinds of work?

Large volume	90% NO
Medium volume	95% NO
Small volume	55% YES

Survey of remodeling contractors
Figure 1-6

Do they have a minimum job they will accept?
Do they have a maximum job they will accept?

	Minimum Job	Maximum Job
Large volume	90% YES	60% YES
Medium volume	80% YES	50% YES
Small volume	40% NO	95% YES

Are you and/or your salespeople trained to design a job, and is it important in percentage of sales closed?

Trained in design	Importance in closing
40%	Little 20%
	Some 6%
	Very 74%

What type of a retail contract document is used by your company?

	Large volume	Medium volume	Small volume
Detailed written specification	16	24	21
Preprinted check-off contract	4	2	
Referring to the plans	14	22	22
Combination of the above	3	16	19

Do you use direct labor, subcontract, or a combination of both

Large volume	Almost 100% say a combination
Medium volume	30% Direct labor
	35% Subcontract
	35% combination
Small volume	35% Direct labor
	25% Subcontract
	40% Combination

What type of a production scheduling method do you use?

	Large volume	Medium volume	Small volume
CPM (or a variation)	6	1	
Flow chart (written)	18	32	28
Progress graph	11	25	18
Magnetic board	2		
By the seat of their pants		8	12
Blackboard			4

Survey of remodeling contractors
Figure 1-6 (continued)

How does the owner (manager) budget his time?

	Large volume	Medium volume	Small volume
Office work	30%	10%	5%
Lead development	10%	5%	1%
Sales	40%	60%	50%
Production	20%	25%	44%

What is the major "repeated" customer complaint?

	Large volume	Medium volume	Small volume
Time delay—job taking too long	19	41	31
Sales misrepresentation	2	4	1
Communication with contractor	6	8	24
Quality of performance	5	6	4
Clean-up	1	2	
High price	2	2	

What is the major management problem?

	Large volume	Medium volume	Small volume
Cash flow	1	4	8
Cost of financing	1		
Final payment from buyer	8	14	12
Getting good subcontractors	19	21	14
Communication		6	4
Side deals by workmen			
Change orders	2	6	2
Customer expects more than agreed	6	13	22

Survey of remodeling contractors
Figure 1-6 (continued)

For now, just see how your business (or your proposed business) compares with the experience of other remodeling contractors. Notice that the most common customer complaint is *delay* for all three volume levels, large, medium and small. Resolve now to leave your jobs on friendly terms with the owner — and do it by avoiding the mistakes other remodelers make so often.

t w o

Prospects?
Almost Everyone!

To be successful, the owner of any remodeling business must be as knowledgeable about marketing and sales as he is about his tools and materials. A good marketing plan, tailored to the capabilities of the company, is an essential tool of business today.

The main difference between successful, average, and below-average remodeling businesses lies in the owner's approach to sales. Without selling skills, even the most capable contractor will fail in business.

Successful remodelers maintain active marketing programs. They set goals, support them with on-going advertising, and have a continuous program designed to generate sales. Average and low-volume contractors, on the other hand, usually rely on passive sales techniques. Their work comes primarily through referrals. A company that's getting plenty of referral business is doing something right. But no remodeler can rely on referrals exclusively. They don't provide a steady workload — the kind of volume you need to keep crews busy and profits on the rise.

Developing Leads

The first step in developing a good marketing plan is deciding how you are going to generate *leads*, the names and phone numbers of people who are prospects for your services. Start by asking yourself some simple and basic questions, such as . . . Who is

Annual Sales Quota: $300,000

Month:	JAN	FEB	MAR	APR	MAY	JUN	JUL	AUG	SEP	OCT	NOV	DEC	Annual Totals
Sales Volume:	Low	Low	Ave	High	High	High	Ave	High	Ave	Ave	Low	Low	
Income:	$15,000	$15,000	$25,000	$35,000	$35,000	$35,000	$25,000	$35,000	$25,000	$25,000	$15,000	$15,000	$300,000
Jobs:	3	3	5	7	7	7	5	7	5	5	3	3	60
Leads:	15	15	25	35	35	35	25	35	25	25	15	15	300
Sales Budget:	$975	$975	$1625	$2275	$2275	$2275	$1625	$2275	$1625	$1625	$975	$975	$19,500
Cost per Lead:	$65	$65	$65	$65	$65	$65	$65	$65	$65	$65	$65	$65	$65

Courtesy: Ira J. Messing, Remodelers, Inc.

Notes: Marketing Budget: 6.5 percent of annual gross
Closing ratio: 20 percent
Average job: $5,000

Sample marketing plan
Figure 2-1

your typical client? . . . Where are they located? . . . What are their remodeling needs? . . . What is the average income for the area? The answers to these questions will help you define your market. Then you can design a program to attract clients whose needs and interests fit your products and services.

The heart of your marketing program is knowing how many leads you'll have to develop to reach your sales goal. To calculate this, you'll need to know what percentage of your leads end up in sales, and how much it costs you to develop each lead.

Often, inexperienced small-business owners will use the "shotgun" approach to marketing. That is, they try to reach anyone and everyone whether or not they are good prospects for the service offered. That's usually an expensive mistake.

The sample marketing plan shown in Figure 2-1 was developed by a successful remodeling contractor. It projects monthly sales goals for the company and the sales personnel, and shows at a glance how many salespeople are needed to meet those goals. The plan can be adjusted to reflect an increase or decrease in sales.

Let's go through the arithmetic to figure how many sales leads we'll need to gross $300,000 annually. If your average job is $5,000, you'll have to close 60 sales a year to reach $300,000. If the closing ratio is 20 percent (you close the sale on 20 percent of the leads), your marketing program needs to generate 300 leads a year. If your marketing budget is 6.5 percent of your projected sales gross ($300,000), your total sales budget will be $19,500. That works out to a cost of $325 per sale (based on 60 sales per year), or $65 per lead (based on 300 leads).

Figure 2-1 uses these figures to project monthly sales, taking into consideration seasonal highs and lows reflecting weather, vacations, type of work, and so on. For example, January is a month of low sales volume. You only need three sales to meet the month's sales quota of $15,000. Low January sales are balanced by the busier summer months such as August, where you'll need 35 leads and seven sales to meet your $35,000 quota. Having determined that the average cost per sale is $325, the sales budget for January is only $975. The sales budget for August is $2,275.

This plan sets up a measurable, controllable sales program. However, it's important that your advertising and promotional efforts be focused toward specific markets. Otherwise, you probably won't be able to meet your sales goals.

Pick Your Market

Housing projects have been around for decades. Before World War II, tract housing consisted of several streets of identical houses. Most projects consisted of 30 to 50 homes. During the 1930s and early 1940s very few projects were built. But when thousands of GIs returned home in the mid-1940s, the demand for housing soared. Large housing projects sprang up around the country. Many projects included 100 to 500 homes. Some were as large as 5,000 homes. Almost every major American city had its share of housing projects. Nearly all of these homes are still occupied. And most of them need remodeling.

Most of the homes built in the late 1940s and early 1950s had very simple floor plans compared to what is offered today, even in low-cost developments. Many of these post-World War II homes were small and "boxy" with a single bath, two bedrooms, and often no garage. But they did have one thing that we rarely see today: a fair-sized lot with room to expand.

Today, there are thousands of these houses around most larger cities. Most of them need every single product a skilled remodeler offers. Many a contractor has become a successful remodeler by concentrating on these homes. Obviously the need was there, but most contractors were content to let the homeowner come to them.

One contractor recognized the vast potential of this market. He knew that some homeowners had the vision, time and skill to remodel their homes on their own. But the vast majority couldn't visualize how attractive their old homes could be and had neither the time nor ability to do the work themselves. They needed to be shown how their homes could be changed or expanded to meet their needs.

He had little scale model homes built so he could demonstrate how these basic homes could be improved through remodeling. When making a sales pitch, he could generate interest and excitement by using the models to show the possibilities. He wasn't willing to wait for his phone to ring. He went out into the community, spreading the word about his service.

Figures 2-2 through 2-4 show some of the models he used for different housing projects during the years he ran this sales campaign. Not only were the models featured in his advertising, they were also put on display in his showroom and sales office. From time to time, salesmen would take them along on sales calls.

The result was hundreds of thousands of dollars worth of sales. Although he's now retired, his unique and creative advertising plan helped make him one of the most successful remodeling contractors in the country.

His success was due to the fact that he identified his market and went after it! He didn't wait for it to come to him. He was active, not passive. Today, hundreds of similar situations exist. You only have to identify them and then reap the rewards.

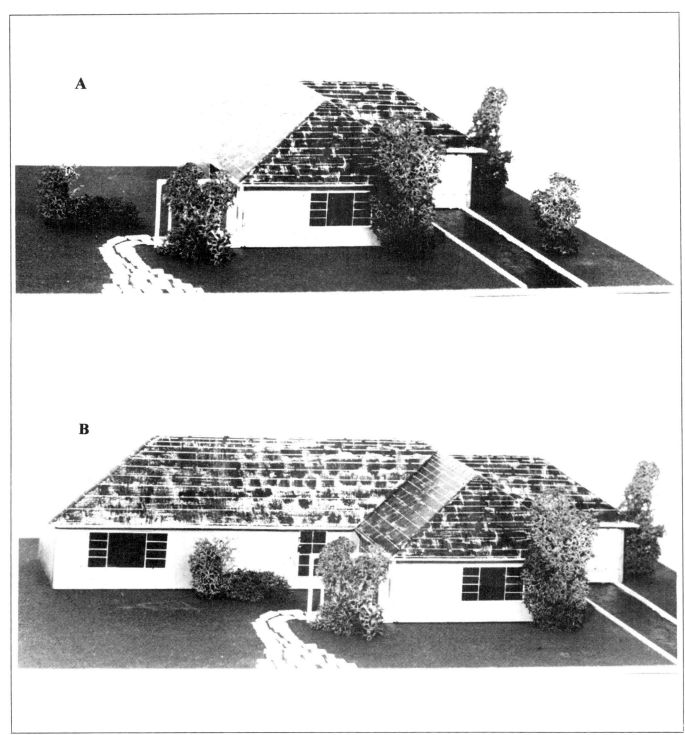

A

B

Courtesy: Ira J. Messing, Remodelers, Inc.

Models show remodeling possibilities
Figure 2-2

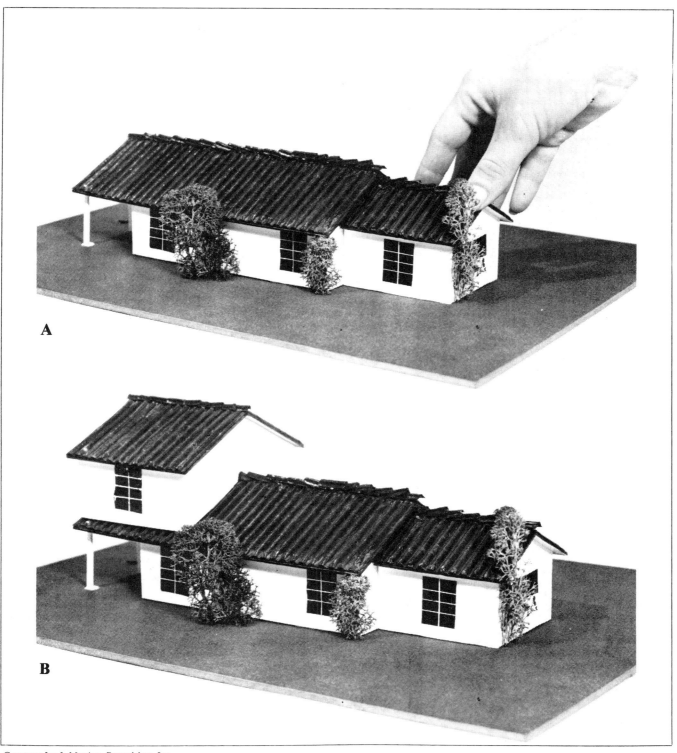

Courtesy: Ira J. Messing, Remodelers, Inc.

Add a second story as well
Figure 2-3

Courtesy: Ira J. Messing, Remodelers, Inc.

Add a new room or new entrance
Figure 2-4

Shell Selling

Don't minimize the importance of the customers doing part of the work themselves. This is often called "shell selling," selling a "bare-bones" room and letting the customer do his own finishing. The "shell" can be carried to various stages of development, depending on the wishes of the customer.

If the work requires a building permit and must comply with the code, the homeowner may not be allowed to complete all work done under the permit that's issued to you. Check with the city building department to be sure what the homeowner *is* and *isn't* allowed to do. If homeowners are permitted to finish the work, be sure they understand what the permit requires and that all work has to comply with the building code. They should also know that the work will be checked by a city building inspector. Spell out in your contract exactly what the homeowner has agreed to finish. That will help absolve your company of any legal liability if the work is not done, or if it's done wrong.

Shell selling has one major drawback. Banks are reluctant to finance work that will be completed by the homeowner. Many people overestimate their skills when it comes to finishing off the shell. They can usually paint and wallpaper — but installing paneling, drywall, flooring, and molding require more skill.

Whether the job is finished correctly or not depends on the homeowner's level of skill and experience. Even if they can complete the work, will the quality of the work be acceptable to the next owner of the home? Time can also be a problem in completing a shell. People often take on more work than they have time to complete. Something comes up, the project is set aside, and it never gets completed. These are the primary reasons why many banks refuse to finance shells. When homeowners first mention having you add a shell that they can finish, *stop!* Ask then and there if they can pay cash for it. Explain that they probably won't be able to finance it with a bank loan.

Professionalism in Sales

Sales are the backbone of your business. Without sales, there is no business. Whether you do the selling, or have marketing personnel do it for you, it's your responsibility to plan sales and deliver the results as planned. If your sales plan isn't working, make some changes. If your own sales skills are the problem, make upgrading those skills a high priority. At the back of this manual is an order form that lists several books that may be of help. If necessary, hire a professional salesperson to carry most of the selling load.

A sale begins with a lead and ends with a close. What happens in between only the salesperson knows. That may sound corny, but it's true. What works for one person may not work for another.

In sales, preparation is two-thirds of the battle in getting the customer's signature on the contract. This means that most of the effort takes place before you meet the client. It means knowing your product and your company thoroughly. It means developing sales techniques that work for you.

Start closing the sale the minute you start your presentation. A good salesperson counters each objection and gets a "yes" at every step in the presentation. Then, when you're finished, it's simply a matter of saying to the customer, "Since we have an agreement, why don't we approve the contract now?" No closing summary is required.

That's low pressure selling. It's one of the most effective ways to sell remodeling work and avoids the hard sell that offends many people. Salespeople are often surprised at how easy it is to sell a good service at a fair price — especially if you're friendly and relaxed. When there's no hard sell, the writing and signing of the agreement is the easiest part. It's welcomed by the buyer, who senses that the seller is a professional. Today, *professionalism* is what sells.

Unfortunately, not every sale can be closed this easily. Some customers won't say "yes" to each step in a sales presentation. Later in this chapter, we'll look at some closing techniques that can help you overcome particular types of sales resistance.

The Good Salesperson

What makes a good salesperson? As you might expect, there's no single answer. One way to judge good salespeople is by the number of leads they close. An outstanding salesperson will close one in five leads in multi-trade remodeling; the average, one in ten; the mediocre, one in fifteen. In single-trade work the closing rate will be higher.

One outstanding trait that all good salespeople share is *creativity.* They can take something ordinary and make it seem exciting. A good salesperson makes every project special. Even the simplest job can be glamorous and exciting in the eyes of the homeowner. Good salespeople share in the excitement of the project, give the owners praise and encouragement, and guide them through their choices.

Other qualities which set good salespeople apart are:

- Knowing their company, their products, and themselves

- Knowing that the low bidder doesn't always get the job

- Representing the business and its products honestly

- Showing confidence, not only in themselves, but in the company

- Not worrying about competition (They know their company is as good as any other.)

- Being able to accept rejection with grace and go on to the next sales call

- Being able to take all jobs in stride, the simple with the difficult

- Not underselling or overselling, but knowing instinctively when the customer is sold

- Leaving homeowners with the feeling that they're getting what they need and want, not just what's being sold

- Having a rehearsed, well-paced presentation which incorporates key selling words, such as *let's* and *we* that emphasize a common effort toward a joint goal

• Leaving every prospect with the feeling that their business is appreciated. Even if the sale isn't closed, a prospect should feel that the salesperson is happy to have had the opportunity to show them what the company does.

Why is developing good salesmanship important? Money! Today it costs you from $50 to $150 for each sales call. Remember, a good salesperson will close just one out of five calls. That's a *minimum* cost per sale of $250 which must be added into each sales contract. A salesperson who closes only one in ten calls can add as much as $1,500 to the cost of the job. Obviously, costs that high will take you out of the competition on most bids. The extra time and trouble spent on a good sales presentation will pay off in the long run, if it means closing more sales more often.

Working the Prospect

A good salesperson writes up a prospect card on every sales lead. This can be as simple as filling out a form like the one in Figure 2-5. Or, it can be a full report including a survey form, the suggested design, and notes on the discussion with a prospective customer. The information recorded depends on how far the sales presentation goes. Keep these notes even if you don't close the sale. Include the reason the sale wasn't closed. And never blame the loss of a sale on the customer. Instead, use it as a lesson on how to do better the next time.

Three steps in making a sale— Every job starts with a sale. From the first phone call to the signing of the contract, you are selling the product. If the customer was pretty clear on what he wanted over the phone, use that as the basis for your first on-site presentation.

Three important steps in making a remodeling sale are:

1) Determine that what the customer wants and needs is possible

2) Determine that the customer has the ability to pay

3) Present the customer with a well-planned design.

When these three points are put together in a professional presentation, you are well on your way to making the sale. Remember, a good salesperson glamorizes the job — making even the simplest "box" seem beautiful.

Know the building code— Always try to set the first meeting in the customer's home and *be on time.* By visiting the home, you can see for yourself if what the customer wants is feasible. As a rule, customers don't know building codes. They may have a misconception about what they can have done. It's your responsibility to know what the building codes do and don't allow so you can help your customers make their decisions. There's no excuse for ignorance in this area. The book *Contractor's Guide to the Building Code* can help you understand what the code requires. You can order one using the order form in the back of this manual.

PROSPECT CARD

Bill Ryan	SALESMAN

NAME						
Larry Smith						

ADDRESS					CITY	
same as below						

REM ADDRESS						
113 Main St.				Flushing		

HOME PHONE				OTHER		
499-6973				Bus. 684-2142		

DATE		SOURCE				
1/20			Daily Herald			

TIME TO CALL						
after 7:00 PM						

OWNER	MTG	CONTRACT	COST	BAL	EMP	OCCUPY
yes	Bk	30 yr.	$78	$24	Sears	Sales
BRICK	**FRAME**	**STORIES**	**FLATS**	**BUDGET**	**MTG**	**CASH**
	X	2		$10	50%	50%
REM	**REPAIR**	**DORMER**	**PORCH**	**BATH**	**KITCHEN**	**ADDITION**
X				X		

REMARKS						
5' x 7' small bath-shower only, new						
commode, lav. & vanity						

APPT	TIME	DAY	DATE
	7:30 PM	Fri.	1/23

Prospect card
Figure 2-5

Ignorance of the building code, zoning restrictions and setback requirements can cause a lot of embarrassment, and worse still, financial losses. Not knowing these ranks high on the list of problems that plague beginning contractors and their sales staff. Too often, the sales staff doesn't understand what is possible and what isn't. Don't offer to build what the building code or government restrictions won't allow. A contract that calls for construction of a family room which extends right up to the property line is worse than worthless if zoning requires a 10-foot setback. That's just simple common sense.

***Keep expectations realistic*—** Many of your prospects won't understand how expensive construction is today. They may have unrealistic ideas about what they can get for their money. This is one of the salesperson's biggest responsibilities: bringing a customer's expectations in line with a realistic price. No sale is made until the clients feel they are getting good value for their money.

Use design as a sales tool— Design is one area that can set your company apart from the rest. First, find out what the customer needs, and how much he's willing and able to spend. Then you can create a unique design that considers wants, needs and costs. Your professionalism and the quality of your work will sell itself.

Your sales team needs confidence in the company's ability to deliver what the prospects are being promised. Your salespeople should take pride in the company they represent and the integrity of company management. That builds confidence, not only with customers, but with those you work with as well.

Preparing Floor Plans

A good salesperson needs to have enough artistic ability to draw a simple floor plan and elevation view. You need to be able to show the homeowner in some detail what the finished project will look like. Too often, salespeople either lack basic drafting skills or don't take the time to prepare a well-drawn floor plan. They may sketch something out on a piece of paper or scratch pad and say to the customer, "See, that's what I've been talking about." Usually, that's not enough.

A salesperson who can help the homeowner visualize the completed job has a much better chance of closing the sale. You should be able to show them a drawing or floor plan and say, "This is what it's going to look like." When the homeowners can "see" what they're getting, they gain confidence in your ability to do the job they want. Not only does a well-drawn floor plan contribute to making the sale, many times it's the floor plan that clinches the sale!

Even someone who "can't draw" can learn to draft floor plans and elevation views. Many community colleges offer architectural drawing class. If you have salespeople who need some help in this area, suggest that they enroll in the appropriate class.

Figure 2-6 shows a well-prepared floor plan and elevation for a remodeling project. In this case, the salesman drew an existing floor plan as well as a floor plan for the new addition on transparent drafting paper. By placing the existing floor plan (A) over the new floor plan (B) and holding both up to the light, the customer can see exactly how the new addition would fit with the existing house. He also included a drawing of the proposed finished exterior (C). It's no surprise that he made the sale.

Follow-Up

Sales can't always be completed in one call. Follow-up plays an important part in every good salesperson's plan. Even if you're turned down at the initial meeting, the potential is still there for a sale. Always follow a sales call with a letter or phone call to thank the customer for taking the time to meet with you. Try to find out in your contact what the customer's objections are and have answers prepared that will overcome the objection.

Arrange a second call or call-back. Reinforce what was agreed on in the first meeting. Then continue from that point to overcome the customer's reservations and close the sale. *Don't let leads go after one call.* Always follow up with two, three or more.

J. Douglas Edwards, a noted authority on selling, did a study on leading salespeople. He found that the best "closers," those with the highest income, averaged their greatest number of closes on their *fifth attempt.*

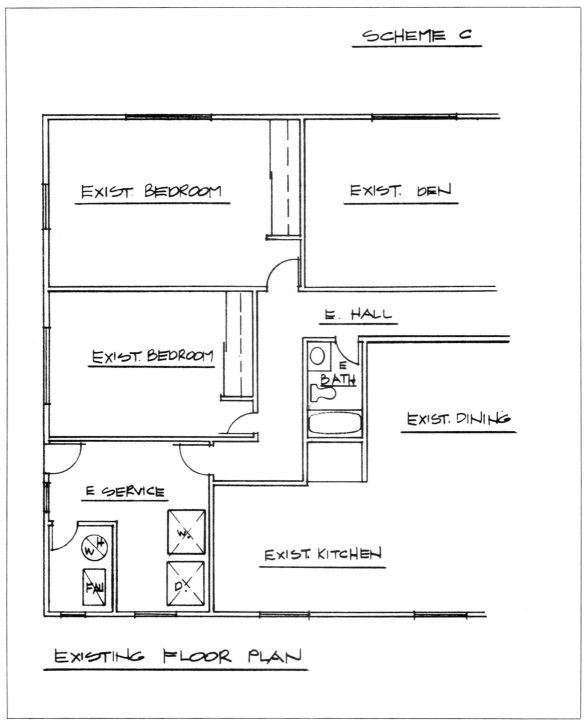

Floor plans and elevation drawn by salesperson
Figure 2-6A

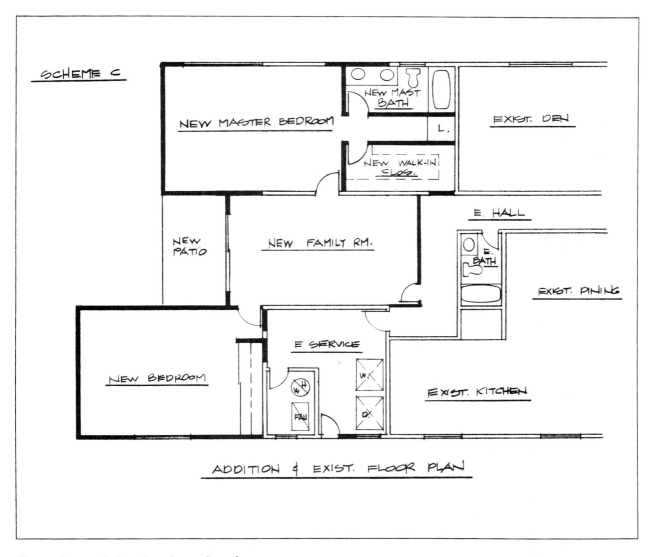

Floor plans and elevation drawn by salesperson
Figure 2-6B

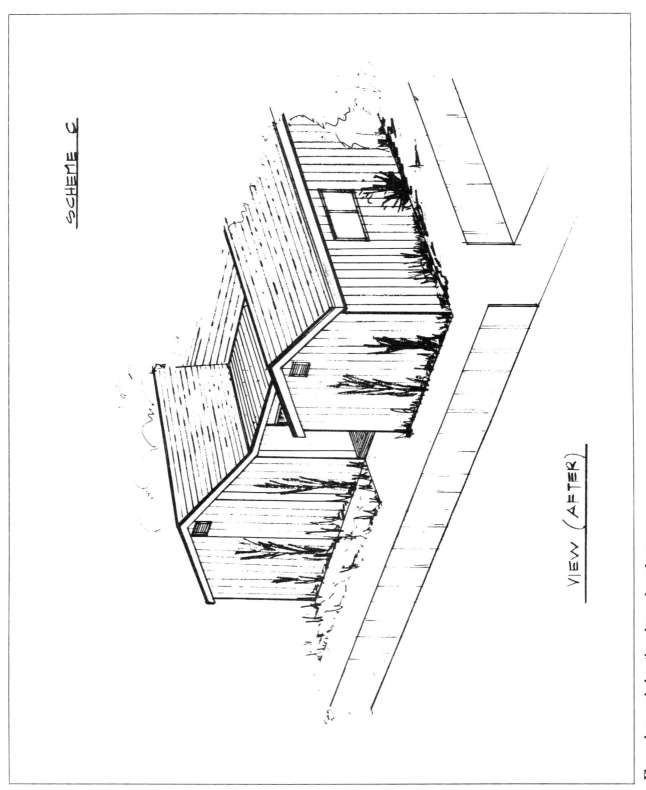

Floor plans and elevation drawn by salesperson
Figure 2-6C

"One-call selling" can be very high-pressure selling. This is especially true with the customer who is afraid to say "yes." Never pressure a customer into an agreement. They should be relaxed and comfortable with the agreement. You want satisfied customers, not highly-pressured victims.

Learn to Listen

Perhaps one of the biggest barriers to effective salesmanship is the failure to listen. We're all guilty of it. First of all, listening is a courtesy you owe your client. But it's more than that. Being a good listener will *help you make the sale.* If you have listened carefully, you can be responsive to the prospect's needs and ideas when it's your turn to talk. You can address his specific concerns. And there's one more advantage: The client will be more inclined to give *you* an uninterrupted audience once he's had his opportunity to tell you what he wants.

Don't interrupt clients to present your viewpoint, even if their request is outrageous, demanding, or not economically sound. Hear them out. Chances are, somewhere in their statement will be one or more points to which you can respond favorably when it's your turn to speak.

Studies have shown that most people (including you) remember only about half of what they hear, even when their memory is tested immediately after listening to someone. This is true even when they thought they were hanging on every spoken word.

Good listening requires a conscious effort. Your prospective client can't pet the dog, play with the children, read a magazine, peek at the TV, and listen to your sales pitch as well. We're all in the habit of listening with only one ear (and paying attention with one-half of our brain). That's human nature. But when it's time for your presentation, you need to give and get undivided attention.

On a sales call, listen carefully to learn what the customer really wants. Maintain good eye contact. Pay close attention. Stay alert. You'll be surprised at how well your attention is reciprocated.

Some of the barriers to good listening are conscious actions. Others are set up unconsciously. What we're thinking about interferes with our ability to hear what other people are saying. Here are some suggestions that will help you develop better listening skills.

• In normal conversation, most of us speak before we think. We haven't made a conscientious effort to think out what we want to say. Often our responses aren't really relevant to what was just said. As a salesman, you must work hard to listen and understand what your customers are trying to convey to you — even if they're not expressing themselves clearly.

• We all have a lot on our minds at any given time. If we don't focus our thoughts, we aren't going to get all the messages transmitted. When you get to a customer's door, silently tell your mind to "turn off" to your problems and give full attention to theirs.

• We like to hear ourselves talk, particularly if the other person isn't interesting. Often we disregard information that doesn't fit our preconceived ideas. Don't fall into this habit — or your customer may feel the same way about what *you* say.

• When you interrupt someone too often, you give the impression that what they're saying isn't important. Even if you feel that way, don't let your customers know it. Be patient and hear them out.

• It's easy to get distracted and lose your concentration. Don't *you* get involved with petting the dog or playing with the children. Give your complete attention to the customer. After all, that's why you're there.

• Too often we jump to conclusions before we've heard the other person out. Don't end up telling the customers what you're going to do for them before you find out what they want or need.

Being a good listener is part of making a good sales presentation. Poor listeners don't make good salesmen. What your customer says is important! Remember, good listeners:

• Give full attention.

• Don't interrupt.

• Don't mentally blank out what they consider irrelevant or unimportant.

• Don't permit distractions.

• Let the customer have the last word.

Good listening starts at the front door and ends only when your car is out of the driveway.

Organize Your Presentation

Professionalism is the key to making a sale. The professional salesperson always makes an organized step-by-step presentation, without "hard sell." Have a smooth, flowing presentation that reflects your professional ability.

Some time during the presentation, make a trial close. For example, "If I could get the whole job done without increasing your payment more than $150 a month, would you authorize me to get started?" The best time to make a trial close is when your prospects are most impressed, usually after you've shown them the sketch of their new kitchen or bathroom or family room. But there are many opportunities to make a trial close. Take advantage of them. If the customer has said "yes" to most of your points throughout the presentation, try closing. Don't be surprised if they say "yes" again.

Even if they say "no," turn it to your advantage. Listen carefully to *why* they say no, or what their objections are. As you resume your presentation, work on their objections so you can overcome their resistance before you come to your final close.

Remember, part of the close comes at every step in the presentation. Try to get a "yes" at each step, instead of waiting until the end. You may still get a "no," but it'll be much easier to pinpoint the customer's objections when you know what he's already agreed to.

Thirty Seconds to Close

Here are the steps that make up an unpressured, logical, organized sales presentation. If you can get a "yes" at each step, the close is automatic. The *longest* time you should devote to each step in the selling sequence is in parentheses.

1) Introduction (10 minutes)

2) Verification (15 minutes)

3) Qualification (5 minutes)

4) Design (30 minutes for multi-trade jobs)

5) Survey forms (30 minutes)

6) Cost breakdown (30 minutes)

7) *Closing (30 seconds)*

8) Financing (1 hour)

9) Writing the contract (1 hour)

That's right: closing — thirty seconds! If you have a "yes" at every step in your presentation, that's all it takes.

Be sure, when you make the presentation, that you have all parties present. If someone who has a voice in the project isn't there, chances are you won't be able to close the sale. If someone is absent, you'll have to repeat the whole presentation. There are two big disadvantages to this. First, the second presentation gives the prospects a chance to disagree with each other, as well as with your suggestions. Second, the person who was there during the first presentation has had time to think about it and develop a list of questions and objections to bring up at the second meeting.

Spell It Out

Remember, you haven't got a sale until it's down in writing. And here's some more advice that we had to learn the hard way. Not only do you write down *what you are going to do,* you also put in writing *what you aren't going to do!*

Why? In most cases, the customer has a pretty specific idea of what he wants before he gives you a call. You're probably not the first contractor to bid the job. Maybe the previous contractor agreed to do something the customer wanted, or made some suggestion about how something could be done differently. Now you come in. Let's say that for economic or design reasons, or perhaps because of the building code, you indicate that this "something" isn't possible. You explain it to the homeowners, and they understand why it can't be done.

But the mind can play tricks. When it comes time to actually do the work, the homeowner may confuse what the other contractor agreed to do with what you agreed to do. He *thinks* you're going to paint the rest of the living room to match the addition, even if you explained you weren't going to do it.

If you didn't spell it out in the contract, you could be in for trouble. You'll lose more of these arguments than you win. And even when you win an argument like this, you lose. The homeowner thinks he's been swindled. He'll question you at every point until the project is completed. These three words are the cause of most problems between a homeowner and a contractor: "But, we agreed . . . ." *Put everything in writing*, especially change orders, and have the homeowners sign a copy of each agreement and change.

Making the Presentation

Here's a plan that will help organize your presentations and establish the needs of each customer. When your customers *approve* the contract, they'll know that what they're receiving has been customized to meet their special interests.

I.   Introduction— The introduction begins with the initial customer contact, whether it's in person or over the phone. Regardless of how the contact is made, it's your job to convince the customer, by actions and words, that your company *can* and *will* do what you say it can. Introduce potential customers to the type and quality of work your company offers. Tell them how long you've been in business. If you've won awards, let them know. Have three or four names of customers who have agreed to let you use them as referrals. (Always ask satisfied customers if you can use their names as referrals for future clients. If you've done a good job, they'll be proud of the project and happy to show it off.)

Show them before-and-after pictures of completed projects, or floor plans and designs that you've used. If the presentation is at your office, have small displays of the materials you use. Stress the quality and *economy* of the materials. "This floor covering is so good, it's worth two dollars more per square yard than I would be charging you." (Don't tell them how much it is, but how much they would be saving!)

The introduction may take some extra time. Catch the interest of your prospects and look for initial objections. Stay with them until you have a "yes" — an acknowledgement that they're interested in your company doing the job.

II.   Verification— Visit the job site. Listen carefully to the customer. *Let them tell you what they want.* Check the site. Look at both sides of the wall and mentally try to look through the wall. What electrical or plumbing lines will have to be moved? Are there any heating pipes, ducts or drains that will require extra labor to remove and replace? You can't be too careful, particularly in older homes.

Sometimes the plans for older homes are on file at the City Building Department or Village Hall. Review any plans you can locate before quoting the job. Try to find the problems before work starts, and make sure that what the customer wants is possible — *before* you make a bid. A major error now will make the difference between a profit and a loss on most jobs.

III.   Qualification— This is where plans and budgets must be reconciled. After finding out how much the customer is willing to spend, make sure the job they want done is within their budget. Can you move this wall and replace that window for this price?

IV.   Design— Design is one of the most important and exciting parts of the sales presentation for most homeowners. It's what makes your company the first choice in the eyes of your customer. A professional remodeling salesperson designs the "right" job for each customer — the perfect blend of what's affordable, needed, wanted, and profitable for your company.

The floor plan in Figure 2-7 was used in making a sales presentation in a home. Normally, the floor plan would be roughed in on the grid which is part of the survey form (Figure 2-8). Draw it to either 1/4 or 1/2 inch per foot scale. Circle your choice of scale at the top of the grid. If the homeowner likes the tentative plan, then you can go ahead and complete the estimate and cost breakdown (Figure 2-9).

In some cases the floor plan drawn on the grid might be all that's required for homeowner approval. Other homeowners may want a more complete and detailed plan. You should draw a plan like that back at your office and then submit it for final approval with the contract.

V.   Survey form— Figure 2-8 shows a survey form developed by a remodeling pioneer. It's been refined and polished over the years to cover the many steps which *must* be considered when pricing most remodeling jobs.

There are sixteen major construction areas involved in remodeling. Any or all of them may be part of your particular remodeling project. In this example, the homeowner wants to add a bedroom and bath. The salesman has made a total survey and a quotation, as required, in every category except miscellaneous.

The survey form describes exactly what you're going to do. It also gives you a basis for pricing each labor and material unit in the project. What you aren't going to do should be listed as an exclusion in the contract. In the example, the salesman has noted one exclusion on the survey form. Under decorating and painting, *sandblasting* has been excluded.

We put two grids on the survey form. One is for the new floor plan and the other, on the back, can be used for an elevation or to sketch out the existing floor plan for a before-and-after drawing.

It's hard to remember everything that must be covered during the sales presentation. The survey form will help you remember what might be overlooked and will eliminate many errors. It also makes you look more professional. Once the survey form is properly filled out, preparing the materials estimate and cost breakdown is a relatively simple task.

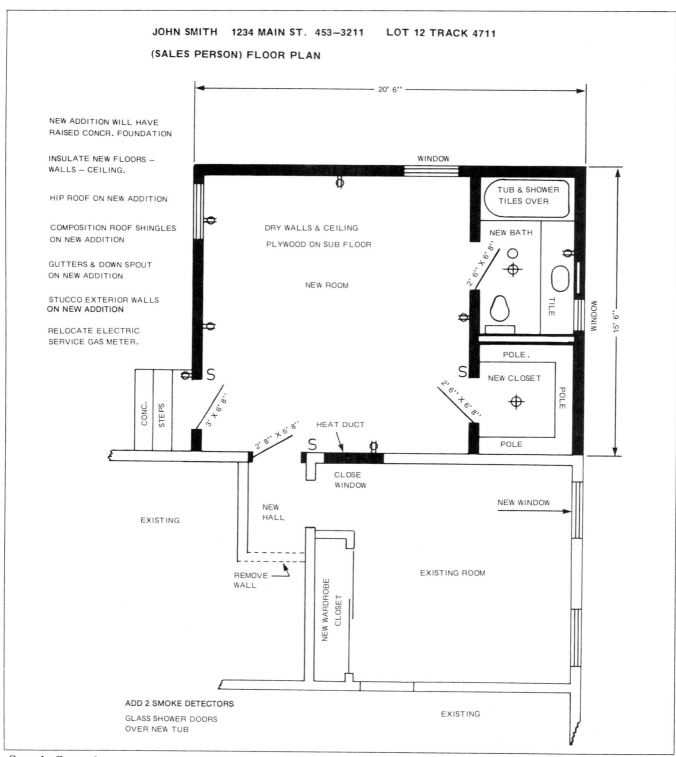

Sample floor plan
Figure 2-7

Job Survey

Appt. Arranged
By: __R.H.__   __25 NOV__   19 __88__

For: Name M/M __JOHN SMITH__   Individual ☐

Address __1234 MAIN ST.__

City __HOMETOWN , USA__   Zip __43421__

Job Location __SAME__

Phone __451-3211__   __655-1843__
         Home   Business   ☑ A.M.

Appointment Date __28 NOV__   __10__   ☐ P.M.

MB: _____

NP	DR CD	TV RD	REF WL	TEL DIR	DR ML	OTHER
						REF

OFFICE __MAIN__
SALES MGR. __D.L.__
COUNSELOR __B.P.__

Remarks __WANTS EARLY COMPLETION DATES.__
__WILL FINANCE THRU OWN BANK.__
__1 BEDROOM — 1 BATH__

☐ Residential   ☑ Addition   ☐ Bathroom
☐ Commercial   ☐ Remodeling   ☐ Kitchen
☐ Industrial   ☐ _____   ☐ _____
☐ _____   ☐ _____   ☐ _____

PREPARATION
1. ☑ Plans _____
2. ☐ Engineering _____
2. ☐ Soil Test _____
3. ☑ Building Permit/Plan Check _____
4. ☐ Survey _____
4. ☐ Variance _____
5. ☑ Bond Disbursement Escrow _____
6. ☑ Blueprints _____
7. ☐ Scaffolding & Staging _____
7. ☐ Temporary Street Block _____
8. ☐ Temporary Power, Gas, Water _____
9. ☐ Temporary Toilet _____
   ☐ _____

DEMOLITION
17. ☑ Interior Demolition _____
17. ☐ Shoring Required _____
18. ☑ Exterior Demolition _____
18. ☑ Site Clearance _____
18. ☐ Remove Slab – Eaves _____
18. ☑ Strip Stucco _____
18. ☑ Remove Wall Section _____
18. ☑ Tree Removal _____
20. ☐ Equipment Rental _____

RELOCATION
19. ☐ Planting Shrubs & Trees _____
55. ☑ Electric Service _____
57. ☑ Electric Outlets _____
60. ☐ Sewer Lines _____
61. ☑ Gas Meter _____
61. ☐ Water Lines _____
62. ☐ Septic System _____
65. ☐ Heat ducts _____
    ☐ _____

ALLOWANCES
10. ☑ Appliances: By Owner (By Contractor)
10. ☑ Appliance Total Allowance $ __1,000 BATH FIXTURES__
    ☐ Cook Tops E G – Ovens E G _____
    Hood – Dishwasher – Disposal _____
    Compactor – Refrigerator IM _____
    Washer – Dryer E G – Electronic Oven ___
    ☐ Other: _____
11. ☑ Bathroom Accessories __$100.00__
12. ☑ Flooring # ____ sq. yds. __200.00 INSTALLED__
13. ☑ Hardware Finish __200.00__

14. ☑ Electrical Fixtures # ___200.00___
15. ☐ Paneling & Trim # sheets _____
16. ☐ Other: _____
16. ☐ _____
16. ☐ _____

FOUNDATIONS – CONCRETE & MASONRY
21. ☑ Excavate and Grade _____
22. ☑ Concrete Foundations _____
22. ☐ Foundation Slab Construction _____
22. ☐ 1 Story Slab _____ 2 Story Slab _____
22. ☑ Foundation Raised Floor – Vents __2__
22. ☑ 1 Story Raised _____ 2 Story Raised ___
22. ☑ Concrete Piers _____ Crawl Hole __1__
22. ☐ Underpin Foundation _____
22. ☐ Foundation for Fireplace – Steel _____
22. ☐ Concrete Footings – Other _____
23. ☐ Concrete Slab for Room: (Size)_____
23. ☐ Concrete Flatwork: (Size) _____
23. ☐ Flashings _____
24. ☐ Concrete Porch: (Size)_____
24. ☑ Concrete Steps: (Width) __5'__ (#) __3__
25. ☐ Concrete Driveway: _____
25. ☐ Concrete Apron – Sidewalks _____
25. ☐ Concrete Curbs _____ ft. _____
26. ☐ Concrete Walls – Waterproofing _____
26. ☐ Concrete Retaining Walls _____
26. ☐ Concrete Planter _____ ft _____
27. ☐ Concrete Cutting _____
28. ☑ Concrete Pumping _____
28. ☐ Concrete Color: – Texture _____
29. ☐ Vapor Barrier _____
29. ☐ Sand _____ Fill _____
30. ☐ Concrete Reinf.: Steel Rods Wire Mesh ___
31. ☐ Masonry _____
31. ☐ Masonry Fireplace_____
31. ☐ Fireplace: Brick _____ Stone Veneer ___
31. ☐ Fireplace: Half _____ Full Height ___
31. ☐ Fireplace Raised Hearth: _____
31. ☐ Fireplace: Width _____ Ft. Overall ___
31. ☐ Fireplace: Wall ____ Corner _____
31. ☐ Fireplace: Standard 30'' Firebox _____
31. ☐ Chimney Height: Standard – Other _____
32. ☐ Masonry Repairs: _____
32. ☐ Veneer Wall: Brick ____ Stone ___ ft. __
32. ☐ Flatwork: Brick _____ Stone _____

Job survey form
Figure 2-8

32 ☐ Precast Stone: _____ Slate _____
32 ☐ Concrete Block: _____
32 ☐ Concrete Cap _____ Coping _____
33 ☐ Asphalt Paving _____
33 ☐ Area Size _____
33 ☐ Repairs: _____
_____

MATERIALS & LUMBER
34 ☑ Lumber Rough _____
34 ☑ Joist & Girders _____
34 ☑ Sub Floor - Plyscore _____
34 ☐ T & G Floor on Girders _____
34 ☑ Exterior Walls _____
34 ☐ Exterior Walls: (Alterations) _____
34 ☑ Interior Walls _____
34 ☑ Interior Walls: (Alterations) _____
34 ☑ Drop Header _____ Flush Header ✓ _____
34 ☑ Wall Sheathing _____
34 ☑ Ceiling Joists _____ Trusses _____
34 ☑ Roof Style: _____ Sheathing _____
34 ☑ Gable _____ Hip ✓ Shed _____
34 ☐ Flat _____ Exp. Beams _____
34 ☐ Mansard _____ Parapet _____
34 ☐ Shoring _____ Bracing _____
34 ☐ Furring: _____
34 ☐ Knee Walls _____ Columns ___ ft. _____
34 ☑ Closets: _____ 1
34 ☑ Trucking & Delivery _____
34 ☐ Extra Lumber _____
35 ☑ Rough Hardware _____
36 ☑ Jambs: Int. # 3 Ext. # 1
36 ☐ Pocket Sliders: # _____
36 ☑ Closet Jambs & Frames # 1
37 ☑ WINDOWS: TOTAL # 2
37 ☑ Wood # 2 Alum. # _____ Steel # _____
37 ☐ In Existing Walls: # _____
37 ☑ New Opening ✓ Existing Opening _____
37 ☑ In New Walls: # 2
37 ☑ Window Sizes: _____ X _____ 3' x 5'
37 ☐ _____ X _____
37 ☑ Style: Double Hung ✓ Side Slide _____
37 ☐ Casement Louver Transom _____
37 ☐ Obscure Glass: _____
37 ☐ Special Window: _____
37 ☐ Prime Windows # _____
37 ☐ Window Inserts # _____
37 ☐ Relocate Customer's Window # _____
38 ☑ Window Screens on: Old # ___ New # 4
38 ☐ Door Screens on: Old # ___ New # _____
38 ☐ Screen Wall Enclosure: _____ lin. ft. _____
38 ☐ Full Height _____ Other _____
38 ☐ Glassene (plastic) Wall: _____ lin. ft. _____
39 ☑ DOORS: WOOD: INT.-EXT. # 2
39 ☑ HC Slab ___ SC Slab ✓ Panel _____
39 ☐ Special Doors: _____
39 ☐ _____
39 ☐ Int. # _____ X _____
39 ☐ Int. # _____ X _____
39 ☐ Ext. # 1 X _____ 2'8" x 6'8"
39 ☐ Ext. # _____ X _____
39 ☐ Relocate Customer's Door: # _____
40 ☐ DOORS – GARAGE:
40 ☐ Wood - Aluminum - Other _____
40 ☐ Single _____ Double _____
40 ☐ Overhead 1 pc. – Sectional _____
41 ☑ DOORS – CLOSET AND MISC. # 1
41 ☑ Bi-Pass ✓ Bi-Fold _____
41 ☐ Hinged _____ Pocket _____
41 ☐ Special Doors: _____
42 ☐ Doors – Sliding Glass Patio # _____
42 ☐ _____ X _____
43 ☑ Doors – Shower & Tub Enclosure: _____
43 ☑ Tub: Glass ___ Plastic ✓ _____
43 ☐ Shower: Glass ___ Plastic _____
43 ☐ Neo Angle: _____
44 ☑ INSULATION: _____
44 ☑ Walls _____ Ceilings ✓ Of New 1 FLOOR
44 ☐ Walls _____ Ceilings _____ Of Existing _____
44 ☐ Roof _____ New _____ Existing _____

44 ☑ Roof _____
44 ☑ Batts ✓ Blown _____ Sheet _____
45 ☑ LUMBER FINISH: _____
45 ☑ Base STREAMLINED
45 ☑ Case _____
45 ☐ Ceiling Mouldings _____
45 ☐ Wainscote _____
45 ☑ Closet Shelves and Poles _____
45 ☑ Closet Pole: Wood _____ Metal ✓
45 ☐ Repairs _____
46 ☐ HARDWARE FINISH: See #13 Allow.
46 ☑ Locksets # 3
46 ☐ Passage Sets # _____
47 ☐ Mill Runs – Special: _____
47 ☐ Railings: Wood _____
48 ☐ SIDING & DECKING MAT'LS, EXTERIOR _____
48 ☐ Type _____
48 ☐ Area _____
49 ☐ Stairways _____
49 ☐ Wood _____ Steel _____
49 ☐ Open Riser _____ Solid Riser _____
50 ☐ Structural Steel _____ Erection _____
50 ☐ Beams _____ Columns _____ Trusses _____
50 ☐ Hot Water Tank Enclosure, Metal _____

CARPENTRY LABOR
51 ☑ Rough Carpentry _____
51 ☐ _____
51 ☑ Patching ✓ Repairing _____ Relocating ✓
52 ☐ Carpentry Siding - Decking (Exterior) _____
53 ☑ Cabinetry Installation _____
53 ☐ Custom Work _____
53 ☐ _____
54 ☑ Finish Trim _____
54 ☐ Install Paneling: By Contractor ___ By Owner _____

ELECTRICAL
55 ☑ Standard Wiring to Existing Service _____
55 ☐ Service Change _____
55 ☐ By Contractor _____ By Owner _____
55 ☑ Relocate Service _____
55 ☐ Enlarge Service: ___ AMP _____
55 ☐ Service to Detached Building _____ ft. _____
55 ☑ Above Ground _____ Underground _____
56 ☐ CIRCUITS: ADDITIONAL _____
56 ☑ 220 V. Outlets _____
56 ☑ Add # _____ Relocate # _____
56 ☑ Home Run 1 Panel _____
56 ☐ Raceway _____ Pole or Mast _____
56 ☐ Overhead Lines _____ Underground Lines _____
57 ☐ TOTAL OUTLETS # _____
57 ☑ Switches: _____ Add # 2 Relocate # _____
57 ☐ 3-Way Switches: ___ Add # ___ Relocate # _____
57 ☐ Dimmer Switches: ___ Add # ___ Relocate # _____
57 ☑ Light Outlets: _____ Add # 4 Relocate # _____
57 ☑ Duplex Plugs: _____ Add # 6 Relocate # _____
57 ☐ Doorbutton: _____ Add # ___ Relocate # _____
57 ☐ Doorbell _____ Chimes _____ Intercom _____
57 ☑ Telephone Jack # 1 TV Outlet # 1
57 ☐ Disposal – Dishwasher Hookup _____
57 ☐ Range Hood – Trash Compactor Hookup _____
57 ☐ Electrical Kills # _____ Repairs # _____
57 ☐ Yard Lights _____ Flush Lights _____
58 ☐ ELECTRIC HEATERS – ELECTRIC FANS _____
58 ☑ Wall Heater # _____
58 ☑ Ceiling Bath Exhaust Fan _____
58 ☐ Ceiling Bath Heater _____
58 ☐ Ceiling Cable Heat # _____ of Rooms _____
58 ☐ Base Board Heaters _____
58 ☐ _____
PLUMBING
59 ☑ TOTAL FIXTURES # 3
59 ☑ Fixtures: White ✓ Color _____
59 ☐ New Location _____ Replacement _____
59 ☐ Toilet: Standard Two-Piece _____
59 ☑ Toilet: One-Piece ✓ Wall-Hung _____
59 ☐ _____
59 ☐ Bidet _____
59 ☐ Urinal: Floor Model _____ Wall Model _____

Job survey form
Figure 2-8 (continued)

59 ☑ Lavatory: Wall-Hung ___ Pedestal _____
59 ☑ Pullman Lav: Oval ✓ _____
59 ☑ Tub: Enclosed _____ Open-End _____
59 ☑ Standard Five-Foot ___ Other _____
59 ☐ Tub: Square _____ Other _____
59 ☑ ___ Steel ___ Cast Iron ✓ _____
59 ☑ Shower Over Tub _____
59 ☐ Fibreglass Tub _____
59 ☐ Stall Shower _____
59 ☐ Hot Mop Shower Pan _____
59 ☐ Pre-Cast Shower Pan _____
59 ☐ Fiberglass Stall Shower _____
59 ☐ Pre-Cast Stall Shower _____
59 ☑ Standard Chrome Fittings _____
59 ☑ Standard Two-Handle Control _____
59 ☐ Single-Handle Control _____
59 ☐ Deluxe Fittings: See Allowance #16 _____
59 ☐ Kitchen Sink: One-Part Two-Part Three-Part __
59 ☐ Bar Sink: One-Part Two-Part _____
59 ☐ Cast Iron ___ W C ___ Stainless Steel _____
59 ☐ Water Heater: E G _____ Gallons _____
59 ☐ Laundry Tray — Washing-Machine Standpipe ___
59 ☐ New Location _____ Same Location _____
59 ☐ Hose Bibb — Sprinklers _____
59 ☐ _____
60 ☑ Sewer Tie-in Under House _____ ft. ✓ _____
60 ☐ Sewer Tie-in Outside Foundation ___ ft. ____
60 ☐ Tie-in Waste to Existing Cesspool _____
60 ☐ New Sewer Line Hookup _____ ft. _____
60 ☐ To Front of Lot ___ To Back of Lot _____
60 ☐ Sewer Changed to Cast-Iron _____ ft. ____
60 ☐ Drainage Tile _____
60 ☐ Plumbing Service to Detached Building _____
60 ☐ _____
  ☐ _____

PLUMBING — OTHER
61 ☐ New Water Service _____
61 ☐ New Gas Line: _____
61 ☐ Heating ___ Cooking ___ Dryer _____
61 ☐ Barb-Que ___ Fireplace ___ HWT _____
61 ☐ Change to Deck Type Faucets _____
61 ☐ Sink Replacement: Lower Waters _____
61 ☐ Garbage Disposal Hookup _____
61 ☐ Sink Replacement: Lower Wastes _____
61 ☐ Install Shower Over Existing Tub _____
61 ☐ Water Line to Refrigerator-Ice Maker _____
61 ☐ Dishwasher Hookup _____
61 ☐ For New Sink ___ For Existing Sink _____
61 ☐ Floor Drain: New ___ Existing _____
61 ☑ RELOCATE: _____
61 ☐ Hose Bibb _____ Softener _____
61 ☐ Sprinkler _____ Water Meter _____
61 ☑ Gas Meter ✓ ___ Pool Equipment _____
61 ☐ New Sprinkler Heads # ___ Cap Heads # ___
61 ☐ Repairs _____
61 ☐ Sewer-Water Lines _____
61 ☐ Fire Hose _____
61 ☐ Fire Sprinkler Heads _____
62 ☐ Cesspools — Septic Tank _____
62 ☐ Remove — Cap and Fill _____
  ☐ _____

HEATING AND AIR CONDITIONING
63 ☐ Gas Wall Furnace: Single ___ Dual _____
63 ☐ Existing Wall ___ New Wall _____
63 ☐ Forced Air Furnace _____ BTU's _____
63 ☐ Gravity _____
63 ☐ Air Conditioner: E ___ G ___ Tons _____
63 ☐ Central Unit _____ Window/Wall Unit _____
63 ☐ Heat Pump: _____
64 ☐ Thermostat: Manual Wall Unitrol _____
65 ☐ Duct Work: Relocate # ___ Extend # _____
65 ☑ New Ducts: # ___ 1
  ☐ _____

ROOFING
66 ☑ New Work Only _____
66 ☐ Re-Roof Entire Building _____
66 ☐ Composition: _____
66 ☐ Hot Mop: Cap Sheet; Rock ___ S ___ L ___
66 ☐ Wood Shingles _____

66 ☐ Wood Shakes: Medium ___ Heavy _____
66 ☐ Regular Zone _____ Fire Zone _____
66 ☐ Tile _____
66 ☐ Slate _____
66 ☐ Other: _____
66 ☑ Roof Tie-in _____
67 ☐ Flashing _____
67 ☐ Coping: _____
67 ☐ _____
68 ☐ Patio Roof: Metal _____
68 ☐ Posts # _____
68 ☐ _____
  ☐ _____

WALLS AND CEILINGS
69 ☑ INTERIOR FINISH _____ ✓
69 ☑ Drywall: New Walls ✓ _____
69 ☐ New Ceiling ✓ _____
69 ☐ Drywall: Existing Walls _____
69 ☐ Existing Ceiling _____
69 ☐ Taped _____ Untaped _____
69 ☐ Ceiling Squares _____
70 ☐ Lath & Plaster: Int. Walls _____ sq. yds.
70 ☐ Lath & Plaster: Int. Ceilings _____ sq. yds.
70 ☐ Acoustic Plaster _____
71 ☑ EXTERIOR FINISH _____
71 ☑ Stucco: Walls _____ sq. yds. 50
71 ☐ Stucco Overhang — 2nd Story — Hillside ___
71 ☐ Aluminums _____
71 ☐ Firewall _____
71 ☐ Colorcote Only: ✓ _____
72 ☑ PATCHING: Drywall ✓ Plaster ___ Stucco ✓
72 ☐ _____
73 ☐ Blown Acoustical Ceiling _____ sq. yds.
73 ☐ Area: _____
74 ☐ Ceiling Squares: _____ sq. ft.
74 ☐ Luminous Ceiling _____ sq. ft.
74 ☐ _____
  ☐ _____

CABINETRY
  Measurement is in linear feet of wall coverage
75 ☑ Pullmans (Vanity) _____ lin. ft. 6
75 ☑ Linens _____
76 ☐ Kitchen Cabinets: Base _____ lin. ft. ___
76 ☐ Kitchen Cabinets: Upper _____ lin. ft. ___
76 ☐ Kitchen Cabinets: Full-Length _____ lin. ft.
76 ☐ Kitchen Cabinets: _____
76 ☐ _____
76 ☑ Custom Made _____ Modular ✓ ___
76 ☑ Door Style: 3/8 Lip ✓ Flat ___ Raised ___
76 ☐ Door Style: _____
76 ☐ Type of Wood Veneer _____
76 ☑ Natural Finish Stained Finish Unfinished ✓
76 ☐ _____
77 ☐ Backs: Upper ___ Lower ___ Full _____
77 ☐ Soffit: Existing _____ New _____
78 ☑ Wardrobes: _____ lin. ft. 8
78 ☐ _____

FINISHING
79 ☑ CERAMIC TILE _____
79 ☐ Kitchen _____ Bathroom _____
79 ☑ Counter Tops: _____ lin. ft. 6
79 ☑ Full-Splash or _____ Inch Splash 10"
79 ☐ Side-Splash ___ Right ___ Left ___
79 ☑ Tub-Splash _____ ft. above tub 5'
79 ☐ Shower Walls: _____ ft. above floor ___
79 ☐ Shower Floor: _____ Shower Jambs _____
79 ☐ Other: _____
80 ☐ PLASTIC LAMINATE — FORMICA STYLE ___
80 ☐ Kitchen _____ Bathroom _____
80 ☐ Counter Tops: _____ lin. ft. ___
80 ☐ Full-Splash: _____ Inch Splash _____
80 ☐ Cove Back _____ Butt Back _____
81 ☐ Marlite Tub-Splash: _____ ft. over tub ___
81 ☐ Marlite Walls: _____
81 ☐ Marlite Other: _____
82 ☐ MIRRORS: SIZE _____
82 ☐ Regular Plate ___ Antique Plate _____
83 ☐ Fencing: _____ lin. ft. _____ ft. ht. ___

Job survey form
Figure 2-8 (continued)

83 ☐ Chain-Link, — Wood, — _____
83 ☐ Gates # _____ Size: _____
83 ☑ **FINISH FLOORING** _____
84 ☐ Flooring Area: _NEW BEDROOM_____
84 ☐ By Owner ✔ By Contractor _____
84 ☐ Remove Existing: _____
84 ☐ Install Underlayment _____
84 ☐ Repair Only: _____
84 ☑ Floor Material: See Allowances #12 _BATHROOM_
84 ☐ Coving: _____
84 ☐ Hardwood Floors: Area _____
84 ☐ Parquet — Other: _____
84 ☐ Refinish Existing Hardwood Floors _____
84 ☐ Terrazzo _____
84 ☐ Diatto _____
84 ☐ Steps: # _____ Landings: # _____
85 ☐ Breakfast Nook: _____
86 ☐ Ornamental Iron: See Allowances #16 _____
86 ☐ Railings — Standard: _____ lin. ft. _____
86 ☐ Columns — Standard ____ # _____
86 ☐ Gates: _____
87 ☐ Sheet Metal Vents: # _____ Relocate - New ____
87 ☐ Vent Bath Fan _____ Vent Dryer _____
87 ☐ Vent Oven _____ Vent Hood _____
87 ☐ Vent HWT _____ Vent Metal Fireplace _____
87 ☐ _____
87 ☐ Metal Fireplace: See Allowances #16 _____
87 ☑ Gutters on: Old _____ New ✔ ft. _50'_____
87 ☑ Downspout: # _1_____ lin. ft. _11'_____
88 ☑ Weatherstripping _____
88 ☐ Doors # _1_____ Windows # _4_____
89 ☑ Cleanup: By Contractor ✔ By Owner _____
89 ☐ Cultured Marble: Area _____
89 ☑ Window Cleaning _____
90 ☐ Other: _____
91 ☐ Describe: _____
91 ☐ House Numbers _____
91 ☐ Doggie Door _____
91 ☐ Drapes _____
91 ☐ Shades _____
91 ☐ Blinds _____
☐ _____

DECORATING AND PAINTING
92 ☑ Sandblast: _____ Exhaust _____
☐ _NOT INCLUDED_____
MISCELLANEOUS
93 ☐ Patching — Floating _____
94 ☐ Pacificote _____
95 ☐ Trim Paint _____
96 ☐ Decorator Materials _____
97 ☐ Supervision _____
98 ☐ Sales Design _____
99 ☐ Overhead Items _____
☐ . _____

NOTES:

Job survey form
Figure 2-8 (continued)

Job survey form
Figure 2-8 (continued)

ESTIMATE AND COST BREAKDOWN

Office_____ S.M._____

_____
Salesman

Owner _____   Date _____

Address _____   City _____ Phone _____

PREPARATION	
1. Plans	$
2. Engineering	$
3. Building Permits, Plan Checks, City Fees	$
4. Survey — Variance	$
5. Control Fee	
6. Lot Book & Blueprints	$
7. Scaffolding & Staging	$
8. Temp Power	$
9. Temp Toilet	$

ALLOWANCES	
10. Appliances	$
11. Bath Accessories	$
12. Flooring sq. yds	$
13. Hardware Finish	$
14. Electrical Fixtures	$
15. Paneling & Trim shts.	$
16. Other	$

DEMOLITION	
17. Interior MD	$
18. Exterior MD	$
19. Tree Removal S M L	$
20. Equipment Rental	$

FOUNDATIONS — CONCRETE & MASONRY	
21. Excavate & Grade	$
22. Concrete Foundations & Piers ft	$
23. Concrete Slab & Flatwork ft	$
24. Concrete Steps, Porches P & S	$
25. Drives, Approaches, Curbs	$
26. Concrete Walls	$
27. Concrete Cutting	$
28. Concrete Pumping	$
29. Vapor Barrier, Sand or Fill	$
30. Reinforcing Steel-Wire Mesh	$
31. Masonry — Fireplaces	$
32. Masonry — Walls, Flatwork, Stone ft.	$
33. Asphalt Paving ft.	$

MATERIALS & LUMBER	
34. Lumber Rough x	$
35. Hardware Rough	$
36. Jambs & Frames	$
37. Window — Sash W A S, Skylights	$
38. Screens & Patio, Enclosures	$
39. Doors — Wood	$
40. Doors — Garage	$
41. Doors — Closet, Misc.	$
42. Doors — Sliding Glass	$
43. Doors — Shower & Tub Enclosure	$
44. Insulation	$
45. Lumber Finish	$
46. Hardware Finish	$
47. Mill Runs — Special	$
48. Siding & Decking Materials	$
49. Stairways W S	$
50. Structural Steel — HWT Enclosure	$

CARPENTRY LABOR	
51. Rough MD	$
52. Siding — Decking MD	$
53. Cabinetry MD	$
54. Finish MD	$
	$
SUBTOTAL $	

ELECTRICAL	
55. Service Change & Relocate	$
56. Circuits, Panels, Raceway, Home Runs	$
57. Electrical Units #	$
58. Electric Heaters, Fans, Smoke Detectors	$

PLUMBING	
59. Plumbing Units & Fixtures #	$
60. Plumbing — Sewer ft.	$
61. Plumbing — Other	$
62. Cesspools — Septic	$

HEATING & A/C	
63. Unit E-G	$
64. Thermostat	$
65. Duct Work	$

ROOFING	
66. Roofing L & M sqs.	$
67. Roofing Extras	$
68. Patio Roof ft.	$

WALLS & CEILINGS	
69. Drywall ft	$
70. Plaster yds.	$
71. Stucco yds.	$
72. Patching	$
73. Blown Acoustical ft.	$
74. Ceiling Squares & Luminous ft	$

CABINETRY	
75. Pullmans	$
76. Kitchen Cabinets	$
77. Custom Work	$
78. Wardrobes	$

FINISHING	
79. Ceramic Tile	$
80. Laminate — Formica	$
81. Marlite — Tile Board	$
82. Mirrors	$
83. Fencing & Gates	$
84. Flooring ft	$
85. Breakfast Nook	$
86. Ornamental Iron & Columns	$
87. Sheet Metal & Gutters, Vents	$
88. Weatherstrip, Waterproofing	$
89. Clean Up lds. & Trash Dump Fees	$
90. Other	$
91. Pickup — Contingency	$

DECORATING	
92. Sandblast sqs.	$
93. Patch	$
94. Labor sqs.	$
95. Trim sqs. extra	$
96. Materials	$

CLOSEOUT	
97. Overhead	$
98. Sales Commission	$
99. Builders Profit	$
100. Contingency Fund	$
COMBINED TOTAL $	

MD = Man Days (Incl. Tax & Insur.)
Concrete: P = Porch, S = Steps
NIC: Not Included

UP = Unit Price (Installed)
Windows/Stairways: W = wood, A = aluminum, S = steel

Estimate and cost breakdown
Figure 2-9

Normally, the only part of the survey form and the estimate and cost breakdown form that the homeowner sees is the floor plan. However, if the homeowners are reluctant to sign the contract because the price seems too high, you could show them the forms to justify the cost estimate. A labor and material cost breakdown may help them understand where their money is going. Giving the homeowner copies, however, isn't recommended. They could use them to get a lower bid from a competitor.

There's a major advantage to using Figure 2-8 and making it part of your contract. The price you quote in the contract covers only the work that's listed on Figure 2-8. If it isn't on Figure 2-8, it isn't part of the job. Here's why that's important. On nearly every job you'll have at least a few costs that couldn't have been anticipated and weren't included in the original estimate. Those should be extra costs for which you get paid extra. They shouldn't come out of your profit.

Here's an example. When excavation started for the job in Figure 2-6, a sewer line from the service porch was discovered running through the area where the new bedroom was to be built. The line had to be relocated at a cost of nearly a thousand dollars. To the contractor, that was clearly an extra cost. To the homeowner, it was just the contractor's bad luck. But absorbing the cost of relocation would have robbed the contractor of nearly his entire profit margin. Did the contractor get paid? In this case he did, thanks to Figure 2-8.

Clearly no sewer line relocation work was shown in the floor plan. However, it *was* shown in item 60 on the job survey form (Figure 2-8). If the remodeler's contract hadn't used the job survey to identify the work included, he may have had to sue to collect for the extra cost, and may not have won in court!

In addition to saving time, minimizing errors and omissions, and preventing costly disputes, the survey form and cost breakdown will serve as a reference during construction.

If you don't already have good forms like these, use ours. There are blank copies in the back of the book. A local printer can reproduce several hundred copies for you at modest cost and bind them into a convenient pad.

VI. Cost breakdown— Because every remodeling project is unique, there are no "average" job costs that make good guides to estimating. You must *know* your material, labor and equipment costs and add the overhead, profit, commissions and contingencies that are appropriate for the work to be done and the competition you have to beat. In our opinion, there's no other way to estimate costs. The estimate and cost breakdown in Figure 2-9 shows what a good bid looks like.

Don't even consider pricing work by the square foot of floor to a customer. It doesn't work. A bid that's based on a cost per square foot of floor invites the homeowner to enlarge or reduce the square footage at the cost quoted. Changes like that can be very expensive, usually much more than the unit cost quoted. We'll explain how to price changes in the chapter on estimating.

Also, avoid pricing each individual item in the job. This can give the homeowner the idea that he can shave costs by buying materials himself or doing some of the work himself:

Customer: "I see you're charging me $89 for the garbage disposer. I saw one advertised the other day for $59.95. I'll pick that one up so you can cut the price by $30.

Maybe I should install that disposer too. I installed one once. It isn't too hard.'' Avoid this problem by keeping the price for each item confidential.

It's best not to develop prices in front of the customer. In fact, some contractors use price codes that only the contractor's staff can use to find the cost of each item in the project.

Your estimates have to be complete, accurate and professional. Your customers must understand that you know your facts and that they can rely on you to be fair. Don't give in to their demand for a price on every single nail, board, and hinge to be used. Stay within the customer's budget, but don't reveal individual prices or offer to shave the price of any particular item. Sometimes that might mean turning down a customer. But that may be better than doing a job at a loss.

When you're ready to give a quote, first give the customers an itemized review of all that they're getting for their money. That makes the price easier to swallow. Don't quote a price until you're sure you're quoting on the exact job that's wanted. Get a ''yes'' at each step in the presentation before asking for the final ''yes.'' If you've had several ''yes'' answers to trial closes during the presentation, the final ''yes'' is easy.

What if you get a ''no?'' One ''no'' wipes out a dozen ''yes'' responses. But don't give up. Restate the reasons why the price is right. Reassure the customer of the kind of quality and value they're going to receive. Mention any awards your company has earned for design or construction. Finally, offer the names of other satisfied customers.

VII. Closing the reluctant customer — We've stressed this throughout the chapter: Closing begins when your sales presentation begins. If the customer says ''yes'' all along, the final and real close is easy. If you've studied what your clients want, if you've prepared a plan that's responsive to their needs and budget, and if you've created a sense of excitement and urgency during the presentation, the final and most important ''yes'' is only a formality.

Most likely, though, there'll be objections along the way and some uncertainty at the end. But every objection has an answer. It's your responsibility to know them all. The key words are *why* and *what. Why* does the customer object? To *what?* Get your customer to state a *specific* objection. When you know what the problem is, you can take immediate steps to remedy it.

You'll hear some objections again and again. Become familiar with them and learn to work around them. Here are some suggestions for dealing with objections. They were developed by J. Douglas Edwards, an authority in selling and salesmanship.

There are many ways to ask a customer to approve a contract. The best way depends on your customer's state of mind. But no matter how you ask the question, whether it's a trial close or final close, ask the question and then *remain silent!* Don't say anything. Wait until the customer answers the question. Because, as Edwards points out, the first person to talk loses!

If you ask a closing question and can't wait for the customer to answer, you'll either answer your own question or worse yet, say something not directly related to the closing question. Then *you* are off the subject and it could take five minutes to bring the customer back to answering the original question.

Here are some examples. We'll identify the moment *you* should stop talking. At that point, the first person to speak *loses.*

The Ben Franklin close: This is a good one to use on customers who can't decide. This is how it goes:

> *"As you know, sir, we have long considered Ben Franklin to be one of our wisest men. Whenever he found himself in a situation such as you are in now, he felt about the same as you. If it was the right thing to do, he wanted to be sure and do it. If it was the wrong thing, he wanted to be sure and avoid it. Isn't that about the way you feel?*
>
> *"Here's what Ben used to do. He would take a sheet of plain paper* (now, you take a piece of plain paper) *and he would draw a line down the middle* (you draw the line down the middle). *On this side he wrote 'yes'* (pointing as you write 'yes' to the left-hand column) *and on the other side he wrote 'no.'*
>
> *"Here,* (pointing to the 'yes' column) *he would list all of the reasons favoring his decision. Here,* (pointing to the 'no' column) *he would list all of the reasons against it. When he was through, he simply compared the columns and his decision was made for him. Why don't we try it and see what happens."*

Now pay attention. The next steps are important. Hand the customer the paper and a pen and say: "Let's see how many reasons we can think of favoring your decision." Give him all the help in the world; "Don't you think this ought to go in?" or "You and your wife particularly liked this." If you're half a salesman, you can plug in twenty or more "yes" reasons.

Then, when you get to the "no" section say: "Now, let's see how many reasons you can think of against it." *Remain silent!* If you feel the urge to talk, excuse yourself and leave the room. Go to your car, the bathroom, or just go out and walk around the house.

As Edwards points out, he has yet to have more than four on the "no" side. Why? Have you ever had prospects write down in their own handwriting all of the reasons they should buy your product? What happens is that after they write down all of the positive reasons, they have trouble thinking of the negative. Starting with the "yes" column makes it hard to switch back to the "no" column. Four is generally the maximum number customers can think of.

All you do now is quickly count the "yes" items out loud — "One, two, three . . . ten, eleven, twelve . . . twenty-three, twenty-four. That's twenty-four on the plus side. Now, let's see what we have on the other side. Hmmm. One, two, three, four . . . the answer is pretty obvious, isn't it? By the way, do I have the correct spelling of your name and the correct address?"

It's a great way to get a decision, but it takes the Ben Franklin validation to make it work.

The call-back close: Edwards agrees that there isn't any good call-back close. But, there's a way to get around that. Most of us, he points out, bow out gracefully when we come up against an "I want to think it over" or "Let us sleep on it" response. We leave and get back to our customer in the next week or so. O.K. so far. Where we get into trouble is when we call back and say, "Did you get a chance to think it over?" *Wrong,* says Edwards.

In a call-back close, it's best not let the customer speak except to acknowledge your "hello." Take control of the conversation immediately. Begin by saying something like, "The last time we met there was something I wanted to tell you." Now, tell him something. It doesn't matter what it is. Say anything. "That picture in your living room really caught my eye.'' Or,''I want to compliment you and your wife on your good taste.'' Say something nice about the the children, the dog, or the landscaping. The point is, you want to disarm the customer. You want his attention on you, or something abstract, not on the decision he or she was making about your proposal.

Then, without giving him a chance to give you his thoughts or comments, continue by saying, ''Let me just briefly review the things we talked about before . . . .'' Give him the *whole presentation* all over again. That's right, the whole presentation. However, as you cover each point this time, don't wait for a response or agreement. Speak for the customer.

You do this by bringing the previous presentation into the present presentation and saying, ''As you remember . . . You will recall . . . We agreed to this . . . .'' Give him the whole presentation, then go into your normal closing sequence. The one thing you don't do, is *ask him if he thought it over.* Chances are he did, and he has a big fat objection!

Edwards calls the next two closes his $10,000 closes. Master these, he says, and your income should increase by $10,000 a year.

The final objection close: More often than not, a customer responds with an objection, rather than a ''no,'' when you offer your closing statement. That's right, an *objection.* You can answer an objection, but here's the trap. Unless you make the customer's first objection his last, he'll bring up another, and another, and another.

To eliminate this problem, Edwards suggests the following:

    1) Hear him out.
    2) Sell him his objection.
    3) Confirm the objection.
    4) Question it.
    5) Answer it.
    6) Confirm the answer.
    7) Close.

Listen to the objection. Say nothing. What you want to do is let the customer hook himself. (This applies throughout the presentation as well as the close.)

After the customer is through talking, *sell him his objection.* You do this by expanding on it, showing that you take the objection seriously. At the same time, appear discouraged. (To be a good salesperson, you'll have to learn how to do some acting.) You say, ''You're right. A picture window overlooking the garden isn't right. Two casement windows would provide the same view and much better ventilation on warm afternoons . . .''

Continue to look defeated. ''Is that the only thing standing between us and this beautiful new room addition — the windows?'' Again, don't talk! Just wait. Keep waiting. And, keep waiting. It may seem like an eternity, but let the customer respond first.

If he says "yes", you're in. Switch the windows and close the sale.

But if he doesn't, what then? Let the customer do the talking. One of several things will come out:

- You'll find out if his first objection was his real objection.

- If he explains his objection in more detail, you can answer it again using the same procedure. Then continue with your close. If you can't answer an objection, the sale is as good as lost.

- In the process of explaining it, the objection may no longer makes sense to your prospect. Most of us have seen this happen or even had it happen to us. When the customer realizes this, you've got the sale.

The "I'll think it over" objection: This is probably the most common excuse offered to delay closing a sale. From cars to appliances, from furnishings to remodeling, it's the one objection all salesmen face, and the most difficult one to deal with.

The problem with the "I'll think it over" objection is that there's nothing specific you can counter it with. It's too vague. What you have to do is *convert it into an objection you can deal with.*

When you get this kind of response from a customer, your answer (according to Edwards) should be: "That's fine, folks. I'm sure you wouldn't waste your time thinking it over unless you're really interested. I doubt if you're saying this just to get rid of me. May I assume you'll give it careful consideration?"

What happens? The customer thinks he's off the hook. You stand up. If you stand up, it looks like you're going to go. The customer agrees that he'll give it careful consideration. Now, are you going to leave and say, "I'll get back to you tomorrow?" No way!

You know there's an objection, but you don't know what it is. "I'll think it over" isn't specific enough. As you put your papers in your briefcase, try to get a specific objection. The customer still thinks he's off the hook, and his guard is down. Ask him, "Just what phase of this project is it you want to think over? Is it this? Is it that?" Continue to shuffle your papers as though you're leaving, but keep up the questions.

If you maintain control over the situation, eventually he'll respond either through desperation or because you've touched on his objection. When he says "Yes, that's it," you finally have the objection. And, once you have that, you know you can close.

Remember, though, you must control the situation. There is one spot in this conversation where, if you stop to breathe, you can lose the whole sale. It's when you say, "What phase of the project is it you want to think over?" If you let him take over he may say, "The whole thing." Then . . . well, there goes the trip to Hawaii!

Just don't let the customer in. Keep offering questions and shuffling papers until you hit on a *specific* objection. When you get it, nine times out of ten, you'll walk away with a sale.

There is a second way to meet the "I'll think it over" response when you sense that there's something the husband and wife want to discuss privately. Excuse yourself and say, "Let me measure the patio wall again," or "I want to get a brochure from my car."

You can use anything as an excuse as long as you leave the house, right now. Even if it's midnight! Go to your car, get a flashlight. Walk around the house and shine the flashlight here and there, stall for a minute, and then go in.

The key thing is to stay out just long enough for them to discuss whatever it is they want to discuss. It's probably going to be an objection. And, when you have a specific objection that you can discuss together, the door is open for a sale.

The final step is to ask your customers to *approve* the contract. You don't ask them to "sign" the contract. Most of us have learned to avoid signing anything until we are absolutely sure that the benefits outweigh the responsibilities. You don't want to give the customer the opportunity to question anything they may still have reservations about. So, ask them to "approve" it or "O.K." it . . . anything but sign. Remember, selling is part acting, part presenting the facts, *and* part psychology.

VIII.   Writing the contract— When you quote a price to a homeowner, it should be based on a specific completion date. All bids are subject to the owner's and your acceptance at that particular time. You can't give a price and leave it open for six months.

That's also a good closing argument. When homeowners are reluctant to make a commitment and want to think it over, give them reasons why they must "buy now." One of the best and most commonly used reasons is that labor and material costs *can and will* change. Therefore, you must have agreement by an established date to guarantee the quoted price.

Be sure your bid is complete, including overhead, contingency and profit. Your profit is the whole reason for doing the job. Don't forget it. Your contract has to be accurate, specific, and written in terms your prospect is going to understand. It should also:

- Show every dimension.

- Show every trade.

- Describe each room and list everything that's going into it.

- Detail all materials, showing the grade, quality, and in the case of fixtures, their make and model number.

- State an allowance for any item not specifically priced out, such as door knobs or other hardware.

- Cover any compromises or trade-offs you've made with the customer to be sure you're providing what the prospects expect. And be careful to list what you *aren't* going to do.

Standard Form Construction Agreement

A. Licensed Contractor
1234 Main Street
Anytown, U.S.A.   Phone 444-6578

Page 1 of 4

License 318-6690

THIS DOCUMENT CONSISTING OF THIS AGREEMENT, PLANS, SPECIFICATIONS, AND "NOTICE TO OWNER", ALL ATTACHED HERETO AND MADE A PART HEREOF, SHALL CONSTITUTE THE AGREEMENT.

__A. Licensed Contractor__ hereinafter called, "Contractor", "Seller" and/or "Beneficiary" agrees to provide the following: labor, materials and construction in accordance with plans and specifications as may be added and initialed by the parties and attached hereto:

(Buyer) __Robert and Mary Homeowner__   Phone __333-4444__

(Residence Address) __4567 10th Street__   City __Anytown__   State __45780__

(Place of business, if any, of Buyer) _____ City _____ State _____

(Job Address) __same as above__   City _____ State _____

Also known as Legal Description: Lot # __34__   Tract # __3347__   Block # __A__

Recorded in Book # __2__   Page # __12__   in the office of the County Recorder of __said county__
State of California, hereinafter called "Buyer", "Owner" and/or "Trustor" agrees to pay therefore the price hereinafter set forth upon the following terms and conditions.

DESCRIPTION OF WORK AND MATERIALS: Purpose: As per the specifications on the attached sheets - to build a new room - bathroom - hallway - two closets and a wardrobe closet to the rear of the house.

Insurance: Contractor carries compensation and liability insurance.

Lien Releases: Contractor to furnish owner with lien releases covering labor and materials furnished up to each progress payment.

NOT INCLUDED: The following items are specifically excluded from this contract and are to be provided by the Owner: Anything - not specifically outlined in this agreement.

ALLOWANCES. The following items, where specific prices are indicated, are included in the Contract Price as allowances for the purchase price of those items to be selected by Owner. Owner and Contractor agree to adjust the Contract Price after verification of actual cost difference if any of said items selected by Owner.

Appliances $ -0-   Light Fixtures $150.00   Bath Accessories $100.00

Floor Covering $100.00 bath only   Hardware Finish $125.00   plumbing faucets   And OTHER $100.00

Finish hardware is interpreted to include all knobs, pulls, hinges, catches, locks, drawer slides, accessories or other items that are normally installed subsequent to final painting. Light fixtures are interpreted to include only those fixtures that are surface mounted. Bath accessories are interpreted to include medicine cabinets, towel bars, paper holders, soap dishes, etc.

TIME FOR STARTING AND COMPLETING PROJECT: Work shall commence within ten days after the last to occur of the following: (1) Receipt by the Contractor of all necessary building permits; (2) Receipt by the Contractor of notice from Lender, Lien Holder and/or Title Company if any that all documents required to be recorded prior to commencement of construction have been properly recorded; (3) Owner has complied with all Terms and Conditions of the Agreement to date; (4) Receipt of all constructions funds by Escrow or Funding Control if any. Subject to adjustment for the above conditions, work shall begin

approximately on __1 May 1988__ and be substantially completed approximately on __15 Sep 1988__ with additional time to be allowed as detailed in paragraph 20 of the Terms and Conditions on the back hereof. Substantial Commencement of work shall be defined as

When permit is secured & excavating for foundation is started.
(Briefly describe type of work representing Commencement)

Contractors failure to substantially commence work, without lawful excuse, within twenty (20) days from the date specified above is a violation of the Contractors License Law.

NOTICE TO THE BUYER: (1) Do not sign this agreement before you read it or if it contains any blank spaces. (2) You are entitled to a completely filled in copy of this agreement. Owner acknowledges that he has read and received a legible copy of this agreement signed by Contractor, including all terms and conditions on the reverse side, before any work was done, and that he has read and received a legible copy of every document that owner has signed during the negotiation. If Owner cancels this agreement after the right of recission has expired, and before commencement of construction, he shall pay Contractor the amount of expenses incurred to that date plus loss of profits.

CONTRACT PRICE AND MANNER OF PAYMENT. In consideration of materials, labor and services, owner agrees to pay contractor in cash sum

of __Thirty two thousand__ DOLLARS is __32,000.00__ payable in progress payments, which do not include finance charges of any kind, according to the following schedule 20% when rough lumber is dropped on job. 20% when foundation is poured & addition is rough framed. 20% when addition is roofed & rough electric and rough plumbing is installed. 20% when addition is stuccoed & drywall installed. Balance payable 30 days after notice of completion.
All payments will be due within five (5) days after billing. Overdue payments will bear interest at the maximum legally permissible rate. If any payment is not made when due, Contractor may keep the job idle until such time as all payments due have been made. A failure of payment for a period in excess of said five (5) days shall be considered a major breach.

Contractor or Owner prior to commencement of construction and subject to lending institution, if any approval, may request funds to be placed in an Escrow or Funding Voucher Control Service prior to commencement of work with funds to be disbursed to Contractor in accordance with the escrow instructions or voucher orders signed by the Contractor. In the absence of an Escrow or Funding Control Service, funds will be paid directly to the Contractor in accordance with the progress payments schedule referred to above. YOU, AS OWNER OR TENANT, HAVE THE RIGHT TO REQUIRE THE CONTRACTOR TO HAVE A PERFORMANCE AND PAYMENT BOND.

By _____
Salesman   Registration #   Owner - Buyer Signature   Date

Accepted by
Contractor Seller _____
Owner - Buyer Signature   Date

"YOU, THE BUYER, MAY CANCEL THIS TRANSACTION AT ANY TIME PRIOR TO MIDNIGHT OF THE THIRD BUSINESS DAY AFTER THE DATE OF THIS TRANSACTION. SEE THE ATTACHED NOTICE OF CANCELLATION FORM FOR AN EXPLANATION OF THIS RIGHT."

Typical contract
Figure 2-10

𝔖𝔭𝔢𝔠𝔦𝔣𝔦𝔠𝔞𝔱𝔦𝔬𝔫𝔰

Plan & Permit: Contractor shall prepare the plans and secure the building permits.

Tree Removal: Remove the tree at the rear of the existing bedroom.

Demolition: Remove the walls between the three closets -- between the two rear bedrooms. Remove the stucco on the outside rear wall of the present rear bedrooms.

Concrete: Excavate for the footings. Pour the concrete footings and foundations at the rear of the present house - starting at the northwest corner of the existing rear bedroom - thence towards the rear 21' - thence turn south 24' - thence return into the rear wall of the existing house. Pour a set of concrete steps 5' wide at the position of the new patio door on the side of the new room addition. Pour a concrete walkway 3' wide from these new steps to the side of the existing rear walkway.

Carpentry: Close the door openings from each existing rear bedroom to the closets that are now changed to a hallway. Remove one window from the rear wall of the existing rear bedroom. Cut an opening on the north wall of this same room and relocate this window and screen. Cut an opening on the rear wall of the existing two rear bedrooms. Install bi-pass wardrobe doors 6'8" high to one of the new closets and a 2'6" x 6'8" hc slab door to one walk-in closet in the new addition. Lay the underpinning, joists, and subflooring for the new addition - prepared for hardwood floors- finished at the same floor height as the existing floor height of the house. Construct the wall and ceiling framing for the new addition: for the new addition to the hallway - the new wardrobe closet for one existing rear bedroom - the new walk-in closet for the other existing rear bedroom - the new bedroom - the new closet - the new bathroom - the new linen closet.

The ceiling height shall be the same height as the existing rear bedrooms. The roof framing over the new addition shall be hip style and spaced sheathing on the roof. Install the following doors: 2'6" x 6'8" to the new bathroom, 2'8" x 6'8" to the new bedroom from the hallway, bi-pass mirrored doors 6'8" high to the wardrobe in the new bedroom. The passage doors interior - shall be hollow core slab (see allowances for finish hardware including door locks). Install a 8' x 6'8" aluminum framed patio door (Seeley or equal) - complete with tempered glass and screen. This patio door shall have a keyed lock. Install the following aluminum frame (Seeley or equal) side slide windows - each with aluminum full frame screens: two 4' x 3' in the new bedroom, one 4' x 2' in the new bathroom. Install a pair of slab lipped cabinet doors on the

(continued on page three of this agreement)

THIS PAGE BECOMES PART OF AND IN CONFORMANCE WITH **PROPOSAL NO.** _____

Submitted by _____ —
(INITIALS)

Job Name _____

Date _____ 19 _____

Accepted by _____ Date _____ 19 ____
(INITIALS)

Accepted by _____ Date _____ 19 ____
(INITIALS)

Typical contract
Figure 2-10 (continued)

Specifications

new linen cabinet in the hallway. After the drywall is installed, case the new openings, and install base and mouldings at all new walls. Fill in the base and mouldings in the hallway where the walls are changed. The new casings and base shall be streamlined, paint-grade lumber. Install shelves and wood poles in each of the new closets and wardrobes. Install shelves in the new linen closet. Install a medicine cabinet, towel bar and soap receptacle set in the new bathroom (see allowances for bath accessories).

Insulation: Install R19 rock wool insulation in all exterior walls and ceiling of the entire new addition.

Roofing: Install medium shake wood shingles on the entire new addition similar to the medium shake shingles on the existing house. These shingles shall be flame retardant. The new valleys shall be metal similar to the existing roof valleys of the house.

Electric: Install a new 150 amp electric service panel. Install the following electrical outlets: new hallway - one light and 3-way switch; new walk-in closet - one light and a switch; new bathroom - two lights, a ceiling heater (Payne No.44), 3 switches and one duplex plug; new bedroom - one light, one switch and 5 duplex plugs; exterior - one light and one switch. (See allowances for light fixtures).

Heat duct: Install a heat duct from the existing forced air furnace to the new bedroom addition.

Stucco: Lath and stucco the exterior walls of the entire new addition. The finish stucco texture shall be similar to the existing stucco finish on the house. Patch the stucco on the north wall of the existing bedroom where the window is relocated.

Dry wall: Install 5/8" drywall sheet rock on all walls and ceilings of the entire new addition. Patch all walls of the two rear bedrooms and new hallway affected by this remodeling. Tape and spackle the joints on all new drywall.

Plumbing: Bring in the waste and water lines to the new addition. Install a 5' recess bathtub (cast iron) with a shower over the bathtub. Install an oval pullman lavatory with a center set faucet. Install a cadet - low boy commode. The plumbing fixtures shall be white color, Crane or equal. (See allowances for tub and lavatory faucets). All new water lines shall be copper. The waste lines shall be connected to the waste line under the existing house. Install a hose bib on the rear wall of the new addition.

(continued on page four of this agreement)

Submitted by _____
(INITIALS)

Date _____ 19 _____

THIS PAGE BECOMES PART OF AND IN CONFORMANCE WITH **PROPOSAL NO.** _____

Job Name _____

Accepted by _____ Date _____ 19 ____
(INITIALS)

Accepted by _____ Date _____ 19 ____
(INITIALS)

Typical contract
Figure 2-10 (continued)

𝔖𝔭𝔢𝔠𝔦𝔣𝔦𝔠𝔞𝔱𝔦𝔬𝔫𝔰

Pullman cabinet: Install a 6′ long pullman cabinet in the new bathroom. This new pullman cabinet shall have a cultured marble top and splash back.

Tub enclosure: Install a metal framed - glass tub enclosure on the side of the bathtub. These doors shall have wire reinforcing in the glass doors.

Ceramic tile: Install ceramic tile (domestic) on three walls over the tub - to the shower head height.

Hardwood floors: Install 1/2" x 1 1/2" oak hardwood floorings in the entire new bedroom. (The wardrobes shall have a plywood floor). Weave in the floors in the hallway where the walls are removed. Sand and polish all new hardwood floors.

Painting: Paint all exterior walls of the new addition with a stuccocote exterior paint material. Paint all exterior wood trim in a flat wood trim paint. Patch the walls where the window is relocated in the existing bedroom. Paint all walls, ceilings, and wood trim on all new walls and ceilings, including cabinets and closets (a prime and two additional coats of flat interior paint). Paint the walls and ceilings of the entire new hallway, and the two bedrooms on the rear of the existing house.

Floor covering: Install a new vinyl floor covering in the new bath. (See allowances for the installed price of this floor covering).

Mirror: Install a plate glass mirror the 6′ length of the pullman from the top of the splash back to the door height.

Cleanup: Remove all debris caused by this work. The job will be left broom clean.

Submitted by _____
(INITIALS)

Date _____ 19 _____

THIS PAGE BECOMES PART OF AND IN CONFORMANCE WITH **PROPOSAL NO.** _____

Job Name _____

Accepted by _____ Date _____ 19 ____
(INITIALS)

Accepted by _____ Date _____ 19 ____
(INITIALS)

Typical contract
Figure 2-10 (continued)

Notice of Cancellation

Date: _____

You may cancel this transaction without any penalty or obligation, within three business days from the above date.

If you cancel, any property traded in, any payments made by you under the contract or sale, and any negotiable instruments executed by you will be returned within 10 business days following receipt by the seller of your cancellation notice, and any security interest arising out of the transaction will be cancelled.

If you cancel, you must make available to the seller at your residence, in substantially as good condition as when received, any goods delivered to you under this contract or sale; or you may if you wish, comply with the instructions of the seller regarding the return shipment of the goods at the seller's expense and risk.

If you do make the goods available to the seller and the seller does not pick them up within 20 days of the date of your notice of cancellation, you may retain or dispose of the goods without any further obligation. If you fail to make the goods available to the seller, or if you agree to return the goods to the seller and fail to do so, then you remain liable for performance of all obligations under the contract.

To cancel this transaction, mail or deliver a signed and dated copy of this cancellation notice or any other written notice, or send a telegram to: _____

_____

_____ not later than midnight of _____

I HEREBY CANCEL THIS TRANSACTION.

_____
Date

_____
Buyer's signature

Notice of cancellation form
Figure 2-11

The customer should read both the front and back of the contract. Your agreement is written on the front. Figure 2-10 is an example of a typical contract and specifications. The front of the contract is often referred to as the ''big print.'' The back of the contract, which is preprinted, is known as the ''small print.'' The small print spells out the legal obligations of both the homeowner and the contractor. A good source for building forms is:

American Building Contractors Association
11100 Valley Blvd., Suite 120
El Monte, CA 91731
(818) 401-0071

Figure 2-11 shows a notice of cancellation form. This form makes it easy for the homeowner to cancel for *any reason* within three days of signing the contract. This cancellation notice is required by federal law. Even if it weren't, it's a good idea. The right to cancel makes it easier to get a signature.

The contract, plus the detailed specifications, the plans and the notice of cancellation form, make up your legal agreement with the customer.

A contract and notice of cancellation form are available at a small cost at many larger stationery and office supply stores. You can also get them through building material suppliers, lumber yards, or companies that specialize in business forms and contracts. If you order several hundred copies at a time, your company name can be printed at the top of the form for a small cost.

If you develop any of your own forms to be used as legal documents, have them reviewed by your lawyer. The law varies from state to state. Be careful to comply with the laws of each state where you do business.

In Summary

The important thing in marketing and selling is to make a plan, then work the plan. Although referrals may play a major role in boosting your sales, you need an aggressive marketing program to keep your business growing and profitable. This means selecting your market, determining how much of the market your company can handle efficiently, and then budgeting to reach your sales goals.

Selling remodeling isn't like selling new cars. You're selling something that doesn't exist yet. It's just a dream you have to develop in your customer's mind. You make that dream become a concrete reality. When you've done your job well, your customers end up feeling that you and your company have done them an invaluable service. That's good for everyone!

three

If You Don't Tell Them ...Who Will?

*A*dvertising and promotion are probably the most useful but least understood tools of the remodeling contractor's business. Most remodeling contractors advertise too little, and often what advertising they do isn't very effective. The reason — advertising and promotion are professional fields. It takes a specialist to create the right message and select the right advertising media to get the best return on your advertising dollar.

It's common for the owners of small businesses, who aren't familiar with the advertising field, to assume that a couple of advertisements, or a few direct-mail letters, will generate enough new business to pay for the cost of the advertising.

Unfortunately, it doesn't usually work that way. A single advertisement, letter or flyer seldom generates enough business to pay the cost of developing the ad and placing it in a newspaper, on radio or on TV. Then the contractor loses faith in the media, or the service producing the promotion, and stops doing it. Pretty soon, he doesn't have enough work to keep his crews busy.

So let's kill one myth about advertising now. Advertisements, brochures, flyers, direct mail, key chains, or TV spots don't *sell*. What they do is create an awareness of the product. *Salesmen sell!* The techniques used in advertising, public relations and promotion are designed to do one thing — create what the advertising profession calls *impressions.* That's all!

However, in creating impressions, they are setting up a chain reaction. By *repeated* exposure, the awareness turns to interest. When sufficient interest is generated, an inquiry takes place, and that's the first step in the sale.

The whole point of advertising is to make the public think about your product, and think about *you* when they do. Advertising opens the door for the salesman. The salesman turns an inquiry into a sale. The contractor turns the sale into a completed job that wins a satisfied customer and earns a profit.

Finding Creative People

The image of public relations and advertising people taking three-hour, three-martini lunches every day is still common. Maybe with the nation's biggest advertising agencies, whose clients are large corporations, such practices still exist.

But today, for the most part, freelance copy writers, artists, and advertising agencies spend very little on entertaining clients. When they do it's for a business meeting, not pleasure. Take a hard look at what the agency or service says it's going to do for you, and just what the cost will be. If you're getting wined and dined, chances are you're paying for it. Don't give your business to an agency that's more concerned with showing you their beautiful offices than showing how successful their programs have been for their other clients.

You don't need a large national advertising agency to get good value for your advertising dollar. Many small or medium-to-small advertising agencies serve small service and manufacturing companies. The Yellow Pages of your phone book probably list several dozen small agencies in your community. A small agency can be a one-person business or from three to five full- or part-time people working together. But they often provide good services at anywhere from 30 to 50 percent less cost than a larger agency. A small agency handles fewer clients and will give you more personal service. Better still, for smaller remodeling companies, there are many freelance artists and writers who work out of their homes and who can do an effective job.

So, unless your advertising budget is a pretty big one, a small agency or freelance agent will give you the best value and most creativity for your advertising dollar.

Another creative source which shouldn't be overlooked is the advertising art departments of your local newspapers. They provide a service at no cost — a price you can afford. Given good direction, they can often produce an excellent ad because they specialize in newspaper advertising.

What to Look For

How do you find good creative people? The best way is to get the recommendation of someone who is pleased with their advertising program. If an agency is good, someone will know about them. Ask other remodeling contractors in your area for a recommendation. If you see or hear an advertisement you like, call the advertiser and ask them who prepared it. The Chamber of Commerce, the Better Business Bureau, or a local industrial or trade association may also be able to recommend someone.

Like a homeowner looking for a good remodeler, you should shop around. Talk to two or three agencies or services before you make a selection. Base your selection on the following criteria . . .

1) Creativity
2) Knowledge about effective advertising techniques
3) Service
4) Price

. . . in that order.

Although you might think that the first step would be to find an agency that has experience promoting or advertising remodelers, that's not always necessary. It may take you a long time to find an agency with moderate rates *and* experience in promoting remodeling sales. Our advice is to find someone who is creative and then teach them about your business.

When you select an agency or service, tell them where you operate geographically, the peculiarities of your trade, and the type of work you're looking for. Explain to them how you've been getting customers previously, and how successful you've been. Give them all the information they need to do a good job, let them know how much you can pay — then put them to work. In other words, *don't tell them how to do their job.* That's what you're paying them for!

Too many advertising programs are misdirected. They're based on a misunderstanding of what the client wanted. The result is like a movie that got good reviews but no paying customers. If you're spending the money, make sure the program is tailored to meet your exact needs, and will bring in prospects that need and can afford what you're ready to provide.

Look for creativity and imagination in your advertising agency. What kind of clients have they handled in the past? How did they solve the needs of their clients? What would they do for you, and how would they do it? Does what they propose meet your budget?

If you can't afford an agency to do a full advertising campaign for you, many will do project work. No long-term arrangement is required for this. Agencies often welcome the opportunity to work with a new business. They know if they can help you become successful, it will mean additional business for them in the future.

Measuring Advertising Results

How do you determine the effectiveness of advertising in any given medium? It's hard to measure immediate results. Determining actual sales months later isn't always possible. Most of the time people responding to an offer don't identify how or where they heard about your company or product. Of course, you can ask. But some people become evasive when they're questioned. They may want to know why you're asking. Maybe they feel as though they're being interrogated. So, if you want to ask, wait until you feel the caller is relaxed and responsive, or bring it up during your first sales presentation.

One way to measure an advertisement is to "code" each medium you use. This way, when an inquiry comes in, you can identify it without asking. How many times have you written to Department 2C or Box A? Department 2C and Box A probably don't exist. They're the advertiser's code for a specific publication.

For example, say you're going to use radio and newspaper advertising. In both cases you're going to give listeners and readers the name of your company, your address, and your phone number so they can call for more information or set up an appointment. You would have the radio ad tell listeners to ask for Department R. And you'd have the newspaper ad tell readers to ask for Department N. The person in your company taking the calls simply notes whether the call is for Department R or N and then gives out the information. The caller doesn't know he or she is being questioned. The person answering the call says that they work for the department requested. Then, it's a simple matter of adding up the number of R and the number of N responses each employee receives.

Another method of tracking calls is to use a fictitious name. There's a national company which advertises heavily on radio. At the close of their commercial they tell the listener to call and ask for "cordial Bob Smith." Of course, every salesman in every one of their sales offices across the country answers to the name Bob Smith, and each of them is very cordial.

The chart in Figure 3-1 shows one simple way of keeping track of where your leads come from. This method does a particularly thorough job of showing the kind of responses received from various types of advertising and how the inquiries are handled.

MONTH APRIL   YEAR 1988

#	Date	G	A	S	R	K	Other	Name	Town	Phone	Rel	S/Man	✓	$	Comments	D	S	Y	M	F	S	R	J	
1	4/17	X						MOORE	JONESBURG	231-7000	5/22	JUB										X		SIGN @ COREY
2	4/17	X						ADAMS	SKOKIE	897-4501	5/22	McCABE								X				
3	4/18	X						NOLAN	PRAIRIE VIEW	712-8000	5/22	McCABE							X					
4	4/18		X					ANDREWS	R.M.	297-7666	5/22	JUB										X		SIGN @ COREY
5	4/22		X					JONES	ECM.	431-2121	4/22	JVB										X		DITTMAN
6	4/21		X					MEYERS	JONESBURG	972-0000	4/21	JVB							X					
7			X					BENSON	ITASCA	444-8888	5/6	BILL B.				X								
8	4/29	X						HOFFMAN	ELMHURST	771-2121	5/1	McCABE			ALREADY BOUGHT FROM OTHERS									
9	4/22		X					GILLETTE	JONESBURG	291-8000	5/2	CHUCK												
10	4/25				X			SMITH	STREAMWOOD	679-0012	5/2	JVB										X		JOB SIGN
11	4/1							JENKINS	JONESBURG	431-2187	4/2	BILL B.				X								
12	4/1	X						JOHNSON	SCH	666-0099	4/10	BILL B.												
13	4/28	X			X			CARLSON	JONESBURG	777-2186	5/1	CHUCK			SOLD HOUSE					X				
14	4/29		X					WONG	PAL	671-7161	5/2	CHUCK										X	X	JOB SIGN
15	4/21	X						BENJAMIN	GLEN HTS.	291-0011	4/28	McCABE								X			X	DIXIT
16	4/25		X					WALLACE	JONESBURG	472-2174	5/1	CHUCK								X				
17	4/28	X						DITMAR	PARK	211-1112	5/1	JVB										X		JOB SIGN
18	4/21	X						KING	MT. PROS.	774-4777	4/28	McCABE							X	X				TRUCK SIGN
19	4/28	X						MARTINEZ	BARTLETT	261-0013	5/1	JVB										X		JOYCE
20	4/6							McGUIRE	JONESBURG	333-1111	4/12	JVB									X			

Courtesy: Drew Builders

Sample telephone inquiry log
Figure 3-1

ROOM ADDITIONS

Custom designed to enhance the value and elegance of your home

- CONSULTING
- DESIGNING
- AFFORDABLE PRICES
- LOW RATE FINANCING
  also:
- **CUSTOM GARAGES**

DREW BUILDERS

"Restoring Value to the American Home"

235 W. Colfax Palatine, IL

FREE ESTIMATES 358-9595

Three Generations of Experience

Courtesy: Drew Builders

Newspaper advertisement for remodeling business
Figure 3-2

Anyone in the office can keep up the chart and tally the results in a short time. At least once a month, review the chart. Based on the responses, you can increase your advertising emphasis in the areas which are doing you the most good, and cut back in those that aren't.

The sample chart shows a good mix of advertising and promotion. The last eight columns list various types of promotional advertising you're likely to use. From left to right they are:

1) Newspaper display advertising

2) A weekly newsless shopper put out by the newspaper. You can repeat the same advertisement used in the newspaper. A sample advertisement is shown in Figure 3-2. You can try various combinations of copy and pictures. The contractor who used this ad found that he got more responses from an advertisement which had a line drawing than he did from one that had a photograph of a room addition. So he started running the line drawing advertisement early in the year and in three months received over 70 inquiries from that source alone.

3) The Yellow Pages

4) Mail-outs. You can use a modified version of the flyers you use at shows.

5) Flyers for shows

6) Shows

7) Referrals

8) Job signs. They're an excellent source of inquiries.

It's important that the chart show all your inquiries. You need a quick way to evaluate the effectiveness of your various promotions.

Other items that you might want to include on your chart are the types of remodeling jobs that are requested, the areas that the inquiries come in from, the salesperson assigned the lead, comments on how the lead progressed, and of course, the name and phone number of the potential customer.

The contractor who designed and used this particular chart was able to increase his business by over 1000 percent in two and a half years! Of course, there's more to his success than keeping track of advertising. But measuring the results of advertising is the only way to get good value for your advertising dollar.

Increasing Advertising Effectiveness

Very few people respond to an offer the first time they see or hear it. Everyone receives hundreds of thousands of advertising messages every week — in newspapers, magazines, on TV and radio. Everywhere people are, there will be advertising messages. We've learned to shut most of them out of our mind so we can deal with our own priorities. How can your message break through the filter everyone uses to exclude nearly every advertising message?

Most people ignore advertising messages that don't meet an immediate need. Remodeling is seldom an immediate need. We say to ourselves, "Sure, I'd like to have the kitchen remodeled, and I'll have it done . . .as soon as the kids' college tuition is paid . . .the air conditioning is replaced . . .or we get new tires for the car . . .then maybe we can afford the new kitchen we've been thinking about." The priority an idea receives depends on the demands being made on the person and their pocketbook at that particular time.

Repeat for Results
When you run just one advertisement, unless the reader takes action then and there, the ad will be forgotten almost immediately. And so will your company, unless you repeat your promotion on a regular basis. Repetition reinforces memory. In advertising, it's essential! You must train homeowners to become customers — your customers!

Advertising is like taking medicine. The reason you take a certain medicine over a period of time is so that it will be effective long enough to get the disease out of your system. You can't just swallow the whole bottle at one shot. It may knock out the disease, but it could also knock off the patient.

Advertising works the same way. One great big dose of advertising may draw more inquiries than you can handle in one day. But next week you'll be forgotten. Advertising in smaller doses over a long period of time is far more effective at reinforcing your image in the minds of potential customers.

What we mean by repetition, however, requires some clarification. With a modest amount of research and planning, any advertising program can be made more effective — and part of that planning is how and *when* to repeat the advertisement. You don't simply repeat the same ad every day or once a week for a year. You carefully select a frequency rate that gives you the best exposure for your money.

Repetition in newspaper advertising may mean that an advertisement runs once every quarter (spring, summer, winter and fall) for three successive days a week, generally Wednesday, Thursday and Friday. Or it can mean three consecutive Thursdays in the Real Estate section, say in February; or perhaps every Sunday in March, April and May.

Radio can be used effectively by many remodeling contractors — especially if you select the right program and time slot. It can also be a complete waste of money. Effective radio advertising requires that you pick the right time slot or program which will reach a receptive audience. It can be 15 seconds every night for a week, or just once a week on Friday for four weeks. Why Friday? Listeners have the weekend to respond. The purpose of your research is to narrow in on those shows or times which will deliver the greatest number of people interested in remodeling, at the least cost to you.

How Much Is Enough?

How much should you spend for advertising? How much is enough and how much is too much?

There's no easy answer. It can be as low as 2 percent of your gross sales to as high as 12 percent. It depends on the size of the city where your business is located, the kinds of media available, and their cost. Another factor to consider is how much competition you have, and how much advertising they're doing. You don't have to match your competition dollar for dollar, but you do have to spend enough to help the public discriminate between *your company* and the others.

The size of your advertising budget will depend on the size of your company and the kind of remodeling business you want to attract. If you're a single-trade contractor, you'll probably have a smaller advertising budget since you're just selling one product. But if you're a general contractor, you offer a variety of services, so you'll need to advertise more.

As a rule, most remodeling contractors don't do enough advertising. If you're just starting out in business and you don't have much capital, you may be tempted to try getting by without any advertising. Don't make that mistake. New businesses, regardless of capitalization, are the ones that need advertising the most.

In the example in Chapter 1, we used a figure of 5 percent of anticipated gross sales (or $30,000) for our advertising budget. We used the funds to buy time and space in five different media. If we coded the media as we suggested in the beginning of this chapter, it's easier to measure the effectiveness of each. The one which produced the greatest number of leads per dollar spent would be the focus of our advertising dollars. That doesn't mean the others should be dropped. Any medium that provides enough leads to pay for itself should be kept. The important thing is to identify the source of each lead so you know the effectiveness of each advertisement.

You also want to keep track of the kind of sales each medium attracts. Different media appeal to different audiences. You may find your advertising dollars are best spent in a medium which brings in five $30,000 jobs rather than one which brings in fifteen $1,500 jobs. Experiment to find the most productive media for your business and your budget. When you find it, stick with it.

Planning an Advertising Program

A good, effective advertising program, one that brings in the right volume of business, must be thoroughly planned and researched. A plan that works for someone else won't necessarily work for you.

Consider the size of your market, the average income and lifestyle, the social structure, your competition, and the amount of work you can reasonably expect to accomplish.
Set the following goals for your advertising program.

- To bring in enough leads to reach your sales goal and earn you a profit — but not so many that you can't follow up on all leads.

- To generate sales within a reasonable distance of your business.

- To reach and attract customers who have the desire and the income to pay for your services.

Most remodeling contractors spend 1.5 percent of their budget or less on advertising. That's fine if it's generating enough business. In most cases, though, it isn't. You need to strike a balance in your advertising budget. Too little and you've wasted your money and your efforts. Too much and you're swamped with too many inquiries to handle. Trying to do too much can drive you to bankruptcy as fast as not having enough business.

It's not *how much* you spend on advertising that's important. It's how *well* your money is spent. More dollars doesn't necessarily mean more customer responses and more business. Selecting the right medium is far more important than the money it costs. Even if a program is expensive, as long as it generates enough business to pay for itself and leads to profits, then it's good business.

Using Demographics

Demographics is the study of the lifestyle and habits of various groups of people. There are studies done on all kinds of social and consumer trends. These include television viewing, the types of newspapers read by the various income groups, and other information which can be helpful in creating an advertising strategy.

A demographic study can give you a profile of your community. It will include information on where people live, their income range, age, how and where they spend their income, family size, home size, number of cars, education, and so on. It can help find the right media for your advertising message.

If you use an advertising agency, a demographic study of your market area should be part of the service they provide. However, if you can't afford an agency, media salespeople can provide most of the demographic information you need.

Timing

Timing is important in advertising. In general, it's more cost-effective to advertise remodeling during good selling seasons. Make hay while the sun shines. Avoid advertising heavily during the slow season. That's the wrong way to fight a sales slump.

However, you can always boost sales with seasonal discounts "to keep the crews busy." Off-season offers like "You Can Cook Your Thanksgiving Turkey in a New Kitchen — Guaranteed" (Christmas Goose, Easter Ham or whatever) are generally effective, provided you can deliver.

It's also a good idea to check into what your competition is doing. For example, if another contractor is taking out huge display ads, you may not want to go head-to-head with him advertising in the same paper. It might be better to select other media that meet your market profile, but aren't being used by your competition. There are several alternatives to choose from. You can stress one medium, or use a combination of two or more, depending on your budget and your success with each.

Selecting the Right Media

Every advertising medium has both advantages and limitations. Remember, though, that the demographics of the audience or readership determine whether it's cost-effective for your business.

Newspapers— Advertising in the Sunday newspaper in metropolitan areas may seem like a good buy because Sunday papers have the largest circulation. But they also have the greatest number of pages. Your 2-column by 5-inch advertisement can easily be lost or overlooked. However, if there is a Real Estate or Home Improvement section, then it might be worth the extra money you'll have to pay for an ad in the Sunday edition. Those sections are read eagerly by people interested in improving their homes.

You can further boost the readership of your ad by asking for a specific position. What's the best position? On the front page of the housing or building section if possible. Generally, though, where there's advertising on the first page of any section,

Courtesy: Kohler Co.

Photographs show the quality of your work
Figure 3-3

it's one-half page, at the bottom. Most of the time it's taken up by a single advertisement. That's expensive, even for a fair-sized remodeling firm. Your next best position is on page 3, or any facing page (right-hand page) in that section. Try to get the last two columns on the right-hand side; as high up on the page as possible. The top right-hand corner is the best position on the page.

Although we read from left to right, studies have shown that when we turn a newspaper or magazine page, our eyes go immediately to the right. If the message that appears there interests us, we'll read it and then go back to the left side and continue scanning or reading.

Keep your advertising copy (the words of your message) simple and straightforward. "Cute" doesn't sell. If you're a single-trade contractor or have a specialty, make it the headline. Always feature your company logo, name, address and phone number prominently. Don't forget the phone number — we've seen ads without it. If your business has won an award, be sure that information is included in your ad.

If you're a general remodeling contractor, you can sharply increase the number of leads by emphasizing the phrases "Add a Room" and "Remodel Your Kitchen and Bath." These are proven lead-generators for remodeling contractors.

Pictures tell more than words. A good, sharp black and white photo of a project or a clear line drawing of your work makes an attractive addition to any ad. A photograph, such as the bath in Figure 3-3, clearly shows the quality of the contractor's work. If your advertisement just says "We are specialists in bathroom remodeling — first-class workmanship," the reader can't visualize the product you're selling. A picture helps readers visualize the bathroom of their dreams.

74

Every Sunday there are dozens of photos and illustrations of new homes being offered by new home builders. But you don't often find advertisements showing completed remodeling projects. A remodeling project is just as important to the homeowner considering improving his home as a new home is to a prospective buyer. So why not show photographs of your completed projects? Don't make the reader guess the kind of product and quality you deliver. *Show them!*

What happens if you go to all the trouble to get space and position in the Sunday Home Improvement section and your response is poor? Probably there's something wrong with your headline, copy, or the design of the graphics. Experiment to find an advertising formula that works for you. When you find the right formula, stick with it. Many contractors, particularly those who specialize in certain types of remodeling, run the same ad once a week for a three- to six-week period every spring. A good ad can bring in customers year after year.

Newspaper supplements— Many newspapers, large and small, have special home improvement supplements several times a year. Stories about home improvement, redecorating, energy savings and remodeling are featured. These sections are often sponsored by a local home building association or remodeling association and may include advertisements from lenders that make home improvement loans. The supplement usually features articles on the benefits of remodeling, how to select a contractor, question and answer columns, as well as information on how to get financing.

These home improvement supplements are usually a good advertising buy because they attract attention from people specifically interested in remodeling.

If your local newspaper doesn't have a home improvement supplement, encourage them to develop one. You and several other contractors may have to pledge advertising support to launch the project. But it may be worth the effort and the expense. A home improvement supplement can be a good service for homeowners, an excellent advertising vehicle for you, and a good source of revenue for the paper.

Radio— If newspaper advertising doesn't seem to work as well as you'd hoped it would, consider radio advertising. The problem with radio is that it has little retention or carry-over value. It also has no visual value. If you specialize in remodeling baths, there's no way a radio commercial can carry the same impact as a photograph can. Words alone just won't do it. Another drawback is that radio doesn't come with a coupon that can be clipped and mailed in. Radio has its limitations.

On the other hand, radio can be very persuasive. It's a human voice delivering a message and may convey a feeling of sincerity or urgency that's hard to duplicate in the printed word. Also, you can say a lot more in a 15-second commercial than you can in a small advertisement or flyer.

With millions of people driving to and from work, "drive time" radio has become a big advertising medium. You have a captive audience. For advertising a remodeling business, evening "drive time" radio is probably more effective than morning. People go to work thinking about their jobs and leave work thinking about home. There's a much greater potential for response from evening commuters.

Even though *evening "drive time"* seems to be a good buy, don't limit your considerations to that time slot. A little research might show that there are other programming times that would be an even better buy. Don't limit your advertising to music and talk shows. Many stations offer special interest shows in the evening and on weekends. Some of these shows command highly identifiable and measurable audiences. Even though the number of listeners may be less, the quality of the individuals listening to those shows may give you a greater return on your investment dollar.

Television— Remodelers with small ad budgets have to be very selective in their choice of media. We've seen remodelers waste money on TV even though they were getting good results from newspaper and magazine ads. A single TV spot, broadcast over an average radius of about 75 miles, can generate several hundred inquiries in a few minutes. For most remodeling contractors, that means someone will be busy for many days following up on inquiries, many of which will be nonproductive. Unless you have several offices that cover the area, TV advertising may reach too broad an audience to be practical.

Aside from the cost of television advertising, there's the difficulty of producing a very short commercial which will sell remodeling. A 15- to 30-second commercial is the most cost-effective length for a TV ad. That's only enough time to deliver two quick thoughts to your audience. One has to be your company name. The other will be your phone number and the department to call. That leaves no time for selling. Also, you miss completely any viewer who doesn't have paper and pencil handy to record your phone number.

In spite of these drawbacks, television advertising can be very effective outside of large metropolitan cities. Small, independent stations can offer you more time at less money than the larger stations can. They also localize your audience. Television is more verbal and graphic than any other media. You can show a picture of what you do and your company name and phone number.

But like radio, the television offer can't be stuck up on the refrigerator for future reference. Your audience has to remember the message. You need something memorable, such as a company logo, to leave a visual impression on your viewers.

If you decide to participate in your own commercials, be sure to get some coaching. Nothing turns an audience off faster than amateurism in commercials. They're used to seeing highly polished professional actors. You want to promote an image of strength and trust. Avoid being the worst performer on TV.

Selecting the proper time slot is very important. Of course you'll reach a greater audience during prime time and early evening viewing (between 5:00 and 10:00 P.M.). But will the business generated be enough to recover both the cost of air time and the cost of production? The commercial will cost the same to make whether it's shown on prime time or late night TV. However, a late-night advertising slot (between 10:00 P.M. and midnight) is much more economical.

Before we leave TV and radio advertising, here's a final point. Both TV and radio should be reinforced with some type of printed follow-up which reaches the same listening or viewing audience. Don't expect any type of broadcast message to bring in all the prospects you need.

Yellow Pages— One medium that's effective for almost any business is the Yellow Pages. It's also the one most favored by remodeling contractors. Many remodelers spend 50 percent of their advertising budgets on Yellow Page ads. It's an effective medium because it stays around the home all year long. Many small contractors use the Yellow Pages as their primary advertising medium. Every large remodeling contractor we know includes the Yellow Pages in their advertising mix.

Nearly every home has a classified telephone directory. It's available all year, offers the widest variety of goods and services and is used by nearly all homeowners.

However, the Yellow Pages also has its drawbacks. According to one contractor, "If you don't have the biggest advertisement there, no one's going to call you." He budgets $800 a month, or one-third of his advertising budget, to Yellow Page ads. His ad is right there on the same page as his arch competitor. Which business a prospect calls first probably depends on the wording and placement of the two ads. If you have a specialty, make sure it's prominently featured so it attracts the reader's attention. Yellow Page advertising works particularly well if your company name is already familiar to potential customers. Prospects are more likely to single out your ad out in the Yellow Pages if they recognize the name of your company.

We know a remodeling company that's been in business for over 40 years and handles well over a million dollars in work every year. Over 40 percent of their business comes from referrals and job signs. The company is well-known in the community and has a reputation for doing quality work. They could probably survive very nicely without doing any advertising. Still, they take two display ads in the Yellow Pages just to maintain their position.

This company's most difficult decision is in which the sections of the Yellow Page they should place their ads. They don't feel the need to advertise in every section and category that applies to their business. That would be too expensive. But they want people to find the company first when they think of remodeling. The current ads are listed under "Roofing Contractors" and "Contractors-Alteration." Roofing has always been this contractor's specialty. See Figure 3-4. The other ad emphasizes the variety of work this contractor handles. See Figure 3-5.

The other 60 percent of the company's business comes from a variety of advertising that keeps the company name before the public. Most prospects have heard of the company and know where to find the telephone number in the Yellow Pages. That's a very potent combination.

Neighborhood newspapers— Local or neighborhood newspapers are very cost-effective for single-trade and smaller remodeling companies. Almost all remodeling contractors should be using local or neighborhood papers — just as they should be using the Yellow Pages. Local papers give you good coverage in a limited geographical area and at reasonable cost.

Courtesy: Motor City Builders

**Yellow page ad under Roofers
Figure 3-4**

Courtesy: Motor City Builders

**Same company's advertisement under
Home Improvement
Figure 3-5**

The important thing in newspaper advertising, even in local papers, is repetition. Repeating a smaller ad several times is likely to be more effective than running a full- or half-page ad once — especially if the repetitions follow a pattern, as we suggested earlier in the chapter. And it probably costs less because of discounts offered for multiple insertions.

Again, if your ad doesn't attract the leads it should, change the copy or get a new illustration. Experiment with it until it works. When it does, keep repeating it. Customers who want to respond may not be able to the first time around.

Direct mail— This type of promotion is popular with remodeling contractors because it reaches exactly the prospect you want — and none other. It can be something as simple as a flyer with a coupon to cut out or an elaborate brochure with a return postcard. Direct mail is most effective when you combine it with a special offer. "Order Within the Next 30 Days and Get 10 Percent Off," or "Order Now and Receive a Free . . . ."

Direct mail has a very low response rate, often only 1 to 2 percent — even if you're giving something away. So don't expect more than 10 to 20 responses from a 1,000-piece mailing. If your sales conversion rate is one in ten, you may get three sales out of 30 leads. When you add the cost of those sales calls to the cost of the mailing, you'll see that direct mail promotion can be very expensive.

On the other hand, if you want to hit a pocket of $250,000 homes where the average sale could be $25,000, direct mail may be the most cost-effective way of doing the job.

Direct mail doesn't have to use the U.S. Postal Service. There are other, often cheaper, delivery systems. Some of these systems cover marketing areas much smaller than a specific ZIP code area. Many so-called "shoppers" go to every single home in a given area. These "newsless" newspapers, delivered free, will include your insert for a modest fee. Usually this is less than the bulk postage rate. With some you can even break the distribution down to a specific 50 to 100 home area. Used regularly or during the best selling seasons, this type of advertising can be very effective.

Building Public Recognition

There are many inexpensive ways to keep your company name in front of the public. These range from wearing T-shirts or hats with your company name on them to donating time or helping out in community projects. The important thing is to have the public associate your company name with the service you provide. When someone needs that service, they should think first of calling you.

Create a logo— A logo is a graphic or artistic symbol used to identify your business. Your company logo will help promote a professional image in the eyes of the public.

A logo doesn't have to be complicated or fancy; in fact, the simpler and neater it is, the better. The company logo in Figure 3-6 reflects quality and professionalism. It's simple, attractive and not too expensive to reproduce. But it personalizes the stationery and adds a touch of quality. It also gives customers an identifying symbol to associate with the business.

If you have a good logo, display it everywhere your company name appears. It should be on your trucks, stationery, contracts, invoices, work-in-progress signs at job sites, and always featured prominently in your advertising and promotion. As time goes by, if you're good, it will become a symbol of quality work and contribute to building your company's image.

There are some logos which have become so well-known that they become symbols for a whole industry. A common logo you'll see in the remodeling industry is "Mr. Build," Figure 3-7. This trademark for a nationwide remodeling chain features the backbone of the industry, a kind of generic tradesman. This is the kind of visual image many people associate with the construction and remodeling industries. This is a good example of the power of association in advertising. If you can come up with a symbol that's easy to remember, you *will* be remembered.

A good and inexpensive way of presenting your logo and advertising your company at the same time is through T-shirts and jackets. Put your name and logo on both. Have your workmen wear the T-shirts in the summer and the jackets in the winter.

Most building and remodeling trade associations have a logo which members can use. They often incorporate the word *trust* in their logo, which serves to inspire public confidence in their members. Using an association's logo implies certain standards and reflects favorably on those who display the membership symbol in their advertising. Many contractors use both their own and their association's logo on all their promotional material.

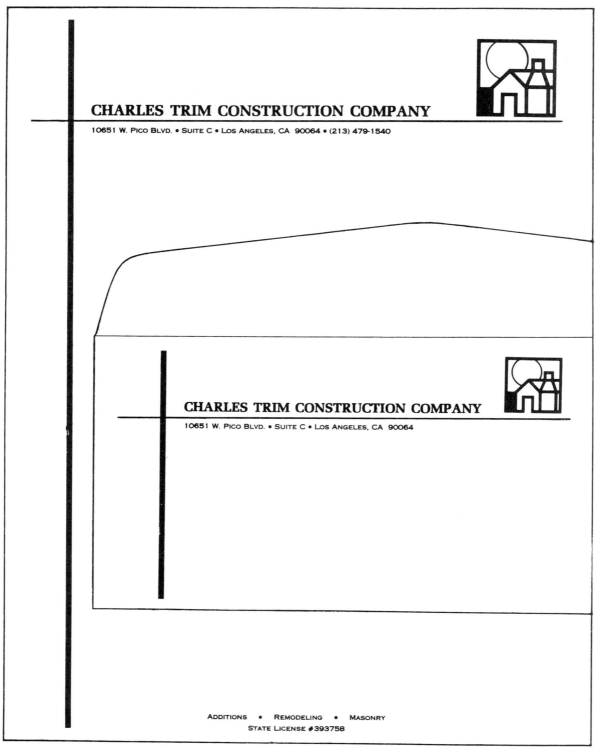

Courtesy: Charles Trim Construction Company

Sample company logo
Figure 3-6

Courtesy: Mr. Build

"Mr. Build" is a familiar logo
Figure 3-7

Job-site advertising—Advertising doesn't stop when you get a job. In fact, the job itself can become an effective advertisement if you promote it properly.

One of the best ways to advertise your work is to put a sign up at every job site. See Figure 3-8. The sign lets people passing by know that this remodeling project is being done by your company. Of course, you'll need the homeowner's consent. The size and quality of signs vary. The sign in Figure 3-8 cost the contractor over $100, and he has six of them. But he feels that the return he gets from his signs is worth the investment.

Many contractors fail to recognize the importance of job signs. They often either display them haphazardly or forget them altogether. Yet, job signs are one of the least expensive and most effective advertising tools you can use. The next time you go by a multi-million dollar construction project, take time to notice the job-site sign. You'll see that it's prominently displayed, and features the name of the contractor and his company. Sometimes there's little on the sign except the contractor's name. The sign probably cost several hundred dollars. But you can be sure the contractor considers it money well spent. If the nation's largest contractors feel it's good business to spend hundreds or thousands of dollars on job signs, you should have a sign on every one of your projects.

Earlier, we discussed the advertising strategy of a contractor who had been working in remodeling for over 40 years. You'll remember that 40 percent of his business was from referrals — at least partially because he insists on putting up a job sign at every work site. Installation and removal is the responsibility of the job supervisor or superintendent. A sign goes up the day the contract is signed and stays in place until the final payment on the job is received.

The superintendent has the task of removing the job sign on completion. This gives him the opportunity to inspect the completed project and see if anything was missed. The homeowners may not see something that an experienced foreman would. This is just one more way of guaranteeing quality work. If corrections are needed, the sign stays up another 24 or 48 hours until all work is finished.

Courtesy: Drew Builders

Job-site signs are good advertising
Figure 3-8

The superintendent also has the opportunity to thank the homeowner for allowing his company to do the work. That's good public relations. Often, homeowners may have friends or neighbors who would like to be contacted about a job. The superintendent can start the ball rolling, and the salesman quickly follows up.

Don't hesitate to ask homeowners for names of possible leads. Some contractors even give homeowners a gift for every lead that results in a sale.

In addition to job signs, consider distributing doorknob hangers on homes throughout the neighborhood where you're working. This calls attention to the good fortune of the family who lives in the home you're remodeling. Everyone in the neighborhood should envy them at least a little — and be curious about the work that's being done.

Your company truck, or trucks, may be one of your best advertisements. Have them painted attractively and *keep them clean.* A shabby truck will reflect poorly on you, and imply your work may be shabby, also. Have your logo painted on them as well as your company name and telephone number.

Showrooms— Figure 3-9 shows the kitchen section of a midwestern contractor's showroom. He does over a million dollars in business a year in a medium-size town. A customer can pick out wall coverings, floor tile, kitchen or bath fixtures from the showroom display. This saves the nuisance of driving to several dealers to make choices. This contractor found that the showroom closed sales faster and created more satisfied customers. The showroom helped his business succeed. In fact, it's worked so well for him that he plans to rebuild and enlarge it. He wants room to display a sample of nearly everything his company installs. Showrooms have worked equally well for many other remodeling contractors.

Courtesy: Motor City Builders

Remodeler's "showroom kitchen"
Figure 3-9

Courtesy: Drew Builders

Display at a home or remodeling show
Figure 3-10

Home shows— If you can't afford a showroom, the next best thing is a display in a home or remodeling show. See Figure 3-10. Home shows *bring the customer to you.* They offer a good opportunity to display your craft. Use lots of pictures. Pass out literature, not only yours, but literature from the manufacturers you buy from.

Increase the effectiveness of your exhibit by making a special offer, or having a "Free Drawing." Give away one or more prizes to the winners. The prizes should relate to your business and shouldn't be too valuable. Otherwise you'll have *lots* of low-quality leads. "Fifteen percent off" on a remodeling project is a good prize to offer, and one that will only attract people interested in remodeling. Use a drawing to get names and addresses of prospects that should be on your mailing or contact list.

Associations and organizations— Join trade associations and service organizations to become better known in your community. Trade associations promote professionalism and ethical standards. They also give remodeling contractors the opportunity to meet and share information. Many large and medium size cities now have remodeling associations.

In addition to local organizations, there are two national organizations. The largest is the *National Association of the Remodeling Industry,* 1901 N. Moore Street, Arlington, VA 22209. The other is the *National Association of Home Builders,* headquartered at 15th and M Streets NW, Washington, D.C. 20005. Both local and national associations offer programs designed for remodeling contractors. These organizations lobby federal and state government for legislation beneficial to the industry, and oppose legislation which could hurt remodelers.

Service organizations, such as Rotary, Kiwanis and Optimists, are composed of local business people. Each organization has a charity which it supports through fund-raising programs and special events. Joining a local service organization offers you the opportunity to meet other people in your business community. Participating in these groups can bring you many business leads, not only through fellow members, but by referrals from fellow members.

Other Promotional Opportunities
No discussion of marketing for remodelers would be complete without mentioning telephone solicitation, novelties, and newsletters.

Telephone solicitation— Of the three, telephone solicitation is probably the least effective. Hundreds of calls by a very capable telephone salesperson may be needed to make one sale. The best time to contact people is in the evening when all members of the household are home. Unfortunately, that's the time of day when people dislike being disturbed. Frankly, you offend too many people to justify the few successes you may get this way.

Novelties— Advertising novelties as a whole are a poor investment. They're reminders of your company name. But no one is going to hire your company for several thousand dollars in remodeling work just because they got your free fifteen-cent ballpoint pen, key chain, or matchbook. Novelties only supplement your regular advertising. They don't replace it. If you're going to use novelties, it's better to give nice items to a few people rather than junk to many.

Newsletters— Newsletters are excellent. They give you an opportunity to showcase your projects. They let you editorialize on every part of your business. But the big problem is that they're expensive and take a lot of time to produce. If you enjoy writing and would like to try doing a newsletter, go ahead. It you have access to a computer with desktop publishing software, preparing the newsletter may be relatively quick and easy.

Cooperative Advertising
Even if your advertising budget is low, there are ways to increase the amount of advertising you do without increasing your advertising costs. Consider cooperative advertising.

Co-op ads have been used for many years. They're available to anyone who advertises. Yet few people are aware of them. Fewer still take advantage of it.

Millions of dollars in co-op advertising credits are available if you know who to ask. Many of your suppliers will help pay for your ads if you promote their products in the ads. You include in your advertising the names or trademarks of the brand name products you use.

Courtesy: Drew Builders
Sample of cooperative advertising
Figure 3-11

In the advertisement shown in Figure 3-11, the contractor used the logos of a lumber company and a window manufacturer. Since he uses their products in his business, both paid him for including their logos in his advertising.

The amount of money that manufacturers pay to have their products mentioned varies. Sometimes it's a fixed amount. Other times it's figured on the amount of space devoted to the product name compared to the total size of the ad. For example, if you devote 25 percent of the space in your advertisement to a manufacturer's product, they'll pay you 25 percent of the total cost of the ad. The rate depends on the manufacturer's policy. But the lowest reimbursement will be about 10 percent and the highest 50 percent.

Co-op advertising has become so big that there's a publication devoted to helping advertisers identify participating manufacturers. It also gives you information on what each manufacturer requires. The publication is the Co-op Source Directory, published twice annually by Standard Rate & Data Service, Inc. The Directory is broken down by classification (such as building materials), by trademark, and by manufacturer.

The Co-op Source Directory tells you who to contact, eligible media, advertising specifications, how to document claims, methods of payment and more. Most advertising agencies and newspapers have a copy of the directory and can tell you how to take advantage of the programs offered. Your local library may also have copies in their business reference section.

Planning Is the Key

The key to a good advertising program is to be selective in the media you use. You also have to be realistic about your markets, and how much of the market you can handle. Advertising helps keep your product and name before the public. Effective advertising makes your company the first to come to mind when your prospect thinks of remodeling.

Here's an outline that should help you create an effective advertising program:

1)   Determine the primary product you're selling, even if you're a general contractor. Is there something you specialize in, such as room additions, baths or kitchens? What does your firm do best? Start there.

2)   Don't try to sell your product or service, sell its *benefit* to the purchaser. Appeal to their emotions and their egos. Don't sell studs and wallboard, sell space, comfort, and convenience. In your copy and headlines, feature what people *want*.

A good illustration of this idea is the story about quarter-inch drill bits. There are enough quarter-inch drill bits sold in the U.S. each year to equal six for every man, woman and child. That's 1.3 billion drill bits. Nobody really needs drill bits. Why are so many sold? *Because people want quarter-inch holes!* Your advertising will be different and better than your competitor's if you feature what people want in your headlines, and then explain how your company can provide it.

3)   Identify your prospects. Determine what kind of home and homeowner are most likely to need your product.

4)   Define your market area. Where are your prospects located? Are they in one area or spread around the city?

5)   Select the media that most effectively reach your marketing area and your prospects.

6)   *Now,* establish a budget that allows you to use those particular media most economically.

7)   Whatever form your advertising takes (radio, TV, newspaper, direct mail, etc.), repeat it over a period of time. When someone thinks of remodeling, they should think of your company first.

8)   Finally, make it easy for every prospect to contact you. All your advertising is wasted if prospects can't reach you quickly and easily.

•   If the phone rings six times and no one answers . . . you've lost them.

•   If whoever answers the phone is vague or puts the caller off . . . you've lost them.

- If your postcard is returned, but they don't hear from you within two weeks . . . you've lost them.

- If the salesman says, "We're busy, can I get back to you?" . . . you've lost them.

When your advertising and promotion program is ready to go, be sure everyone in your organization is prepared to answer every inquiry as soon as it's received. Otherwise, all the money and effort you've put into your program will be wasted. Immediate follow-up is essential if you're going to convert leads to sales.

four

Design:
The Sales Clincher

*M*any remodeling contractors and their subcontractors don't participate directly in the design process. Far too often they leave this all-important responsibility to someone else. They simply build the plan agreed upon. That makes the job easier for the contractor, but it reduces the creativity and usually limits the profit margin available. When all the competitive contractors bid on the same design and plan, the work usually goes to the lowest bidder.

If you want the sales and recognition of a truly successful remodeling contractor, the design and plans you bid should be your own.

Compare what happens when you prepare plans for a remodeled kitchen, bath or room addition. First, you're the only contractor bidding those plans. If the owner likes your design, the work won't go to the lowest cut-rate dealer in town. Second, you can design what you build best and include the materials you want to install. Third, if your design catches the fancy of the owners, they'll want to build what you suggest even if the cost is higher than the competition is offering. Finally, good design is the sales clincher. It's much more effective than any list of materials, contract document, verbal description or book of samples could be. When you help the homeowner visualize how pleasant it will be to work in the beautiful, convenient new kitchen you've designed — you've made the sale.

Obviously, we feel that it's important for every remodeling contractor to offer a design service. In this chapter we'll suggest some principles of good design and include a number of examples. We'll also explain the design procedure. If you haven't done any mechanical drawing and don't want to learn, don't worry. Most communities have designers who work for reasonable fees. Maybe you know someone who enjoys drawing or planning the use of color and texture. If they would like to learn about space planning and interior design, perhaps you could enlist their services on a project basis for a moderate fee.

Good Design vs. *No Design*

Any time you see a remodeled home, take a minute or two to think about design. Is it good design or bad design? What would you have done differently? For example, good design reflects the character of the whole house. It should add to the house, without appearing to have been added on. Is the addition or the change in proportion to the rest of the house? Does it carry out the same style and provide enough space for the function intended? Are the colors and textures used in harmony with other colors and textures in the home? What are the traffic patterns? How about lighting, use of windows and privacy?

Be sensitive to design requirements. In many ways, *design makes the difference.* A well-designed remodeling project doesn't just close the sale. It brings in referral jobs as well.

When you go into a home to make a sales presentation, you have a lot of competition. Customers will compare your designs to the work of other contractors. They'll also compare them to designs they've seen in model homes, newspapers, and the latest decorator magazines.

It's your job to balance their expectations with practicality and offer them a finished product that's both realistic and pleasing . . . but, different.

Regardless of how impractical their "dreams" are, never make the mistake of talking down to a customer. They probably know far less than you do about construction. But frequently they've read magazines, books and newspaper articles about remodeling and may be a lot more knowledgeable than you expect.

Many homeowners have a pretty good idea of the amount of space they need and how they want to use that space. Some even know exactly what kind of fixtures, cabinets, appliances, and floor coverings they want. In fact, they've probably done some research. They're generally familiar with brand names, have an opinion on what's good or bad, and have a fair idea of prices.

What they don't know are the costs involved in moving walls, plumbing and electrical services, or installing new services. You and the homeowner must decide if the changes are possible and whether they can be done for a price you both can live with.

Even if their goals are unrealistic or uneconomical, hear them out. You may be able to direct their thinking along more practical lines.

If possible, offer something a little different, but maybe even nicer than what they had originally wanted. Always try to give the customer something *more*. Not necessarily bigger, but better. It doesn't always have to cost less, but it should be something which provides better value for the dollar. Offer more efficient use of space, more charm, more light, more beauty.

If you can't produce what they want for the price they want, explain it to them in those terms.

An example of a different approach to remodeling is in Figures 4-1 and 4-2. This was a disorganized, dingy little kitchen, with only one window. In the process of remodeling, the designer turned it into a showcase of efficiency without really expanding it. It's perfect for the couple who own the home. Both work and they need a convenient, though not necessarily large, kitchen.

The design required knocking out the rear wall to make room for a spacious bay window and window seat. The sinks, which had been located on that wall, were replaced by an island unit with fold-down countertops. Complementing this, the designer added an unusual custom-made pedestal table, shown in Figure 4-2. It provides additional work space and a convenient eating area.

The bay window increased light and made the room appear much larger. The problem of cramped work space was solved with the tiered table. Each of the three tiers rotate and slide out, allowing the table to assume several different positions and heights. The couple can prepare meals together, without getting in each other's way; and they can work standing or sitting, which is especially nice after a long day at the office. Moveable track lights mounted on the ceiling direct lighting where it's most needed. All this was done in very little space. The homeowners, needless to say, were delighted with their new kitchen.

Design Influences Sales

Pictures, we all agree, can sell more than ideas and promises. When your customer sees a nicely prepared floor plan and an elevation showing how the finished project will look, your chances of making the sale will go up about 75 percent. But, your design must be good if it's going to beat out the competition. Even before you settle on cost, if the customer doesn't like the design, you'll lose the sale.

Today's homeowners are more sophisticated than they were even ten years ago. They won't settle for conventional solutions. A new sink, new cabinets and new floor covering just aren't enough. They want something original and fresh. If you do each new project the way you did the last project, sooner or later you're going to run out of customers. No one wants to walk into their neighbor's house and find a remodeled kitchen that looks the same as their remodeled kitchen. This mistake is made by far too many remodeling contractors.

If something works well once, don't keep doing it again and again. This gets boring for you and the customers alike! Don't be conservative. Challenge the homeowner, and don't be afraid to rock the boat. When people see your completed projects they shouldn't say, "It looks very nice." You want them to say *"Wow! It's even better than I expected!"* Plan to give your customers something different and exciting. The referrals will come rolling in.

Courtesy: Armstrong World Industries, Inc.

New kitchen: not bigger, just better
Figure 4-1

Courtesy: Armstrong World Industries, Inc.

Custom-made pedestal table adds convenience
Figure 4-2

Some people think there's a lack of creativity in the remodeling business today. An article in a leading residential remodeling magazine warned homeowners against settling for the first remodeling contractor they talk to. It said that what most contractors want to do is what they've done before. If you're dealing with a homeowner who's up on the latest trends and ideas, you'd better have something good to offer. If you don't, someone else will.

Give Something Extra

Don't try to sell change for the sake of change. Listen to what your customer says . . . give them what they want and need. But don't just rearrange what they have. Create a design that gives them more space or convenience, plus (we say it again) something extra. Give them a design that's within the budget, but unique. Something as simple as adding a chair-rail and moldings can set your designs apart from your competitors. It costs very little, but the effect is striking.

A design that meets the criteria for being unique, creative, and very functional as well, is the garage home in Figure 4-3. It shows just how much living space can be packed into a small area.

The home, complete in every way, retains the original dimensions of the garage, just 24 by 22 feet. It's loaded with space-stretching ideas which can be used in practically any building or remodeling project. It has nearly 700 cubic feet of storage — as much as some homes three times its size!

Notice in Figure 4-4, that the floor plan is diagonal. The room was separated into a living, dining and sleeping area (called the main living area); a combination entry, den and office; a bathroom; and a kitchen with an adjacent utility room which functions as a pantry, storage area and laundry. There's no wasted space. All corners are used to expand the living area in the open space.

Since manufacturers now make scaled-down appliances and fixtures to meet the needs of smaller homes, this home has every modern convenience. In addition to what you might expect in an ordinary home, there's also a fireplace, skylight, a greenhouse corner off the kitchen which serves as a pleasant bar, and a complete apartment-size laundry.

An illusion of space is created by walling off only the utility room and bath, leaving the rest of the space open. At night, a sliding partition (fixed to a track in the ceiling) can be closed to screen the queen-size bed from the rest of the main living area. During the day, the Murphy bed tucks up into its own closet. If preferred, it can be left out and fitted with a slip cover to serve as a sofa.

The skylight, sliding glass doors, corner windows, and use of light colors on the interior all add to the spacious feeling. Blond and rattan furniture add to the general light atmosphere. A single floor pattern was used throughout to tie everything together.

Notice two other unique features. One is the island in the kitchen. It can be used for eating as well as food preparation and storage. It has ten drawers for silverware, utensils, and linen, and can be fitted with two center leaves to become a 45- by 60-inch dining table. It also rolls on casters, and can be brought into the living area and used as a game, sewing or hobby table.

Courtesy: Armstrong World Industries, Inc.

This home *was* a garage!
Figure 4-3

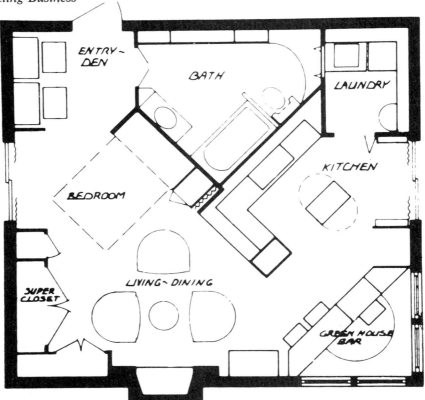

Courtesy: Armstrong World Industries, Inc.
Diagonal floor plan for garage home
Figure 4-4

The second feature is the "supercloset." Inside are shelves, drawers, and six clothes rods. Attached to the doors are receptacles for small items such as jewelry, scarves and handbags. The doors, which are mirrored on the inside, fold out and around to form a mini-dressing room.

Don't think that only trained designers could do this well. You can use any of these ideas! In fact, many manufacturers offer ideas like these to builders and remodelers free for the asking.

Learning From Doing

"Boss" Kettering, the genius behind many of the developments in the automotive industry and the father of modern refrigeration, once said: "If you're still doing it the same way you have always done it, you're probably doing it wrong."

Kettering didn't believe in fixing things if they broke or weren't working properly. He went right to the root of the problem and changed the design to make them better. In the early days of the automobile, the only way to start the car was to crank it by hand. Sometimes the car backfired though, with painful results. A member of Kettering's family suffered a broken arm while starting their car. So Kettering, instead of redesigning the cranking mechanism, developed the electric starter.

Kettering believed that each time we do something we should learn from it, and apply what we learn to future work. Many of us fail to do this. We get into ruts and keep repeating the same old routines. Those who do make their new knowledge work for them are constantly upgrading the quality of their work, and their lives. They aren't just getting by.

Design vs. *Redecorating*

There's a type of remodeling contractor, however, who makes a business out of just getting by. He's the one who has no design capability or experience, and doesn't try and develop any. Such contractors *survive* because of the type of homeowner they deal with.

This kind of homeowner wants to *"remodel"* simply because they're tired of looking at the same old kitchen. What they really want is a handyman to put in some new cabinets, wallpaper, paint, and maybe a built-in microwave oven. It's the same with the bathroom. There's no shower, or the tub and commode are old, so let's put in new ones.

This contractor doesn't need a floor plan, let alone a design. All he needs is the right price. Since he generally has two or three suppliers with several levels of quality (meaning *price*), he can come up with the right ticket and the homeowner is off on the road to happiness.

That's not remodeling! That's upscale redecorating. And if the price is a little too high, the homeowner will probably do the job himself. The difference between a "hired hand" and a "do-it-yourselfer" is about $100. The minute anything is $100 more than the homeowner wants to spend, they're going to do it themselves.

True remodeling means tearing out whatever you're going to remodel, redesigning it, and then putting it back together. Replacing walls, windows, doors, fixtures, appliances, wiring, plumbing, and improving the general quality of the home — that's remodeling. And to do these things takes planning and a knowledge of design. You can't ask a homeowner for $10,000 to $20,000 for a project, unless you come up with a design that justifies the cost.

In a true remodeling job, designing within a budget is what sells the job. If you want to improve your business and the quality of your work, learn more about your business . . . all phases of the business, but especially design. Each job you take should offer a new challenge, a new opportunity to develop and refine skills. Don't look at a project as another routine kitchen change-out — be creative. Imagination doesn't cost, but it sure can pay!

Design Needs Selling

Even good design, however, doesn't stand on its own. It may take some selling. But if the design is truly outstanding, any homeowner will be pleased. All of the headaches, frustrations, and costs that come with most big remodeling projects will be forgotten when the job is finished. Then, you're the winner.

Every client is different and should get a unique design. Everyone has their own outlook and style. It could be that the tried and true approach you've used in the past may be the only answer. But before you go down that road, try something fresh and original. Just using different materials such as the glass block in Figure 4-5, can give the most conventional job an unconventional look.

Courtesy: Armstrong World Industries, Inc.

Glass block is both creative and functional
Figure 4-5

Glass block was popular during the forties and early fifties. Then it fell out of favor. Now some enterprising designers have brought it back into fashion again. You can see in the photograph how glass block can be used for design as well as a structural element. It provides light, insulation, and security. Try and break it!

In the family room, shown beyond the kitchen, the contractor replaced the windows with a block wall. He also enlarged the window area over the kitchen sink. The room now has a more spacious look and feel. The windows had looked onto another building, so the owners haven't lost anything, but instead improved the general atmosphere of the rooms. They seem to sparkle.

The design didn't stop there. Glass block was used as support for the kitchen island and for the divider in the left foreground. The crowning touches included a light in the base of the island for nighttime illumination, and a circular neon ring at the window over the sink. This kitchen wasn't just modernized. It became a trend setter.

Look Ahead

When it comes to designing, in addition to "looking over, under, around and through the wall," add "look ahead." How old are the homeowners? How long do they plan to live there? Do they have children? If so, what ages? How do they see their life style changing over the next five years?

Today, as it has been for many years, the most desirable housing configuration in this country is a three bedroom, two bath home with a two-car garage. It should come as no surprise then, that most remodeling projects involve four areas: redoing the kitchen, adding another bedroom, adding on or redoing a bath, or building a garage.

In designing a remodeling job, determine the customer's needs and wants first. Save what your client really needs, then eliminate their whims. To do this, you need to be both a psychologist and a salesman.

If a homeowner can't give you a clear idea of what they want, you'll have to help them. Ask them as many in-depth questions as you can think of. This will help you come up with a plan that meets both their needs and their interests.

Suppose you're going to remodel a kitchen. First you'll have to find out which style the homeowners prefer: modern, traditional, country, provincial, or colonial. Perhaps none of these. Maybe they have something very different and personal in mind. You have to listen carefully to what they tell you, and mentally picture what they like.

How are they going to use the kitchen? Just to cook in, or will they eat some or all of their meals there as well? Are the meals to be formal or informal? Do they want a counter or a separate table?

Do they both like to cook? Does more than one person work in the kitchen at the same time? What kind of foods do they like to cook? What kind of appliances do they use or want to use? Do they need more than four burners and two ovens? Do they want a separate freezer in the kitchen?

How about entertaining? How many people do they have in as a rule? Do their parties seem to gravitate to the kitchen? Is the kitchen to be used as an entertainment center?

Do they have children who like to use the kitchen for play or study? Should there be a desk or special work area? Should it be located near the phone? Are the laundry facilities separate? Do they want to keep them separate or can they be put in the kitchen?

Is anyone in the family left-handed? Is anyone physically handicapped or in a wheelchair? If so, they may need lower counters, ramps instead of steps, or easily accessible appliances, fixtures and switches.

Make a list of questions to ask homeowners. Cover everything that may change your design. You don't want to find out too late that something has been left out. Here are a few more questions you may want to ask:

1) Do they have any hobbies which require use of the kitchen? What are they? Do they require any special appliances or additional outlets?

2) If there isn't a door to the outside, should one be included? Will they need a place to hang coats or other outerwear?

3) If there's an existing door, is it next to the sink, refrigerator or range where it may interfere with food preparation? Should it be closed or moved?

4) Is the traffic pattern into and out of the kitchen efficient? Should it be rerouted?

5) Would they like a pass-through cut into the wall to make serving in the dining room or the patio more convenient? Would it "open up" a smaller kitchen?

6) Do they want to install a phone in the kitchen if they don't have one already? Should there be a counter for notes or storage drawer for phone books?

7) Ceiling fans are both decorative and functional. Would one be appropriate?

8) Which would be more effective . . . light fixtures, fluorescents, or indirect perimeter lighting? Would an under-cabinet light be useful?

9) Do they like to barbecue? Would an indoor stovetop or island grill be cost-effective?

10) Are drinks for entertaining prepared in the kitchen? If so, would a separate wet-bar serve a useful purpose?

11) What type of storage would be most functional? What kind and how many utensils do they have?

12) Is everyday china and good china and silver stored together in the kitchen? If they are, is utilization of space efficient? If not, can it be improved?

13) Would they like a walk-in pantry?

14) Should there be a separate closet for brooms, vacuum, and cleaning products?

15) What type of floor covering . . . linoleum, parquet, tile, hardwood or carpeting?

The answers to these questions will help you determine the design of that particular kitchen. As you can see, they cover many items or situations which the homeowners may not have even considered. The answers to some of these questions can solve a lot of design problems. Develop your questions based on the type of remodeling you do. If you're a general remodeler, you should also have one for each area of your work: kitchens, baths, room additions, room conversions, and so on. Revise and improve your list as you gain experience. Once you have a good one, include it in your sales estimating book. But never stop revising and improving it.

Always keep in mind that although the homes may be similar, no two families are alike. To some, a kitchen may be the cozy center of family life; to others, it may be the center for their entertainment, an elegant showplace. Either way, it's the kind of detail you get from your questions which will provide you with the key to giving the homeowner something special; something tailored just to their personalities and lifestyle.

Design Today

Good design in remodeling can solve many problems in a home. It can add living space; increase the function of a room; bring the outside in with windows, skylights or a greenhouse; add lighting for utility or dramatic effect; create space for new appliances and fixtures; or offer the opportunity for energy savings.

Any remodeling contractor who has a flair for design has a competitive edge. Offer what people want: built-in or space-saving appliances, entertainment and computer centers, exercise rooms, hot tubs, saunas and more. Offer more convenience and utility in less space. Give good value for the money spent and you'll have no trouble building a thriving remodeling business.

Interior design is becoming a separate specialty in the construction hierarchy. An interior designer is just as much a part of the team as the architect, engineer, and draftsman. With all this emerging emphasis on design, it was only a matter of time before it spilled over into remodeling.

It's unfair to point a finger at many of today's remodeling contractors and say they aren't designers. Most of them didn't start out to be. They were expected to be able to take existing space and modify it to suit the homeowner's needs and budget. Ten years ago, most remodeling projects simply involved modernizing or bringing a home up-to-date.

Today, you're not only expected to bring the home up-to-date, but take it into the future.

Keeping Up with Trends

It's important that you stay current on trends in interior design. Fortunately, that's easy today. You have easy access to volumes of material on trends and fashion in home design. Nearly every magazine stand has at least two or three shelter magazines. Buy or subscribe to several. Ads in these magazines will promote other books and periodicals that can help you develop design skills.

Most remodeling projects involve kitchens or bathrooms. These are the two rooms most influenced by trends, as well as the ones most often remodeled. Trends run in cycles and have an average life of about ten years. Of course, some fade at five years while others go on for fifteen or even twenty.

Inflation and the economy have almost as much influence on design as function. The more money people have to spend, the larger and more spacious they want their homes. Those with less money want more convenience and utility from the space they have.

To satisfy these opposing interests, designers develop different styles. For the more affluent, you have the big, oversized kitchens which feature the European look and European products; smooth, sleek, expensive and more often than not, white. Why white? Simple. White denotes cleanliness. And, if there's one area we want clean, it's where our food is prepared. Although wealthy people may not eat or entertain in the kitchen, they want it to look clean.

Even homeowners of modest means can have a sleek, smooth, contemporary European look. However, it's smaller and it's American designed and manufactured. As for how clean it is, they'll know, because they do the cleaning. They may choose white, because it's stylish, but can just as easily go with another color.

Regardless of the style your customers select, they'll probably be influenced by a trend started by a designer or an architect. That's why it's important to follow trends. Once a trend gets started, homeowners are going to read about it, see it, and want it, and *you* want to know about it first. If you can't provide them with the latest ideas, they'll go to someone who can.

Figure 4-6 shows an example of a trend popular in the mid-1980's. The theme is fitness and health. The designer updated an older home, transforming two small bedrooms and a cramped bath into a large and luxurious exercise and health "spa."

Of course, not everyone wants or can afford something like this. But with one out of every four people in the country involved in some type of fitness program, it's certainly going to stimulate ideas. When people consider remodeling, they won't necessarily say to themselves that they want that particular design. But when they see something often enough, they begin to think they might like something similar.

Design Sources

Your training and experience is in construction, not design. But you still have to provide plans that use good design principles. What do you do? How do you come up with creative ideas that will capture the imagination of your customers? If you or your salespeople have experience in design, you don't have a problem. But if not, you'll have to get some help.

Where can you get help with design? Easy! Here are some other sources:

***Hire trained people*—** If your business is growing and you'll be hiring additional salespeople, look for applicants who have some type of training in interior design (not decorating).

Finding trained designers can be difficult. You may have to hire someone who's not trained but who is willing to learn. If you find a qualified candidate who doesn't have formal design training, offer to enroll that person in a design course.

Courtesy: Kohler Company
Design a health spa in the home
Figure 4-6

Libraries— Your local library will probably be a good source of information. There you'll find many periodicals and books on the subject. Although a lot of the design information published today is aimed at new construction, most of it can be applied to remodeling as well. You can even pick up good ideas from books and articles for "Do-It-Yourself" projects.

You may find the most current information in the periodical section of the library rather than in books. Although the business and trade sections of neighborhood libraries are growing, the number of books available on interior design are limited. Call your library and ask for the reference section. Tell them what you're looking for. They'll tell you how many books they have in stock on building and design, and whether they have access to additional books from nearby libraries. If so, they'll borrow them for you.

Shelter magazines— Subscribe to several shelter magazines through your business. Some of these are free or very low-priced. They're an invaluable source of information.

There are two types of shelter magazines, consumer publications and trade publications. If you can't find a particular magazine, check with the publisher if you know who puts it out. If you don't know, a bookstore can probably help you find out. The consumer publications can generally be found on newsstands or where magazines are sold. The trade publications are by subscription only. We recommend the following:

Consumer Publications

Better Homes and Gardens/Special Interest Publications:
 1) *Bedroom and Bath Ideas*
 2) *Building Ideas*
 3) *Country Kitchen Ideas*
 4) *Home Plan Ideas*
 5) *Kitchen and Bath Ideas*
 6) *Remodeling Ideas*

(Meredith Corporation, Locust at 17th, Des Moines, IA 50336. Ph: 515-284-3000)

Colonial Homes
(The Hearst Corporation, 1790 Broadway, New York, NY 10019. Ph: 212-830-2900)

Decorating Remodeling
(New York Times Co., 110 5th Avenue, New York, NY 10011. Ph: 212-463-1000)

Family Circle
(Family Circle Inc., 110 5th Avenue, New York, NY 10011. Ph: 212-463-1000)

Fine Home Building
(Trauton Press Inc., P.O. Box 355, 63 S. Main Street, Newton, CT 06470. Ph: 800-243-7252)

Home
(Home Magazine Publishing Corp., 9800 La Cienega Blvd., Inglewood, CA 90301.
Ph: 213-410-9546)

Home Owner
1001 Home Ideas
(Family Media Inc., 3 Park Ave., New York, NY 10016. Ph: 212-340-9200)

House Beautiful
(The Hearst Corporation, 1700 Broadway, New York, NY 10019. Ph: 212-903-5000)

Practical Homeowner
(Rodale Press Inc., 33 E. Minor St., Emmaus, PA 18098. Ph: 215-967-5171)

Woman's Day
(Diamandis Communications, 1515 Broadway, New York, NY 10036. Ph: 212-719-6749)

Other publications by Diamandis Communications:
    Home Improvements (semiannually)
    Kitchens & Baths (quarterly)

Trade Publications

Kitchen and Bath Design News
(KBC Publications Inc., 2 University Plaza / Suite 11, Hackensack, NJ 07601.
Ph: 210-487-7800)

Kitchen and Bath Remodeling
(A Chaners Publication, P.O. Box 5080, 1350 E. Touhy Ave., Des Plaines, IL 60018.
Ph: 312-635-5800)

Newspapers— Many newspapers run regular columns or sections on home remodeling.
Newspaper articles will usually be about the latest trends. If you see something like
"Sleek European Styling Slips Through the Kitchen Door" or "Designer Client
Relationships: Whose Responsibility Is What?" you'd better pay close attention. Your
customers are reading the paper too!

Magazines for remodeling contractors— Newspapers and the shelter magazines don't
usually deal with the mechanics of design and construction. But magazines for
professional remodelers and interior designers do. Here are the ones you should be
receiving:

Professional Publications

Builder
(Published for the National Association of Home Builders. Hanley-Wood Inc., 655 15th
St., N.W. Suite 475, Washington, DC 20005. Ph: 202-731-0717)

Fine Home Building
(Taunton Press Inc., P.O. Box 355, 63 S. Main Street, Newton, CT 06470.
Ph: 800-243-7252)

Qualified Remodeler
(QR Inc., 20 E. Jackson Blvd. Suite 700, Chicago, IL 60604. Ph: 312-922-5402)

Remodeling
(Hanley-Wood Inc., 655 15th Street, N.W. Suite 475, Washington, D.C. 20005.
Ph: 202-737-0717)

Magazines are a great instant resource if you're uncertain about the design for a particular project. Most have color photos covering rooms from every angle, as well as floor plans, elevations, wash-drawings, and before and after illustrations. Some also detail the placement of fixtures, electrical outlets, appliances, windows, doors, light fixtures and use patterns. They're literally packed full of design ideas.

Bookstores— If you're in a bookstore, take a few minutes and go to the reference section and see what you can find on construction. In addition to the standard books which cover specific trades, you should find at least ten or fifteen books dealing with design. They should cover the latest designs in baths, kitchens, bedrooms, living rooms, sunrooms, patios, recreation rooms, room additions, and how to finish off an attic or basement.

Find a bookstore that has a construction and building trades section. If they have a large selection, but don't have what you're looking for, ask for help. If you don't see what you need, go to the *Subject Guide to Books in Print*. It lists all books available by subject area. If what you're looking for isn't in stock, many bookstores will order it for you.

Specialty publishers— Many publishers specialize in publishing for particular markets. If you find one book on construction or remodeling you like, check the name of the publisher. Then call or write and ask what other books they have in print. They may have several that are of interest to you or apply to your business. The publisher of this book, Craftsman Book Company, is one such company. An order form bound into the back of this volume lists many good books that will help you make a better living in your field.

U.S. Government— One of the largest sources of information on construction, and the one most overlooked, is the U.S. Government. There's a catalog printed monthly of all government publications. You can find it in the reference section of your library. You can also send away for an annual list of government publications for consumers. Or you can contact the Federal Information Center (FIC) in your area for information on construction and remodeling. There should be an 800 number listed in your local telephone directory. Take advantage of this source. After all, you paid for it.

Product design programs— Many manufacturers of building materials offer brochures and literature which include good design ideas. These companies have staff designers paid to develop floor plans that make effective use of their product. These designs are usually very creative, dramatic and effective.

Manufacturers of bathroom fixtures, windows, kitchen cabinets, floor coverings, roofing, siding and doors are just a few of the companies to contact regarding this kind of information. The best way to determine what is available and which company offers brochures is to contact their nearest sales office. Tell them you're looking for floor plans and design ideas which utilize their products. Ask if they can supply the literature, or if not, who to contact within their company for this type of information. Some companies even offer seminars to promote their products. These aren't always publicized, so ask to be put on their promotion or advertising mailing list.

Other sources— Other sources of information on building and design include the National Association of Home Builders (NAHB), and (NARI) the National Association of the Remodeling Industry (The addresses for these associations were given in Chapter 3). If you're not involved with either, you should be.

Outside Design Help

Interior design is important now and will get more important as your customers become more aware of the difference that good design makes. When you're bidding on high ticket, high margin jobs, consider hiring an outside design service. It's much easier to hire skilled design professionals than it is to learn the principles yourself. Of course, good interior design talent doesn't come cheap. You'll have to weigh the advantages against the cost before you take this step.

At the time this book was written (1988), we were paying between $500 and $700 for an architect or designer to do a simple floor plan and elevation. If it's a complex job with several rooms involved, the fee is higher. If mechanical and electrical details are required, add ten to fifteen percent.

When the total cost of the job is more than $6,000 or $8,000, you can probably justify adding $500 for professional design. That's less than eight percent of the job cost. But what if the job is $3,000 or less? If you add a $500 design fee to your bid, you've increased the cost by more than sixteen percent! At that level, hiring a professional designer might be a luxury that makes your bid unattractive when compared with the competition — even if your design is superior. You'll probably lose that job to a lower bidder.

Some remodelers absorb half the design fee as a cost of doing business. They would add only $250 to the bid, taking the other $250 out of their profit. But if you come out of the job with little or no profit, what's the point? You should make more than wages on every job. Any skilled tradesman can make good money in the remodeling business without accepting the risk and responsibility that remodeling contractors are forced to assume.

Who Pays?
The design of a particular project, whether it's done in-house or by an outside designer, is a cost which should be paid by the homeowner, not the contractor. Establishing the cost, outlining the terms, and preparing a contract for the design costs should be done by the salesperson as a separate transaction. It is prepared separate from your bid and before the bid is finalized. See Figure 4-7.

HOME IMPROVEMENT CONTRACT

THIS DOCUMENT CONSISTING OF THIS AGREEMENT, PLANS AND SPECIFICATIONS, IF ANY, AND NOTICE OF CANCELLATION, NOTICE TO OWNER, ATTACHED HERETO AND MADE A PART HEREOF, SHALL CONSTITUTE THE AGREEMENT.

THIS AGREEMENT IS BETWEEN

CONTRACTOR/ SELLER/ BENEFICIARY	NAME Best Contracting Co.				DATE 8/15/1988
	ADDRESS 3456 First St.	CITY Anytown, USA	STATE	PHONE 479-1540	LICENSE NO 699-2156

BUYER/ OWNER	NAME Mr. and Mrs. Robert Homeowner			
	RESIDENCE ADDRESS 1234 Main St.,	CITY Anytown,	STATE USA	RESIDENCE PHONE 344-9286
	PLACE OF BUSINESS (If Any)	CITY	STATE	BUSINESS PHONE

Hereinafter called "Buyer", "Owner" and/or "Trustor" agrees to pay therefore the price hereinafter set forth upon the following terms and conditions.

CONSTRUCTION PROJECT

PROJECT ADDRESS – STREET 1234 Main St.	CITY Anytown,	STATE – PROVINCE USA	ZIP CODE 655-6187

Also known as Legal Description: Lot# _____ Tract# _____ Block# _____

Recorded in Book# _____ Page# _____ in the office of the County Recorder of _____
State of California.

DESCRIPTION OF PROJECT: CONTRACTOR WILL CONSTRUCT THE IMPROVEMENTS IN THIS AGREEMENT AND DESCRIBED GENERALLY AS FOLLOWS

Prepare working plans and specifications for certain additions and alterations to the dwelling. This shall include plot plan, floor plans, construction and mechanical specifications and elevation views (6 sets of prints).

☐ Buyer acknowledges receipt of notice to owner form.
☐ Buyer acknowledges receipt of notice of cancellation form.
☐ Are there plans, if so who will provide — owner ☐ contractor ☐.
☐ Check here if this space is insufficient for complete specifications (staple additions to original and each copy).
☐ Check here if there are plans (staple plans to original and each copy).
If checked, additional specifications or plans are attached to and incorporated in this Agreement.

NOT INCLUDED: THE FOLLOWING ITEMS ARE SPECIFICALLY EXCLUDED FROM THIS CONTRACT AND ARE TO BE PROVIDED BY THE OWNER

(Engineering, soil tests, permit service of permits fees.)

ALLOWANCES: The following items, where specific prices are indicated, are included in the Contract Price as allowances for the purchase price of those items to be selected by Owner. Owner and Contractor agree to adjust the Contract Price after verification of actual cost difference (if any) of said items selected by Owner.

APPLIANCES $ _____   LIGHT FIXTURES $ _____   BATH ACCESSORIES $ _____

FLOOR COVERING $ _____   HARDWARE FINISH $ _____   AND "OTHER" $ _____

Finish hardware is interpreted to include all knobs, pulls, hinges, catches, locks, drawer slides, accessories or other items that are normally installed subsequent to final painting. Light fixtures are interpreted to include only those fixtures that are surface mounted. Bath accessories are interpreted to include medicine cabinets, towel bars, paper holders, soap dishes, etc.

TIME FOR STARTING AND COMPLETING PROJECT: Work shall commence within ten days after the last to occur of the following (1) Receipt by the Contractor of all necessary building permits; (2) Owner has complied with all Terms and Conditions of the Agreement to date; (3) Receipt of all construction funds by Escrow or Funding Control (if any). Subject to adjustment for the above

conditions, work shall begin approximately on 2 weeks from / date of agreement and be substantially completed approximately on 4 weeks from start date. with additional time to be allowed as detailed in paragraph entitled "Delays" of the Terms and Conditions on the back hereof. Commencement of work shall be defined as

(BRIEFLY DESCRIBE TYPE OF WORK REPRESENTING COMMENCEMENT)

Contractors failure to substantially commence work, without lawful excuse, within twenty (20) days from the date specified above is a violation of the Contractors License Law.

CONTRACT PRICE

PAYMENT: Owner agrees to pay Contractor a total cash price of $ 1,500.00 OWNER represents that this agreement is a cash transaction where in no financing is contemplated and contractor acts in reliance on said representation.
The payment schedule will be

(1) Down payment of $ 500.00   (2) Payment schedule as follows: $1,000. when plans are delivered to owner.

The plan shall become the property of the owner when final payment is paid (THE COST OF THE PLANS SHALL BE CREDITED AGAINST THE CONTRACTORS BID PRICE IF BEST CONTRACTORS CO. IS SELECTED TO DO THE WORK WITHIN 90 DAYS.)

All payments will be made within five (5) days after billing. Overdue payments will bear interest at the maximum legally permissible rate. If any payment is not made when due. Contractor may keep the job idle until such time as all payments due have been made. A failure of payment for a period in excess of said (5) days shall be considered a major breach.

Contractor or Owner prior to commencement of construction and subject to lending institution (if any) approval, may request funds to be placed in an Escrow or Funding Voucher Control Service prior to commencement of work with funds to be disbursed to Contractor in accordance with the escrow instructions or voucher orders signed by the Contractor. In the absence of an Escrow or Funding Control Service, funds will be paid directly to the Contractor in accordance with the progress payments schedule referred to above.

NOTICE TO THE BUYER: (1) Do not sign this agreement before you read it or if it contains any blank spaces. (2) You are entitled to a completely filled in copy of this agreement. Owner acknowledges that he has read and received a legible copy of this agreement signed by Contractor, including all terms and conditions on the reverse side, before any work was done, and that he has read and received a legible copy of every document that owner has signed during the negotiation. If owner cancels this agreement after the right of recission has expired, and before commencement of construction, he shall pay Contractor the amount of expenses incurred to that date plus loss of profits.

TERMS AND CONDITIONS

The terms and conditions on the reverse side are expressly incorporated into this Agreement. This Agreement constitutes the entire understanding of the parties. No other understanding or representations, verbal or otherwise, shall be binding unless in writing and signed by both parties. This Agreement shall not become effective or binding upon Contractor until signed by Contractor or a principal of Contractor. By his signature below, Owner acknowledges receipt of a fully completed copy of this Agreement.

NOTICE

Contractors are required by law to be licensed and regulated by the Contractors' State License Board. Any questions concerning a contractor may be referred to the Registrar Contractor's State License Board, 3132 Bradshaw Road, Sacramento, California. Mailing address: P.O. Box 26000, Sacramento, California 95826.

You, as Owner or Tenant, have the right to require the Contractor to have a Performance and Payment Bond.

You, the buyer, may cancel this transaction at any time prior to midnight of the third business day after the date of this transaction. See the attached notice of cancellation form for an explanation of this right.

SALESMAN	REGISTRATION#	OWNER – BUYER SIGNATURE X Robert Homeowner	DATE 8/21/88
ACCEPTED BY CONTRACTOR - SELLER SIGNATURE X William Best		OWNER – BUYER SIGNATURE X	DATE

FORM 213A

Prepare a separate contract for plans
Figure 4-7

Contractors don't have to pay for professional design services out of pocket before they have an agreement with the owners. You should offer to have prepared plans and elevations at cost — the designer's fee. The plan becomes the property of the homeowner, but the cost is credited against the remodeler's bid price if that remodeler is selected to do the work.

Here's something else to consider when hiring outside design help. When you draw the plans, you include the materials you want to install and the construction detail you want to build. When a design professional working for a fee draws the plans, you'll probably have higher material costs and more labor expense. Some designers want to buy the cabinets, fixtures, and appliances they include in their designs. When they do, they add at least a fifteen percent markup to the cost. You'll have to pass that on to the customer.

Be aware of these problems. Adding five percent to your bid will make your proposal five percent less attractive to the owners — unless that increase adds at least five percent to the value of the completed job.

Here's our final point about hiring design professionals. Don't get the impression that we're opposed to charging $500 for good design on a small job. We've had some $2,500 jobs where charging $500 for good design was money well spent. Some owners consider design more important than price. If "cost is no object," then by all means, use a design service.

How Much Help Do You Need?

When selecting a designer, consider the type of job. On large projects, as in Figures 4-8 and 4-9, get an experienced professional. You'll need the best help available to be competitive. Consider a job like this an opportunity to show what your team can do. Work as shown in Figures 4-8 and 4-9 will produce both satisfied customers and referrals for many years. It's permanent advertising if you do it right. These two projects were completed for about $40,000 each. The elevation drawings show the kind of work you should expect from an outside service, not only in drawing, but in planning as well. Quality work creates a visual impact that turns prospects into buyers.

Drawing elevations— Many remodeling contractors can visualize what the project should look like but can't draw an elevation view that's acceptable. If you don't have a gift for drawing, find an artist or drafting student who can draw an elevation or perspective view for you. Many students would be happy to have the experience and will work for a reasonable fee.

Drawing floor plans— The amount of detail to include in a floor plan depends on the drafting skill of the salesman or contractor and the size of the project. If you're moving walls, adding windows or doors, or making other major changes in the house, a drawing is essential. It's the only way to capture the look and feel of what you're proposing. A project in the $40,000 range should always be thoroughly detailed and include a perspective drawing.

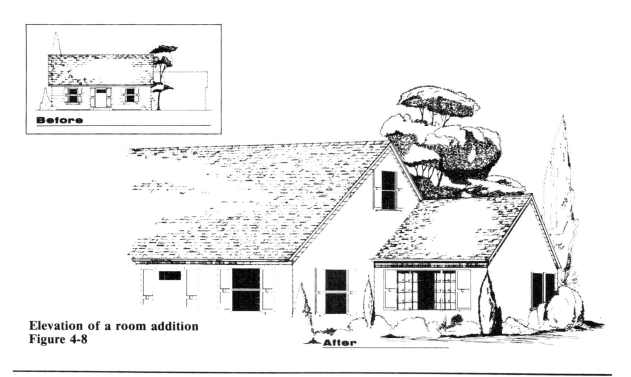

Elevation of a room addition
Figure 4-8

Quality elevations create a visual impact
Figure 4-9

Some contractors deliberately limit the amount of detail in a floor plan to confuse the competition. If they think a homeowner is going to show a competitor their floor plan, they'll leave out important details so the competitor can't use it to underbid them. A competitor who knows all the details in your bid can usually figure some way to offer a lower price. It's dangerous to leave the plan with your customer until you've got a signed contract. Some homeowners will shop the plan all over town trying to get a better deal — usually fibbing a little on the price you quoted. Avoid leaving any plan with your customers unless, of course, your customer has bought and paid for it. Then the plan belongs to the customer. He or she can do anything with it. But any plan you've produced at your own expense still belongs to you.

Before and after— A good floor plan should always include before and after drawings. This way the customer can see and appreciate what you're going to do. It can also help you spot problems before they occur, such as in the placement of doors, windows, and fixtures.

If you do only a new floor plan, the homeowner has to mentally compare a room or area that exists to one that exists only on paper. With a before and after floor plan, the homeowner can compare one drawing to the other. It makes the changes you're proposing easier to understand. Use vellum or tracing paper so your customer can lay the old over the new to see how changes fit into the floor plan. Make it easy for your customer to understand your proposal and you've made closing the sale easy.

Look at Figures 4-10A, 10B and 10C. The contractor had the designer prepare a before view (floor plan A). Notice how much easier it is to visualize the changes in floor plans B and C when floor plan A shows the existing design. Almost every room in the house was involved in this remodeling project. Every complicated job like this needs a complete plan before the homeowners are asked to sign the agreement.

Before remodeling
Figure 4-10A

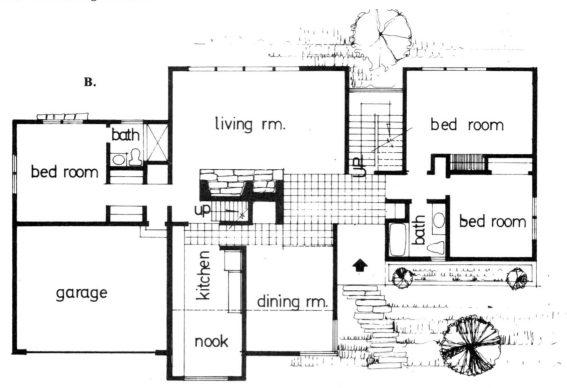

First floor after remodeling
Figure 4-10B

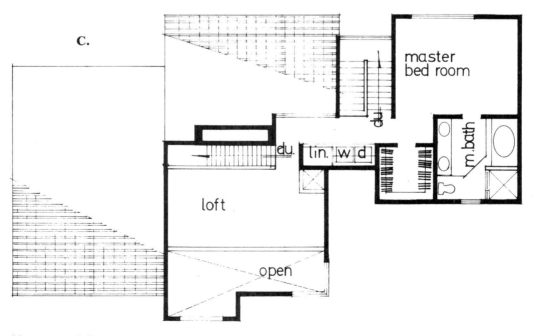

New second-floor addition
Figure 4-10C

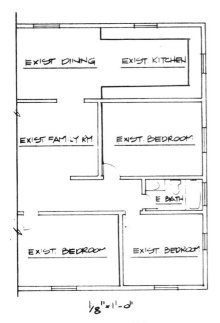

Simple one story addition
Figure 4-11A

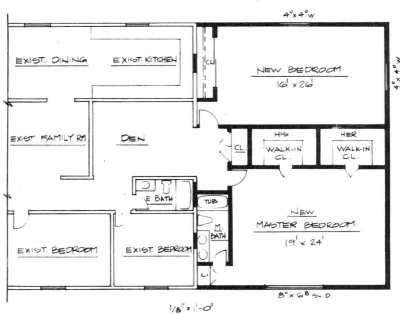

Addition with existing floor plan
Figure 4-11B

Preparing a Design

A good design for a simple project should take about thirty minutes. If the design takes longer, do it in your office. If the customer's at your place of business, do it after they've gone.

The next two sets of floor plans show a new addition and a remodeled bath. The addition in Figures 4-11A, 11B and 11C is quite complex. It includes adding a new wing with two bedrooms and a bath, and converting an existing bedroom to a den. A project as extensive as this requires considerable planning. You'll need a well-designed floor plan to sell the homeowner on what will be a very expensive addition.

There's too much room for error on a project of this size to prepare a design on the spot. Draw plans like this at the office, and make sure the contractor and salesperson review them. Expect many questions from the homeowner about space allocation and costs.

View (after)
Figure 4-11C

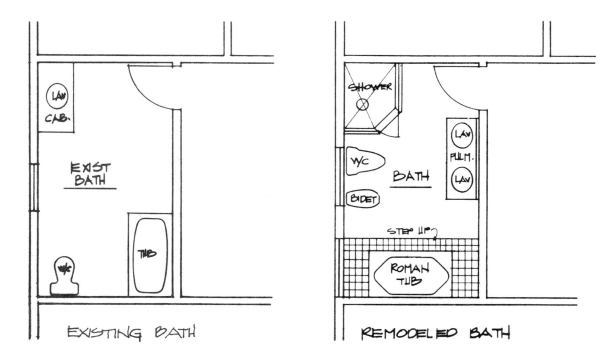

Bathroom remodeling plan
Figure 4-12A

On the other hand you can, and should, prepare simple projects like the one shown in Figures 4-12A and 12B in front of the customer. It gives the buyer a feeling of participation — and that makes getting their approval easier.

The design for the bath in Figure 4-12 was done in the customer's home. When you're remodeling baths, the size of the existing room is always a limiting factor. You may have to move interior walls to gain space, especially if you're adding additional fixtures. That can take more time than the half hour limit. But the contractor who designed this one proposed a totally new and elegant bath in exactly the same space.

He was able to rearrange the room to make space for the new fixtures. As a result, the design took only about twenty minutes to draw. The customer liked the plan, and the salesperson left with an approval.

Both of the above plans were drawn to scale, although the contractor who did the bathroom plan didn't include the scale. Since the room size didn't change, you could look at the drawings in Figure 4-12A and say no scale was needed.

But look at Figure 4-12B. It's very misleading. It creates the illusion that the bath will be much larger than it is. The customer could be disappointed with the completed job. Put the scale on every plan, no matter how small or simple it is. Draw perspectives carefully to illustrate the project's actual appearance and size.

Do the finished elevations or perspective in your office. Take time to do them accurately and to scale. Present them to the clients when you meet to sign the contract. Finished elevations and perspectives help sell the job.

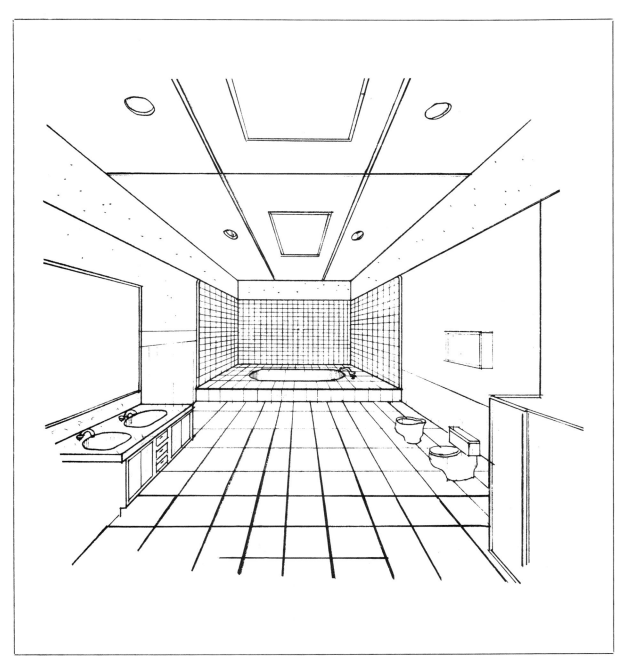

View (after)
Figure 4-12B

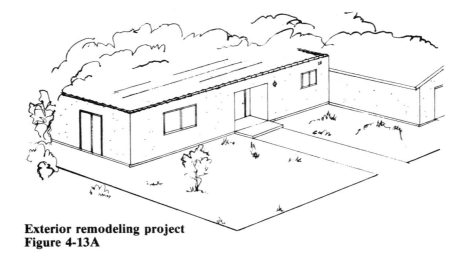

Exterior remodeling project
Figure 4-13A

Remodeling home exteriors— Figure 4-13A and 4-13B are elevation views that helped close a sale. Exteriors of older homes are "bread and butter" work for a skilled remodeling designer. It's easy to suggest improvements that will make the home a much more attractive, comfortable place to live. Here are some prime examples:

• New roof styles

• New styles or positions for windows and doors

• New exterior siding or finish

• New fencing, walks, patios and trim

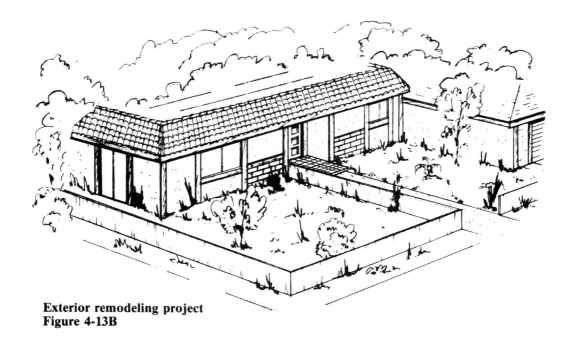

Exterior remodeling project
Figure 4-13B

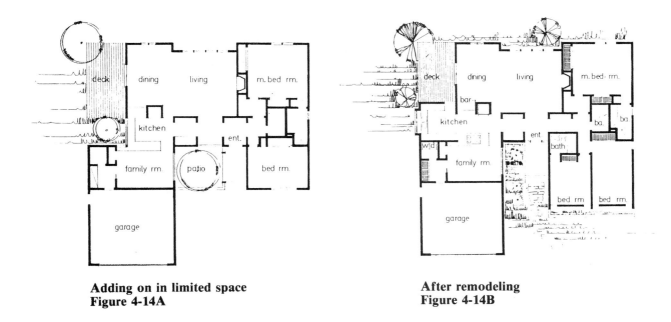

Adding on in limited space
Figure 4-14A

After remodeling
Figure 4-14B

Figure 4-13B is a simple elevation showing how new trim and roofing will look. A drawing like this both helps sell the job and avoids complaints when the job is finished. A customer who's surprised or disappointed by the materials you install is worse than no customer at all. You'll either have to redo the job or threaten suit to collect. Either way, you've made an enemy.

Note that accurate scale isn't important here. But be sure the before and after renderings are the same size.

Adding on in limited space— The project in Figures 4-14A and 4-14B, involved major changes. The homeowner wanted to enlarge the kitchen and add a bedroom and bath. The job required some creative planning by the contractor because there wasn't much space available. He had to move old walls, add new ones, and change the entrance to the house. Although the before and after plans are well drawn, without a scale and dimensions for the remodeled areas, you can only guess at how much larger the home will be. It's also hard to tell how much space remains for the entry and the front patio.

If the plans showed dimensions, the homeowners could pace off the new patio area and see how much space would remain. They would know at a glance if the kitchen and bedrooms would be too big or too small or about the right size. These are very important points. How happy will the homeowners be if they sacrifice one nice 15 foot by 18 foot bedroom for two tiny bedrooms and a bath that aren't big enough to turn around in. If the new rooms are going to be small, show on the plans exactly how small *before* construction begins.

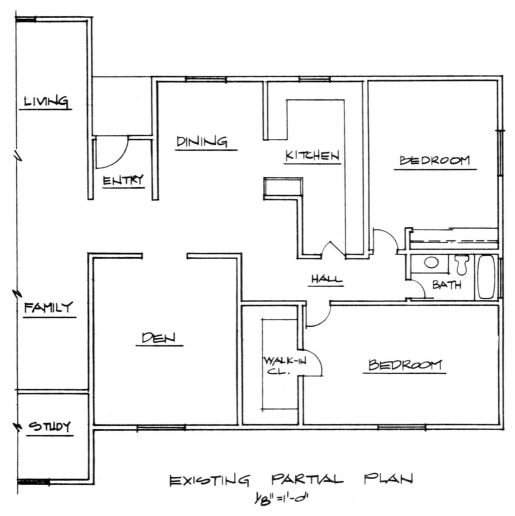

EXISTING PARTIAL PLAN
⅛" = 1'-0"

Floor plan with scale shown
Figure 4-15A

Adding a second story— Figures 4-15A through 4-15E show a large second-story addition. The homeowners wanted and needed considerably more room. In fact, they needed three more bedrooms, two baths, and the closet space to go with them. The least expensive way to add that space would have been to add rooms at ground level. But the lot was too small for that. So the contractor had to build up rather than out.

In a project this size, there's always the question of how big everything is. To help the homeowners, the contractor put the scale, ⅛" = 1'0", on his first drawing, Existing Partial Plan (Figure 4-15A). All the other drawings were made to the same scale. He also showed dimensions for the new second-story rooms so the homeowners could *visualize* how big the rooms and windows would be. The dimensions are shown on the "Second-story addition plan" (Figure 4-15C).

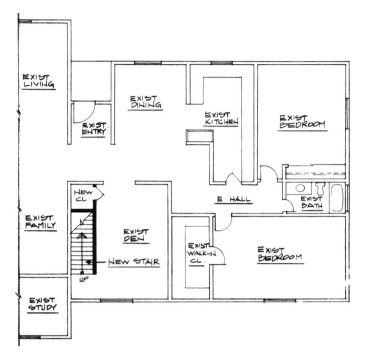

Remodeled first floor plan
Figure 4-15B

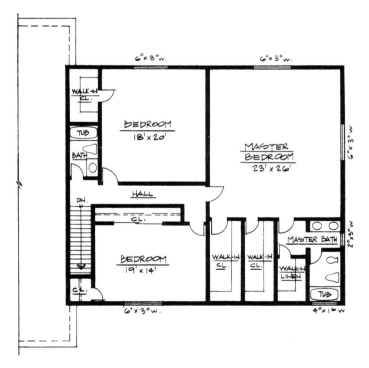

Second-story addition plan
Figure 4-15C

Exterior view (before)
Figure 4-15D

Exterior view (after)
Figure 4-15E

Sell the Design

As you're drawing the design for a remodeling project, sell it to your clients. Explain what you're doing and why you're doing it. For example, if your project includes a room addition which faces south, explain that south-facing windows save energy in cold weather. There's a reason for everything you suggest. Explain that reason and the alternatives you considered and rejected. That reinforces your credibility as a design professional. It also make a sale harder for the competition.

Always sell energy savings. Every homeowner wants the most economical warmth in the winter and the most economical cooling in the summer . . . with optimum comfort in both seasons. Good insulation works as well for the homeowner against the heat of summer as it does against winter's cold.

Energy-efficient fixtures and appliances can pay for themselves in just a few years. If you have to move any older fixtures or appliances, suggest they be replaced. Tell your client what the pay-off period is. For instance, suppose you replace an old toilet with a new one that saves 2.5 gallons of water per flush. If it's flushed 20 times a day, you'll save 18,250 gallons of water in a year. Depending on water cost, savings in two or three years could pay for the toilet. Imagine the savings over 15 or 20 years! Any smart homeowner will say "yes." And point out, of course, that the labor cost to put the old one back in is the same as to put a new one in.

Detail and Accuracy Are Important

Good remodelers make both before and after floor plans. That's extra work, we know, but it's worth the trouble. But don't try to make your plans works of art. It's far more important to make a plan that's accurate than one that's artistically impressive. An elevation like Figure 4-16 looks good, but it's not essential. A clear, accurate floor plan and elevation will be enough.

Poorly executed drawings and plans cause two types of problems. The first is with the homeowner. If the plans and elevations you draw don't present a clear picture to the homeowner, you're going to have a dispute when work begins, or worse, when it's finished.

Anything and everything you're going to move or change in a project should be included in the finished floor plan. This means every window, door, appliance, cabinet and fixture involved in that particular project. This reinforces your sales presentation and can also help later if the customer wants to make changes.

Let's say the customer wants to move an electrical outlet. Unfortunately, the framing makes that nearly impossible. Sometimes, what appears to be a minor change to the homeowner is actually a major revision. If you and the homeowners have reviewed all proposed changes, you could explain why the outlet needs to be where it's shown on the plans. They may still insist on the change, but at least you've identified the problem. Write a change order, spelling out everything that's added, moved or eliminated.

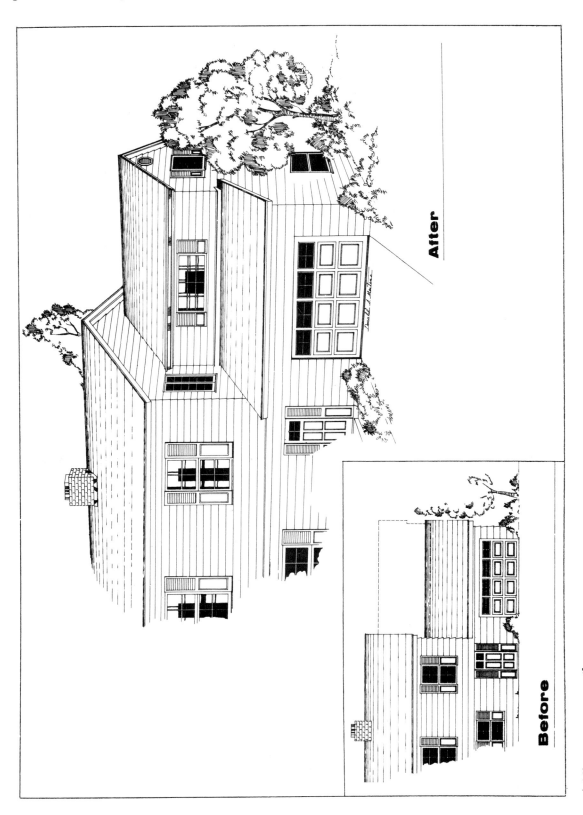

Adding a room over the garage
Figure 4-16

The second problem with poorly drawn plans is that they encourage poor workmanship. Tradesmen can't be expected to read your mind. If the plans are vague, expect errors. Work you give to subcontractors must be shown clearly in the plans or described accurately in the specifications. Otherwise you'll have errors, extra charges and disputes with your subs. Your plans have to show every detail. If the plans don't show where the toilet paper hanger gets installed, don't complain if it's hung four feet from the toilet.

If your drafting skills aren't up to par, it's easy to learn the basics. Many schools offer daytime and evening classes in both drafting and art for remodelers and designers. If you can't attend a class, books are available that teach drafting.

You don't need a lot of expensive equipment to draw a good plan. A kitchen table, a good T-square, two pencils, and one or two triangles work nearly as well as a professional drawing board with built-in square, triangles and fancy drafting pens. The most significant difference is the cost.

Use Proper Scale and Symbols
Good drawings are prepared to the proper scale and use standard symbols.

Scale— Although practices vary somewhat across the country, the scales shown below are the ones most commonly used. They're easy to read and don't require oversized sheets of paper which are expensive and difficult to duplicate.

You'll get a clear picture of the plan or elevation on either letter size (8½'' x 11'') or legal size (8½'' x 13¼'') paper. Both sizes can be copied on any copy machines. Anything bigger may require a special copy machine or a blueprint machine. The best scales to use are 1/2'' or 1/4'' to 1 foot. Anything smaller than 1/4'' is too hard to read and will be too cluttered with detail.

Plan	Scale
Plot	1'' = 20'
Foundation	¼'' = 1'
Floor	¼'' = 1'
Elevations	¼'' = 1'
Sections through building	⅛'' = 1'
Details	1½'' = 1'
Cabinet elevations	¼'' = 1'
Fireplace elevations	¹⁄₁₆'' = 1'
Floor framing	¹⁄₁₆ to 1'' = 1'
Electrical	½'' = 1'

- Draw elevations smaller to minimize the number of sheets.

- Elevations that show only a part of the job can be drawn to a larger scale so more detail shows.

- Depending on the size and type of floor plan, the scale can be 1/4'' up to 1''. The larger the better, as long as it all fits onto a single sheet of paper.

- Electrical work can be included on the floor plan. However, if it's complicated, a separate plan should be drawn so that the electrical contractor can see exactly what work needs to be performed for his bid.

Symbols— You'll eliminate most questions and errors on materials if you use the standard symbols shown in Figure 4-17. When you're putting in your comments or instructions, the following abbreviations can save you time and space. These are the ones most commonly used and understood in the industry. Spell out all other words.

&	....	And, as in sand & gravel
@	....	At, as in 2'' x 10'' joists @ 16'' o.c.
C	....	Center line
Conc	....	Concrete
O.C.	....	On Center, as in 16'' o.c.
W/	....	With, as in w/6'' conc slab over

Specialists vs. *General Contractor*

Remodeling jobs can be divided into two categories: specialty projects and multi-trade projects. Designing and contracting for each type of job has its limitations and advantages.

If you're a general contractor dealing in multi-trade jobs, you may find yourself at a disadvantage bidding on a single kitchen project against a contractor who specializes in kitchens. A general contractor will usually charge more and make less on a specialty job than the specialty contractor. The contractor who just remodels kitchens can do the work much faster and more efficiently than a contractor who only does an occasional kitchen. He may also have more design experience in that area and more ideas to offer the customer.

This doesn't mean that general remodeling contractors should avoid bidding against single-trade or room-specialty contractors. Many jobs start simple and grow more complex as the homeowner begins to see the possibilities. Whenever there's a multi-trade job involving carpentry, concrete, plumbing, electrical, heating, roofing, siding or other trades, a general contractor is in a better position to take on the entire job. Most homeowners prefer to deal with one contractor who can coordinate the whole project. They want one contractor responsible for the whole job. They want someone they can go after to make good on the mistakes any tradesman made.

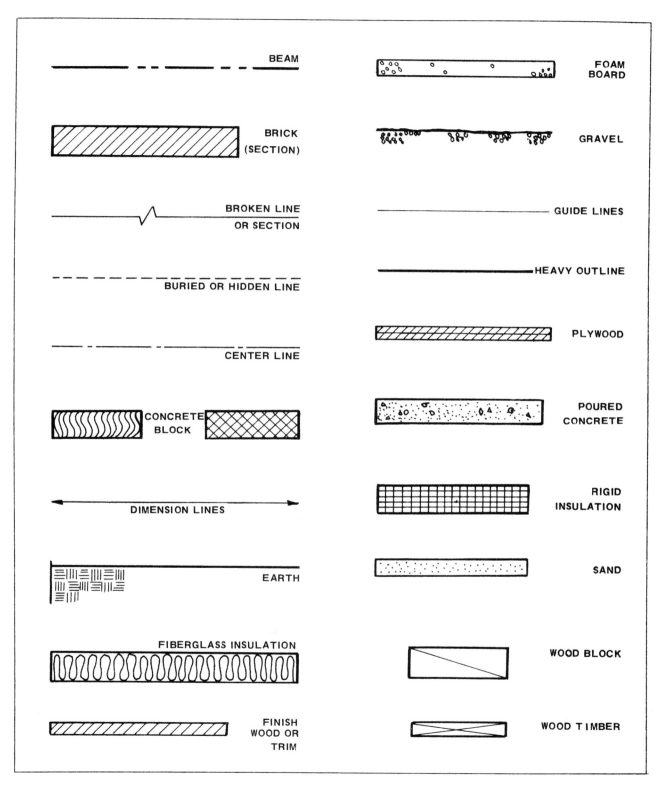

Common construction symbols
Figure 4-17

Some homeowners try to save a few dollars by acting as their own general contractor, subcontracting each trade on the project. The concept is sound. But in practice we've never seen it work as planned. Every subcontractor knows enough to bid higher to a first-time builder (the homeowner) than to a regular customer. Extra money paid to the subs is usually more than a general contractor would have cost.

Problem Jobs

Jobs that cause the greatest number of problems are the ones that take the longest and involve the greatest number of trades.

When you're working on a large and complicated job, the homeowners can be the biggest problem that you have to deal with. They're worried about how long the job is taking, among other things. The best way to overcome anxiety is to keep the project on schedule. That's not easy in multi-trade jobs. But the delays will be more tolerable if you explain the situation to the homeowners: every trade takes a certain amount of time and there could be delays between trades. In any case, keep homeowners informed about job progress.

Murphy's Law usually applies on larger jobs: *If something can go wrong, it will.* Although no contract can be written to cover all situations, the Standard Form Agreement in Chapter 2 will help minimize the confrontations. A well designed and thoroughly explained plan is another big asset in difficult situations.

The Economics of Remodeling

Well designed home improvements can add more to the value of a home than they cost. Stress this point when making your sales presentation. Emphasize that every dollar spent on improving the home can add a dollar or more to the resale value, especially if the other homes in the neighborhood are of equal or greater value.

Sometimes you'll be asked to make improvements on homes that are already worth more than most of the other homes on the block. Usually the homeowners are aware of this fact but want the improvements anyway. If they don't plan on selling the house, they may not be too concerned about recapturing their investment. For them, the quality or comfort of living in their home is more important than justifying the cost of remodeling.

What should you do if you're in a situation where the homeowners *don't* realize that the proposed project is an over-improvement? Even if they have the money to pay for the remodeling, *you have an obligation to advise them that they probably won't get their investment back when they sell.*

Some home improvements are a matter of personal preference and aren't expected to add as much value as they cost. For example, a swimming pool and spa will add pleasure for the homeowner even though the return on investment is low. That's a personal decision — and one you shouldn't make for someone else. When you're faced with this situation, it's always better to explain facts honestly. Your prospective clients may go ahead with the job, cut it back, or drop it altogether. But it should be *their* decision.

Here's something else to consider when dealing with "over-improvements." If the homeowners are over their heads in debt and can't afford the project, it's even more important to advise them carefully. You may not get *your* investment back! A contractor who sells a job that the owners can't afford is doing a disservice both to his or her company and the remodeling industry as well. Good business should always promote ethical standards.

Containing Remodeling Costs

Here's a rule of thumb we follow: If your customers want to recover the remodeling cost at the time of sale, limit improvements to no more than 25 percent of the present home value.

There are two reasons for this. First, most financial institutions set the limits of financing home improvements at 25 percent of the home's present value. Second, most realtors agree that it's hard to sell a home for $250,000 in a neighborhood where most homes sell for $150,000 — even if the improvements justify the price.

Recoverable Improvements

Realtors are usually a good judge of what adds value to a home and what doesn't. Most would agree that modernizing a kitchen is the best home improvement investment, providing the cost doesn't exceed 25 percent of the present home value. Another high-value improvement is the addition of a bath. If the home had only one bath, the recoverable cost of adding a second bath should be about 100 percent; a bath-and-a-half, 80 percent; two baths, 50 percent.

Adding a third bedroom to a two-bedroom house should add nearly as much value as you charge. A garage addition falls in the same category, especially in a neighborhood where overnight street parking is limited or prohibited and the lighting is poor. In this case, figure the recoverable costs at 75 to 125 percent of your price.

Here are a few more improvements that will give homeowners a good return for their dollar investment. The percentage following each type of remodeling project shows the typical recoverable cost.

Air Conditioning: If it's central air, 75 to 100 percent.

Basement Recreation Room: 15 to 65 percent.

Exterior Repainting: A fresh coat of paint will do more to sell a house than anything else. Recoverable costs run from 100 to 300 percent or even higher. The variation in the percentage reflects other factors such as the location of the home and its workmanship.

Exterior Siding: 75 percent or more.

Fireplace: If it contributes to the heating and saves energy, up to 100 percent. If it's just a decoration, almost nothing.

Family-Room Addition: This depends entirely on how much it cost and how the price of the home compares with other homes in the neighborhood.

Heating System: Probably nothing. Most people take a heating system for granted.

Interior Decorating: Also probably nothing. Interior decorating is a matter of personal taste.

Landscaping: Anywhere from 10 to 50 percent, depending how extensive it is. Low maintenance is always a plus.

Patio: Depends on the cost in relation to the rest of the house, from 25 to 75 percent. (Ask the buyer who likes to cook out!).

Swimming Pool: A pool can be a real selling point to a family with older children. But it can scare off buyers with small children. Many people see them as a maintenance nuisance — which they are. A lot depends on the climate and the area. Figure the recovery rate at up to 40 percent.

The Last Word on Design

Successful remodeling contractors know that design is an important part of the service they provide. Good design makes a home more attractive, more comfortable and provides more of the conveniences that modern homes are expected to have.

If you're more comfortable working on site than laying out a new floor plan, don't be concerned. After all, most remodelers got into the business by working on construction projects. But, if you're losing business or not selling jobs because your designs aren't acceptable, it's time to sharpen up your design skills.

Even if your skills are fairly good, you may want to use outside design help occasionally. A good designer will be worth the cost if you get the job. Even if the designer's fee eats into your share of the profit, completing a job that's a real knockout can bring in referral business for many years.

Design carries as much weight as cost, sometimes more, in the minds of many homeowners. Most good designs will sell themselves. If you feel your design is right for your customer, have enough confidence in your judgement to sell it to the homeowners. If you can give a client something different, exciting and affordable, more often than not, you're going to get the job.

Develop a Price/Estimating Book

*L*earning to be a good estimator is a "hands-on" process. It takes knowledge and experience to estimate the time and materials needed to complete a particular job. When you're just starting out, estimating can be the most intimidating part of a remodeling job.

Your task is to assign a dollar cost to each item, add in your indirect and overhead costs, and most important, figure in your profit!

As an estimator, you're dealing with one known fact and several unknown ones. You *know* you're going to add a room or redo a kitchen or bath. Your job is to establish what the *unknowns* are. What's best suited to this particular project? Do you want to use 2 x 4s or 2 x 6s? Should you order board feet, square feet or cubic feet? What are the installation costs for the materials you want to use?

That's a lot of responsibility. And if you make a mistake or miss something, or your subcontractors' estimates are off, you and your company can come up short. That's why experience is so important. No two jobs are alike. Each one has its own potential problems. You must know how homes were built yesterday as well as how they're built today. When you take a wall down or a roof off, you need to have a pretty good idea of what you're going to find. Otherwise, you may be in for some expensive surprises.

Know Past and Present Construction Methods _____

Every good estimator should be able to identify the age of a house and know the construction techniques used when the house was built. The way a house was built can have a major influence on the cost of remodeling.

For example, several years ago, in some parts of the country, homes were built with single-wall construction, flat studs, or even no studs. Floor and ceiling joists were underspanned, by today's codes. Electrical service and wiring was inadequate compared to current electrical standards. The same is probably true of the plumbing, heating, and insulation. Only recently have some codes required that floors, walls, and ceilings be insulated.

Today's building codes require construction that is both more durable and safer for all of us. The saying "They don't build them like they used to," is certainly true. We can't. We couldn't get yesterday's construction past today's building inspectors.

Homes and apartments built today are much better than homes and apartments built thirty, fifty, or more years ago. They're better not only because building codes require it, but because construction techniques, tools and materials have improved over the years. Whether you consider today's designs better or worse than designs of the past, we can all agree that most homes built today have to meet higher standards than homes built as little as ten or twenty years ago.

As a contractor, you can take pride in the fact that what you build today is built to last at least as long as those splendid old Victorian homes you see in older sections of some cities and towns.

When you go into a home to estimate remodeling costs, you have to look past the exterior and anticipate the problems. If it's a fairly new home, the problems may be minor. The older the home is, the more cautious you need to be.

One contractor we know found himself in a bad situation because he wasn't aware of past building requirements in his area. As part of a project, he had to remove the concrete apron in front of a garage. Based on his construction experience, he estimated that it would take one day for two men to break up the slab by hand and remove the debris. Unfortunately, when the house was built in the 1950's, aprons had to be reinforced with No. 3 rebar. It took his crew two days using a jackhammer and compressor to get the job done.

The homeowner wasn't willing to pay for the extra work. After all, the contractor had agreed to remove the apron for a set price. This caused friction between the contractor and homeowner that continued through the entire job. Most people are a little more understanding. But estimating mistakes happen all too often in the remodeling industry.

Starting Out As an Estimator _____

Construction cost estimating is an art, not a science. There is no single price that will be right for every contractor bidding the job. Every estimate has to be custom-made for the project at hand and for the crew that will be assigned to do the work.

There are good estimates and, unfortunately, *bad* estimates. Good estimates are prepared in a logical, orderly, step-by-step, consistent process. They're based on a good working knowledge of the construction trades involved and include every cost in a project that can be anticipated before work actually begins. Bad estimates occur when you guess, take shortcuts, rush the job because you're under pressure, or don't ask for help when you find yourself in unfamiliar situations.

How can someone without experience learn all the ins and outs of estimating? The best way is to join a local or national remodeling association. Local remodeling associations and local chapters of national associations frequently hold seminars on estimating. They're usually conducted by experienced estimators and local contractors. Annual remodeling association conventions often include estimating seminars and workshops as well. Through these associations you'll meet experienced contractors who can give you advice and help you avoid the more common estimating mistakes in your area.

Another way to gain experience is to become a franchisee of a national remodeling company. They usually provide training programs that will help you sharpen construction, management and estimating skills. As a franchisee you'll meet other franchise holders who have overcome the same problems you're wrestling with. Franchise operators also distribute newsletters with helpful tips for running your business more effectively and efficiently. They're extremely helpful to people just starting out. Of course, you'll have to weigh the cost of buying a franchise against the potential benefits you'll receive.

Develop a Price/Estimating Book

Every estimator needs a book of reference material for use when compiling estimates. We'll call it your *estimating and pricing book*. It's your own collection of material costs, labor required, and reference data used for estimating. It should be your personal bible. You and every person in your organization who does estimating should keep an estimating and pricing book.

It would be convenient if you could send away for an estimating and pricing book that provides all the information you need. Unfortunately, that's not possible. Building codes, labor and material costs, construction methods and designs, differ from state to state, from city to city, even from job to job.

No matter how many published estimating books or tables you've collected, your own price book will be the best guide to your labor and material costs. Find the estimated cost of work on new jobs by comparing actual costs from similar jobs already completed. Using historical cost information will make your estimates more accurate and save hours of time on the telephone and looking through catalogs.

One of the early pioneers in franchised remodeling businesses explains how he opened 150 offices in cities across the country. The basis for his success, he says, is the estimating price book he created for each city. He would call on 20 to 30 subcontractors in each city to gather information for his book. These cost books became the foundation for his cost estimates and contributed to the success of his company.

These books covered only the most common items. Every remodeling job includes many items and installation conditions that wouldn't be found in even the most extensive labor and material cost guide. That's where judgement becomes important. Construction and estimating experience is needed to adjust prices to the job at hand. A good, complete estimating price book is very valuable, but it's no substitute for good judgement and sound estimating practice.

Start your personal estimating price book with your first job. Record every material and cost in the job. Keep notes on costs for all the trades and materials you use. You'll also want it to include incidental costs such as scaffolding, hoists, chemical toilets, and dumpster rentals. Remember to list charges for licenses, special fees, and bonds.

The size and layout of your estimating price book depends on your needs and the type of work you handle. You may want it to be pocket-sized so you can carry it easily, or a standard 8½ by 11 size. The larger size has room for listing more information on each page. Either way, always use a loose-leaf binder so you can add new pages and remove outdated material.

Use your estimating price book as a guide — not as the final cost authority. Compile labor and material cost estimates for each job. Then check those costs against your estimating price guide. If your estimate looks high or low compared to actual costs on similar jobs, keep checking. There's probably a mistake somewhere. Recheck your math. Look for something that was left out.

No two remodeling contractors prepare estimates the same way. So no two estimating price books will be the same. Your specialty, the number of people on your payroll, and the amount of work done by subcontractors will determine what's in your price book.

Figures 5-1 and 5-2 are sample pages from estimating price books used by two different contractors. You can use these as examples to compile your own price book. This particular price/estimating book is used by a large general remodeling company which operates in more than one state. Because they emphasize stick estimating, the book is very detailed and comprehensive. It's 54 pages long, and kept together in a standard loose-leaf binder. Since they deal primarily with large projects, most pricing is done in the office. This estimating price book isn't normally taken into the field, so its size isn't a problem.

The prices in the book are left blank. This permits salespeople and estimators to write in their own prices based on local costs. This is important, because the book is used in several different areas, and prices vary.

Figure 5-2 shows a book used by a contractor who concentrates on kitchens and baths. His business is small and his work is somewhat repetitive. He has worked out his own unit pricing system based on past experience.

He uses a pocket-sized loose-leaf binder. His salespeople usually figure a "ballpark" price in front of the customer, which he confirms when he gets the customer's signed agreement. He only reviews his prices about every 90 days. He feels that's enough to keep up with price increases and stay profitable.

Estimating Methods

There's no single correct way to estimate remodeling costs. Of course, some methods will provide better or more complete figures than other methods. Most good estimators combine several estimating techniques. They've developed a unique estimating style that helps them anticipate problems and recognize unique situations that will affect construction costs.

Materials
34. Lumber (rough)
The cost of lumber is computed by the board foot. To define a board foot - a board foot equals a piece of wood 12" x 12" x 1" thickness. To compute lumber for an addition, use the following methods:

Floor: For floor area on a normal raised foundation, compute 3 board feet for each square foot of addition.

Walls: On slab or raised foundation, figure 9 board feet for each lineal or perimeter foot of interior or exterior wall. Include all walls as solid walls.

Ceiling: For ceiling area, figure 2 board feet for each square foot of addition (regardless of roof style).

Roof: For flat roof (ceiling and roof the same), 2 board feet per square foot.
For exposed beam ceiling 2½ board feet per square foot of addition (for 1" sheathing). If 2" sheathing figure 3½ board feet per square foot of addition.
For gable or hip roof style, figure 2½ board feet per square foot of addition.

_____ ¢ per board foot of lumber - cost of construction grade lumber.

$_____ Added for waste and roof tie-in for all additions.

$_____ per SF Redwood decking (2 board feet/square foot)

$_____ per SF Slab - flat roof

$_____ per SF Slab - gable or hip roof

$_____ per SF Raised foundation - flat roof

$_____ per SF Raised foundation - gable or hip

$_____ extra lumber for gable or hip tie-in

$_____ per SF Second story _____

Price estimating book for large contracting company
Figure 5-1

34C. **Building Paper 15#**
Building paper is used under wood siding.
Building paper is used to protect floors.

$_____   100 ft. x 3 ft., roll of 15# - covers 300 sq. ft.

$_____   500 sq. ft. - plastic membrane off.

35. **Hardware (Rough)**

$_____   Approximately for average room.

Cost includes nails, bolts, vents, teco clips, etc.

36. **Jambs and frames**
Cost of frames is included in windows.

$_____ each.   Interior door.

$_____ each.   Exterior residential door.

$_____ each.   Pocket door.

$_____ each.   Exterior residential door, metal.

37. **Sash - Window**
Aluminum and Steel
Cost of windows includes clear or obscure glass and an aluminum screen at the openable portion of the sliding glass window.

$_____   per SF of window. Price includes cost of screens, but not installation.

Cost is the same for obscure glass.

38A. **Screens**
$_____   per screen for all size windows

$_____   average size screen door

Price includes labor, material, but not installation.

Price estimating book for large contracting company
Figure 5-1 (continued)

BATHROOM REPAIRS

Bath 7 x 5

Plumbing-replace fixtures (add $50. for color on fixture)

White std. grade	$1030.
Colored std. grade	1125.
Tub only white	562.
Lav. only white	280.
W.C. only white	218.
Bowl for vanity	187.
Shower stall metal std. grade 36x36	470.
Medicine cabinet w/fluorescent light	
Std. grade incl. elec.	45.
Std. grade no lights	45.
Replace door w/h.c. door	150.
move door location, add	65.
D/H windows replace, same opening	155.
Wd. change to glass block 32x32 w/16x16 vent brick wall	375.
frame wall	345.
Wall ceramic tile per sq. ft.	9.
Drywall for walls, W.R. (water resistant)	250.
Add for ceiling	95.
Perfotape area above tile, average 4"	95.
Perfotape ceiling w/wall (add)	45.
Plywood floor 5/8" C.D.X	155.
Shower enclosure on tub, stand grade	125.
Chrome accessory - 3 rod, soap dish, glass holder,	
toilet tissue holder, tub dish	75.
Remove and reinstall owner radiator	90.
All baths, add for prep. walls	125.
Electric ceiling fixture, replace std. grade	35.
Electric ceiling fixture, new location	75.
Electric ceiling fixture, wall receptacle and switch	90.
On unusual jobs, see F.M.S or sales manager	
For soffit above tub	125.
For bulkhead at end of tub	125.
Vanity 24"average w/top including plbg. bowl and trim	
for larger sizes figure accordingly	400.
For tile V.A. average bath floor	100.
Floor tile ceramic w/wall work (sq. ft)	9.
Floor tile without wall tile (min)	175.
Debris	100.

(All of the above includes labor)

Sample price estimating book for small remodeling business
Figure 5-2

Stick Measuring

On most estimates, the first task will be to figure the cost of demolition and removal of walls, fixtures, doors, windows, or whatever will be taken out before construction begins. Visit the jobsite with tape measure in hand. Measure how much material will be removed. List that quantity on your estimate sheet and assign a dollar value to each step.

Then break the project down into parts, probably by trade, such as rough carpentry, electrical, plumbing, heating, drywall, and so on. Figure the quantity of each material needed for each trade and for each part of the project.

Total each type of material, such as linear or board feet for lumber; number and kinds of electrical outlets; the square feet of drywall, plywood or paneling; the number of plumbing fixtures, and the length of piping. Also include the linear feet and size of warm ductwork and cold-air returns, including floor and wall outlets.

Assign a dollar value to each material listed. Be sure to allow a percentage for waste and coverage. Add the cost of supplies such as nails, screws, and sandpaper. Transfer the total cost of materials to your estimate sheet.

Now, you're ready to figure the labor costs. If you've already started your own price or estimating book, you can use it to determine how much labor is required for each step in the installation. If you don't have your own figures, you'll have to rely on the prices quoted by your subcontractors.

When you figure your labor rates, you'll have to add into the hourly rates an additional cost for your *labor burden* (also known as taxes and insurance). This can add 25 percent or more to the base hourly rate. Included in these costs are:

- Worker's Compensation Insurance

- Liability Insurance

- Social Security (FICA) and Medicare

- State Unemployment Insurance

If $18.50 is the average hourly rate for rough carpentry, you'd add at least $4.63 per hour (25 percent of $18.50) to that to cover your labor burden. So the actual rate for rough carpentry would be $23.13 an hour.

Also keep in mind that the insurance rates differ from trade to trade (for example, roofers cost more to insure than carpenters), and from state to state. Have your accountant or tax lawyer help you determine the proper amounts for your area.

There are some disadvantages to stick measuring. Because you measure each item individually, it takes longer than some of the other methods. If you get distracted while you're doing the estimate, it's easy to miss something. And when you're transferring figures from one sheet to the next, the likelihood of making a mistake or leaving something off is quite high. Stick measuring doesn't include a factor for human error. Other methods take this into consideration. But if you don't make any mistakes, it's the most accurate method of estimating, because each item is figured separately in a careful, step-by-step procedure.

Unit Pricing

Unit pricing is one of the newer methods of estimating used today. With the unit pricing method, every material in a remodeling project is converted to standard measurements or units. Materials are defined in terms of linear, square, or cubic feet. Purchased or manufactured items are described in individual units: sink, tub, stove, cabinet, and so on. Be careful not to confuse unit pricing with the term "price per unit," meaning the cost of an individual item. Unit pricing involves much more than the single unit.

When you use a unit pricing system, all labor, material and miscellaneous costs associated with installing each unit are combined to make figuring easier. For example, the labor cost would include time spent looking for tools, setup and layout time, coffee breaks, and cleanup. Material costs consider everything used in the installation of each unit, including glue and sandpaper. Then an allowance for waste is added.

Your subcontract costs are based on establishing a fixed price for the installation of standard items, such as heating ducts, kitchen and bath appliances, or circuit breakers. So, your unit price includes literally everything involved in providing each particular unit, whether it's a new roof, drywall, or kitchen cabinets.

The advantage of unit pricing is that it takes into consideration the waste and inefficiencies peculiar to remodeling. Contractors who use this system insist that it saves time and eliminates many mistakes. Even a person inexperienced in construction can verify the estimator's figures because all the costs are built in. This may be exaggerating a bit, but not entirely.

However, there are variables that can't be built into a pricing system. This is why many contractors don't use unit pricing as their only estimating procedure. For example, it's easy to reduce wall framing costs to a simple cost per square foot of wall. But what happens when you're going to add a window or door? Now you have to deduct so many square feet of rough framing and add in the unit cost of installing a door or window. You're going back to more traditional stick by stick estimating.

Change orders can also present a problem in unit pricing, particularly when the change requested affects only a portion of the unit.

For most jobs, you'll have to combine estimating systems. There's nothing wrong with that; it's what most good estimators end up doing. No one method can cover everything.

Figures 5-3A to E are an example of a remodeling project for a bedroom with closet and adjoining bath. It includes before and after floor plans, exterior view, specifications, and the estimate and cost breakdown. All of these items are included when you figure your estimate. The contractor has described the project in the specifications (Figure 5-3A), given the customer before and after plans showing the proposed changes (Figures 5-3B and 5-3C), and broken down all his costs for his estimate (Figure 5-3D).

This contractor likes to combine estimating methods when working up his figures. (All estimates in unit prices are marked *up.*) He figured his direct labor (carpentry, demolition, excavation, grading, concrete and masonry) in *man days*. Man days include hourly wages, taxes and insurance. The rough carpentry he estimated to take 10 man days. At $200 per day, that makes a total of $2,000 for rough carpentry labor costs.

He used stick measuring to estimate most of his material costs, such as concrete and rough lumber. For example, he estimated he would need 2,800 board feet of rough lumber. The cost of rough lumber was $400 per thousand board feet. So he figured the cost, $1,120, plus $72 tax, and $50 delivery charges, for a total of $1,232. He rounded it up to $1,240 for his estimate.

𝖘𝖕𝖊𝖈𝖎𝖋𝖎𝖈𝖆𝖙𝖎𝖔𝖓𝖘

General Purpose: To build a room, bath and closet to the house. (Scheme F).

Plan: Contractor shall prepare the plan for the work described herein.

Permit: Contractor shall secure the building permit for the work described herein. (Owner will reimburse contractor for plan check for the permit, city fees and the building permit).

Tree removal: Contractor shall remove one medium size tree and bushes at the position where the addition is to be built.

Concrete foundation and slab: Dig the footings for the concrete footings and foundation - starting at the northwest corner of the existing rear bedroom - thence west to a point in line with the west line of the existing house - thence return into the northwest corner of the existing northwest bedroom. Install the steel bars in the footings. Install a vapor barrier under the concrete slab floor. Install the wire reinforcing mesh in the slab floor. Pour the concrete footings, foundation and slab for the new addition - at the same floor height as the existing house. Install a 4′ wide concrete walkway from the patio door position of the new room - 8′ in length.

Carpentry: Remove the exterior lathe and stucco on the existing walls where the new addition is to be built. Construct the framing for the new bedroom, bathroom and wardrobe. The ceiling height shall be the same height as the existing rooms of the house. The roof framing on the new addition shall be hip style, blended into the existing house roof. The roof sheathing shall be plywood. The roof eaves shall match the existing house. The bath shall be framed 5′ x 14′. The wardrobe shall be framed the full room width. Remove the window in the existing rear bedroom and close this opening. Cut an opening from the existing hallway and install a 2′8″ x 6′8″ door. Install a 2′6″ x 6′8″ door to the new bathroom. The new inside doors shall be fir slab - hollow core. (See allowances for finish hardware). Install a 4′ x 2′ double glazed (obscure glass) aluminum frame side slide window (with screen) in the new bath. Install a 8′ x 6′8″ aluminum framed patio door (with screen) in the new room. This patio door shall have tempered double glass. After the drywall is installed - case the new openings, and install base at the new walls of bedroom (similar to the casings and base in the existing house). Install a wardrobe closet in the new room - wall to wall - with bi-pass wardrobe doors. Install a wood shelf and wood pole in the new wardrobe. Install an 8′ long pullman cabinet in the new bathroom with 6 drawers and 2 sets of cabinet doors opening to storage area. Install a medicine cabinet and a towel bar and soap receptacle set in the bathroom (See allowances for bath accessories). Install a chrome curtain rod on the tub shower.

Plumbing: Bring in the waste and water lines to the new bath. (Use copper water lines). Install one bathtub, a shower over the tub, a toilet and two sinks. (See allowances for plumbing fixtures).

Heating: Install a heat duct to the new room connected to the existing forced air heating furnace in the house.

(Continued on page two of this agreement)

Submitted by _____
(INITIALS)

Date _ _____ 19 _____

THIS PAGE BECOMES PART OF AND IN CONFORMANCE WITH **PROPOSAL NO.** _____

Job Name _____ Mr. & Mrs. Homeowner _____

Accepted by _____ Date _____ 19 ____
(INITIALS)

Accepted by _____ Date _____ 19 ____
(INITIALS)

Specifications for remodeling project
Figure 5-3A

$\mathfrak{Specifications}$ Page No. ___2___ of ___2___ pages

(Continued from page one of this agreement)

Electric: Install the following electric outlets - connected to the existing electric service panel. (There is no change to electric service panel). New Bedroom - 2 lite outlets, 2 switches and 5 duplex plug outlets. New Bath - 2 lites, 1 ceiling heater, switched. Two switches for the lites and one duplex plug outlet. One outside flood lite, switched. (See allowances for light fixtures and bath heater).

Tile: Install a ceramic tile top and splash back on the bath pullman cabinet. Install ceramic tile on the walls (over the bathtub) to the shower head height. Install ceramic tile on the bath floor and one row of tile base in bath. (See allowances for bath tile material). Install quarry tile on the exterior walls of the new room, at the same height as the quarry tile on the existing rooms. Install quarry tile on the exterior corner of the new room and frame the new patio door. (See allowances for quarry tile material).

Exterior lathe and stucco: Lathe and stucco the exterior walls of the new addition, with a similar texture finish as the existing exterior walls.

Drywall: Install drywall on all new walls and ceiling of the new addition. Patch the opening in the existing rooms affected by this remodeling. Tape and spackle the new drywall.

Mirror: Install a plate glass mirror over the new pullman cabinet in the bathroom - the width of the new pullman, door height.

Gutters - downspouts: Install GI gutters and a 2 downspouts from the roof of the new addition.

Cleanup: Remove the debris caused by this work.

Allowances included in this agreement: plumbing fixtures $1,500.00-- ceramic tile (material) $3.00 per ft.-- quarry tile (material) $2.50 per ft.-- bath accessories (materials) $200.00-- finish hardware (materials) $150.00-- electric fixtures & electric heater $250.00.

Not included: painting (interior or exterior) --floor covering (other than ceramic tile in bath) -smoke alarms - any other items not specifically included herein.

Insulation: Install rock wool insulation in the exterior walls and ceiling as per the R value required in the codes for the city.

Roofing: Install composition roofing shingles on the new roof addition similar to the roofing on the existing roof of the house.

Submitted by _____
(INITIALS)

Date _____ 19 _____

THIS PAGE BECOMES PART OF AND IN CONFORMANCE WITH **PROPOSAL NO.** _____

Job Name _____ Mr. & Mrs. Homeowner _____

Accepted by _____ Date _____ 19 _____
(INITIALS)

Accepted by _____ Date _____ 19 _____
(INITIALS)

Specifications for remodeling project
Figure 5-3A (continued)

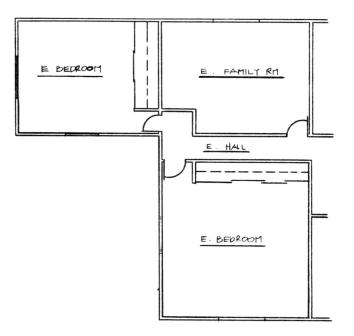

Existing floor plan
Figure 5-3B

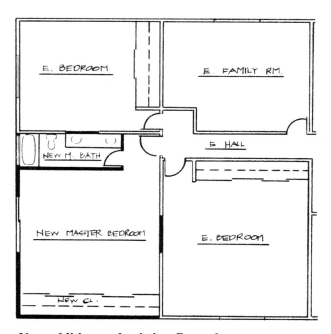

New addition and existing floor plan
Figure 5-3C

ESTIMATE AND COST BREAKDOWN

Office_____ S.M._____

Salesman_____

Owner **Mr. & Mrs. Homeowner (Scheme F)** Date _____

Address _____ City _____ Phone _____

PREPARATION			ELECTRICAL			
1. Plans	$	400.00	55. Service Change & Relocate		$	
2. Engineering	$		56. Circuits, Panels, Raceway, Home Runs	UP	$	60.00
3. Building Permits, Plan Checks, City Fees	$	Owner	57. Electrical Units #	UP	$	510.00
4. Survey — Variance	$		58. Electric Heaters, Fans, Smoke Detectors		$	
5. Control Fee		Owner	**Smoke Detectors**			
6. Lot Book & Blueprints	$	35.00	PLUMBING			
7. Scaffolding & Staging	$		59. Plumbing Units & Fixtures # 3	UP	$	1,200.00
8. Temp Power	$		60. Plumbing — Sewer ft.		$	150.00
9. Temp Toilet **Use owners facility**			61. Plumbing — Other		$	
			62. Cesspools — Septic		$	
ALLOWANCES						
10. Appliances **Plumbing fixtures**	$	1,500.00	HEATING & A/C			
11. Bath Accessories	$	200.00	63. Unit E-G		$	
12. Flooring sq. yds.	$		64. Thermostat		$	
13. Hardware Finish	$	150.00	65. Duct Work	UP	$	250.00
14. Electrical Fixtures **& Bth Elec Heater**	$	250.00				
15. Paneling & Trim shts.	$		ROOFING			
16. Other **Tile Ceramic (Material)**		425.00	66. Roofing L & M 8 sqs.	UP	$	1,000.00
Tile (Quarry) "		300.00	67. Roofing Extras		$	
DEMOLITION			68. Patio Roof ft.		$	
17. Interior MD	$					
18. Exterior MD **@ $150.00**	$	300.00	WALLS & CEILINGS			
19. Tree Removal (S) M L **UP**	$	150.00	69. Drywall 1220 ft	UP	$	1,220.00
20. Equipment Rental **Dumpster**	$	200.00	70. Plaster yds.		$	
Abestos Removal			71. Stucco 40 yds.	UP	$	880.00
FOUNDATIONS — CONCRETE & MASONRY			72. Patching	UP	$	100.00
21. Excavate & Grade 1 md @ $150.00	$	150.00	73. Blown Acoustical ft.		$	
22. Concrete Foundations & Piers ft 3 md &	$		74. Ceiling Squares & Luminous ft		$	
23. Concrete Slab & Flatwork ft **Materials**	$	1,050.00	**Glazing**			
24. Concrete Steps, Porches P & S **Walk**	$	150.00	CABINETRY			
25. Drives, Approaches, Curbs	$		75. Pullmans	UP	$	750.00
26. Concrete Walls	$		76. Kitchen Cabinets		$	
27. Concrete Cutting	$		77. Custom Work		$	
28. Concrete Pumping **UP**	$	150.00	78. Wardrobes	UP	$	450.00
29. Vapor Barrier, Sand or Fill	$	150.00				
30. Reinforcing Steel-Wire Mesh	$	50.00	FINISHING			
31. Masonry — Fireplaces	$		79. Ceramic Tile	UP	$	750.00
32. Masonry — Walls, Flatwork, Stone ft.	$		80. Laminate — Formica		$	
33. Asphalt Paving ft.	$		81. Marlite — Tile Board		$	
			82. Mirrors	UP	$	150.00
MATERIALS & LUMBER **del.**			83. Fencing & Gates		$	
34. Lumber Rough 2,800 x$400.+tax/	$	1,240.00	84. Flooring ft		$	
35. Hardware Rough	$	120.00	85. Breakfast Nook		$	
36. Jambs & Frames	$	80.00	86. Ornamental Iron & Columns		$	
37. Window — Sash W A S, Skylights	$	210.00	87. Sheet Metal & Gutters, Vents	UP	$	220.00
38. Screens & Patio, Enclosures **Incl.**	$		88. Weatherstrip, Waterproofing		$	
39. Doors — Wood	$	110.00	89. Clean Up 3 lds. & Trash Dump Fees		$	200.00
40. Doors — Garage	$		90. Other		$	
41. Doors — Closet, Misc. **See wardrobes**	$		91. Pickup — Contingency		$	1,000.00
42. Doors — Sliding Glass	$	840.00	**Quarry Tile**	UP		450.00
43. Doors — Shower & Tub Enclosure	$		DECORATING			
44. Insulation **UP**	$	690.00	92. Sandblast sqs.		$	
45. Lumber Finish	$	175.00	93. Patch		$	
46. Hardware Finish **Other**	$	50.00	94. Labor sqs.		$	
47. Mill Runs — Special	$	120.00	95. Trim sqs. extra		$	
48. Siding & Decking Materials	$		96. Materials		$	
49. Stairways W S	$					
50. Structural Steel — HWT Enclosure	$		CLOSEOUT			
Skylights -Greenhouse Windows			97. Overhead			$7,478.00
CARPENTRY LABOR md **Inc. Tax & Insur.**			98. Sales Commission			$4,680.00
51. Rough 10 MD $200.00	$	2,000.00	99. Builders Profit			$4,681.00
52. Siding — Decking MD	$		100. Contingency Fund			$1,869.70
53. Cabinetry ½ MD $200.00	$	100.00				
54. Finish 2MD $400.00	$					
	$					
SUBTOTAL $			COMBINED TOTAL $			39,263.70

MD = Man Days (Incl. Tax & Insur.)
Concrete: P = Porch, S = Steps
NIC: Not Included

UP = Unit Price (Installed)
Windows/Stairways: W = wood, A = aluminum, S = steel

Estimate using combined estimating techniques
Figure 5-3D

He used a flat unit price when figuring clean up and tree removal using his own crew. The rest of the work was subcontracted out and estimated using unit pricing. Those prices include materials, labor, and miscellaneous costs, and were supplied to him by his subcontractors. You can see how well these various techniques worked in figuring this estimate.

Unit price estimating may be able to save you valuable time. But don't think of unit price estimating as a shortcut. Every estimate, whether stick by stick or based on composite unit prices, has to include everything in the job. There's no substitute for finding every cost item in a job and then covering that cost with a price — labor, material, equipment or overhead.

If you want to try estimating with composite units, experiment on a job you've already completed and where you know the actual costs. Compare the price you get using this method to the actual job cost. If unit price estimating seems easier and more accurate, try it on a job you're currently estimating.

First, estimate the job the way you usually would. Then, do a second estimate using unit prices. If costs come out about the same and if you find it faster and just as reliable, consider making unit price estimating your usual procedure.

Formula Estimating

Formula estimating is generally less accurate than unit price estimating. Formula estimates use assumed costs for each part of a project: a square foot of wall, floor or ceiling, for example. Most single-trade contractors can develop square foot or linear foot or cubic yard prices for most of the work they do. This is where formula estimating is most useful. A contractor who specializes in one trade long enough should know what his costs are for most of the work he does. Of course, unusual conditions or uncommon details will still have to be estimated carefully.

Contractors who use formula estimating like to refer to building costs in terms of "a linear price for a kitchen," "a square foot price for a room addition," or "a unit price for a bathroom." You'll find, however, that most remodeling jobs include special conditions that make formula estimating dangerous at best. For example, the cost of remodeling a 5 by 6 foot bathroom could be anywhere from $6,000 to $12,000. That's a broad price range: $200 to $400 per square foot. Don't try to bid remodeling work with rule-of-thumb methods. It won't work.

But if you get a bid from a reliable subcontractor that's based on some price formula, you can probably accept the bid at face value. In a year that subcontractor will complete many jobs just like the one he's bidding for you. He knows that some of those jobs will be completed for less and some will cost more. He also knows that at year end he'll have a nice profit if he sticks to the formula he's using. It simply isn't worth his time to estimate every single cost item in every job.

Many experienced contractors use a formula for estimating some of their work. They do this because it's worked successfully for them in the past and they know where the pitfalls are. If they're getting formula bids from subcontractors, it's usually because they have a long-standing relationship with them.

Most successful contractors and subcontractors estimate costs by identifying every cost item in a job. They find every material that will be needed and how much, figure the installation cost based on their labor rate, and then add a reasonable allowance for overhead, contingency and profit.

Commercial Estimating Books

Many estimating reference books are published every year. Some are listed in the reorder form at the back of this manual. None of these books is designed to be used as your only source of information for bidding. Instead, use them to verify prices you've developed for labor and material, to confirm bids received from subcontractors, to develop preliminary estimates, and to price some minor item when there's no time to get a quote from a dealer.

Even if you've been in remodeling for many years, you'll see items that are new to you in many jobs. That's when it's nice to have one of the commercial estimating reference books on your desk. These books can save you time and money, provide practical tips to make your work easier, and improve both your estimating and building skills.

Estimating books are organized in various ways. Some are divided into residential and commercial construction, with the building materials and trades for each section listed alphabetically. The material and labor costs are broken out and listed separately. That makes unit pricing easier.

Other books cover remodeling by type of project, listing costs by type of project: kitchens, baths, room additions, and so on. The projects are divided into interior and exterior work. Each step of each installation is described, and then the amount of material required and the length of time it takes a particular tradesperson to install that material is listed. That makes it easy to develop your own material and labor costs.

For example, if you're going to remodel a kitchen and your customer wants folding pantry doors, you would check under *Kitchens, Interiors,* then *Doors*. One of the subheadings of *Doors* would be *Folding*. After the unit is described, the book will give you the labor rate. It might say something like "A single carpenter can hang a four-panel bi-fold door, including installing the tracks, in about 2.3 hours at the following cost per installation:

	Hours	Rate	Total	Rate	Total
Carpenter - - - - - - -	2.3	————	————	$20.60	$47.40

The figures show typical costs and the blanks are left so there's room to insert your own numbers.

Most estimating books include a table of factors that permit modifying national average costs from the book to your own region or city. For instance, if the Department of Labor determines that the average hourly rate for carpentry work is $22.00, contractors in Indiana would multiply that rate by 0.98 to get the average local rate of $21.56 per hour. In Illinois, the multiplication factor would be higher. There you would multiply the national average by 1.04 to get a local rate of $22.88 per hour.

If you use an estimating reference manual, be sure to modify the labor cost for your own wage rate. Wages vary widely from city to city. If the wage listed in the book is $30 per hour and you're paying only $15 per hour, labor costs in the book should be divided by two when used in your estimates.

Beginning an Estimate _____

It's hard to estimate construction on remodeling projects if you don't understand the whole construction process. Estimates for multi-trade jobs are rarely simple. Begin by estimating small jobs having one or two trades. These usually have fewer problems.

Visit the Site

The first step in putting together an estimate is to visit the site. *Never give a firm price over the phone* — even if you have absolutely no business on the books and your creditors are holding a gun to your head. No one can compile an accurate estimate from a word description of what has to be done.

Sometimes you'll have to deal with callers who are shopping by phone and insist on an estimate. Without seeing the job, you know your estimate will be nothing more than a wild guess. But if you want the business, you're going to have tell them something so you'll be invited to visit the job site.

If this is the case, let the customer know that you can't give a valid price by phone. After they explain what they want, give them a price *range* that you think may be in the ballpark, but be sure to stay on the high side. (For a bathroom job you might say between $15,000 and $20,000. That gives you $5,000 of flexibility to work with in your estimate. Your customers will be pleased when your actual bid is lower.) Make a pitch for your company. Mention jobs you've completed, offer to supply references, and ask for a meeting. Chances are, if your prospects are serious, you'll get one.

When the contractor discussed the bathroom remodeling project in Figure 5-4 with the customer, he allowed a 25 percent spread in his figures over the phone, quoting $15,000 to $20,000. In addition to references, he also discussed similar projects that he had recently completed. As a result, the customer decided to let him bid.

After visiting the site he was able to come in with a bid of $18,573.45. This was right in the middle of his ballpark estimate. He got the job. Although it was a small job, there was a considerable amount of detail involved which he never could have guessed by the phone conversation.

Estimating is detailed work. Watch those details! Anything that's missed could cost you thousands of dollars or the goodwill of a customer. Is there enough protected storage space to allow for advance delivery of materials? Or will they have to be brought in as needed? Can concrete be poured directly from the truck, or will it have to be pumped to the pour site? Are doorways and stairwells large enough to allow fixtures and appliances to be brought in, or will you have to tear out a wall to get the fixtures inside?

Will you need special ladders or scaffolding? Are existing heating ducts, electrical and plumbing systems compatible with the ones you plan to install? You'll have to answer these questions and many more before you can prepare an accurate and profitable estimate.

Figuring Demolition

Most remodeling work begins with demolition and removal. These costs are just as important to your estimate as the figures for the new construction.

Once you arrive at the job site, begin assembling the information you'll need. Be careful to note any part of the job that's unusual or that might require special handling.

ESTIMATE AND COST BREAKDOWN

Office_____ S.M._____

_____
Salesman

Owner **Mr. & Mrs. Happy Owner (Scheme N)** Date_____

Address _____ City _____ Phone _____

PREPARATION			ELECTRICAL			
1. Plans	$	300.00	55. Service Change & Relocate	UP	$	150.00
2. Engineering	$		56. Circuits, Panels, Raceway, Home Runs		$	
3. Building Permits, Plan Checks, City Fees	$	Owner	57. Electrical Units # 16	UP	$	640.00
4. Survey — Variance	$		58. Electric Heaters, Fans, Smoke Detectors		$	
5. Control Fee		Owner	Smoke Detectors			
6. Lot Book & Blueprints	$	30.00	PLUMBING			
7. Scaffolding & Staging	$		59. Plumbing Units & Fixtures # 6	UP	$2,400.00	
8. Temp Power	$		60. Plumbing — Sewer ft.		$	
9. Temp Toilet	$		61. Plumbing — Other 1 ¼ MD		$	400.00
			62. Cesspools — Septic		$	

ALLOWANCES (SEE PAGE 2 SPECIFICATIONS

10. Appliances	10% fee to contractor only incl.	HEATING & A/C			
11. Bath Accessories	in allowance items $	63. Unit E-G		$	
12. Flooring sq. yds	$	64. Thermostat		$	
13. Hardware Finish	$	65. Duct Work	UP	$	250.00
14. Electrical Fixtures	$	ROOFING			
15. Paneling & Trim shts.	$	66. Roofing L & M sqs.		$	
16. Other	$	67. Roofing Extras		$	
Asbestos Removal		68. Patio Roof ft.		$	

DEMOLITION					
17. Interior MD	$	WALLS & CEILINGS			
18. Exterior MD	$	69. Drywall ft		$	
19. Tree Removal S M L	$	70. Plaster yds.		$	
20. Equipment Rental	$	71. Stucco yds.		$	
		72. Patching	UP	$	600.00
FOUNDATIONS — CONCRETE & MASONRY		73. Blown Acoustical ft.		$	
21. Excavate & Grade	$	74. Ceiling Squares & Luminous ft		$	
22. Concrete Foundations & Piers ft	$	Glazing			
23. Concrete Slab & Flatwork ft	$	CABINETRY			
24. Concrete Steps, Porches P & S	$	75. Pullmans		$	
25. Drives, Approaches, Curbs	$	76. Kitchen Cabinets		$	
26. Concrete Walls	$	77. Custom Work		$	
27. Concrete Cutting	$	78. Wardrobes		$	
28. Concrete Pumping	$				
29. Vapor Barrier, Sand or Fill	$	FINISHING			
30. Reinforcing Steel-Wire Mesh	$	79. Ceramic Tile Granite	UP	$1,920.00	
31. Masonry — Fireplaces	$	80. Laminate — Formica		$	
32. Masonry — Walls, Flatwork, Stone ft.	$	81. Marlite — Tile Board		$	
33. Asphalt Paving ft.	$	82. Mirrors		$	
		83. Fencing & Gates		$	
MATERIALS & LUMBER		84. Flooring ft		$	
34. Lumber Rough x	$ 250.00	85. Breakfast Nook		$	
35. Hardware Rough	$ 30.00	86. Ornamental Iron & Columns		$	
36. Jambs & Frames	$	87. Sheet Metal & Gutters, Vents	UP	$	125.00
37. Window — Sash W A S, Skylights	$	88. Weatherstrip, Waterproofing		$	
38. Screens & Patio, Enclosures	$	89. Clean Up 2 lds. & Trash Dump Fees	UP	$	120.00
39. Doors — Wood	$	90. Other			
40. Doors — Garage	$	91. Pickup — Contingency		$	450.00
41. Doors — Closet, Misc.	$				
42. Doors — Sliding Glass	$	DECORATING			
43. Doors — Shower & Tub Enclosure	$	92. Sandblast sqs.		$	
44. Insulation	$	93. Patch		$	
45. Lumber Finish	$ 25.00	94. Labor sqs.		$	
46. Hardware Finish	$	95. Trim sqs. extra		$	
47. Mill Runs — Special	$	96. Materials		$	
48. Siding & Decking Materials	$				
49. Stairways W S	$	CLOSEOUT			
50. Structural Steel — HWT Enclosure	$	97. Overhead		$3,380.00	
Skylights - Greenhouse windows		98. Sales Commission		$2,066.00	
CARPENTRY LABOR		99. Builders Profit 10% Fee on allowances is			
51. Rough 7 MD	$ 1,400.00	projected estimated costs			
52. Siding — Decking MD	$			787.00	
53. Cabinetry ½ MD	$ 100.00	100. Contingency Fee		884.45	
54. Finish 1 MD	$ 200.00				
SUBTOTAL $		COMBINED TOTAL $		$18,573.45	

MD = Man Days (Incl. Tax & Insur.)
Concrete: P = Porch, S = Steps
NIC: Not Included

UP = Unit Price (Installed)
Windows/Stairways: W = wood, A = aluminum, S = steel

Estimate for bath remodel
Figure 5-4

If you're going to move walls, doors, or windows, try to get the original building plans before you begin the demolition estimate. That will help you avoid surprises that might cost time and money later. You don't want to discover too late that there's an unexpected standpipe or some needed electrical wiring or plumbing inside a wall that you've just torn down.

If you're working on a tract home, the housing plans may be on file in the city Building Department. If it's a custom home and the owner doesn't have the original plans, the architect who designed the home may still have a copy. The time spent in locating the plans should be the first cost entered on your estimate. Don't spend a week hunting up old plans. But make a few phone calls, especially if the work you plan involves structural framing, the electrical system or the mechanical system.

When estimating demolition, determine what can be salvaged and reused, either on this project or on some other project. For example, with a little care, most architectural millwork (moldings, beams, arches) can be salvaged and reused. If you can't salvage the old material, matching the existing designs may be a serious problem. Custom millwork shops can duplicate most millwork, but the price will be much higher than lumber yards charge for standard items.

Remember to include the cost of removing debris from the building site. If there's a lot of material to be taken away, it may be less expensive to rent a dumpster than make several trips to the dump site. Truck, driver and dump fees are all part of the demolition costs.

Pricing Subcontract Work

Pricing subcontract work can be a complex problem. First, collect quotes from several subs. When you've received the bids, go over them item-by-item. Determine exactly what each bid includes and excludes. Include in your bid to the owner only what the subcontractors have included in their bids. Then add your markup for supervision. Some trades require more supervision than others. Add your markup accordingly.

There's another reason to review subcontract bids very carefully. If you know the estimated cost for each item in a subcontract bid, you can estimate the cost of similar items in the future. Average the bids for each work item and list those prices in your estimating book. Of course, you'll want to take advantage of discounts and savings whenever possible. But your book should show the usual or most common estimated costs.

When you've compared the bids from several subcontractors for several different jobs, you'll have a good idea of the going price for most work. After a while you'll feel comfortable including these prices in your bids without actually getting a quote from a sub.

Of course, it's always good practice to get a quote on large or unusual jobs. But for most bids, if you can predict what the sub's bid will be within a few dollars, why bother?

Even if you feel it's good practice to get bids on every job that involves subcontracted work, the figures in your price book will help spot bids that are out of line or have omitted something.

Subcontractors often use the unit price method for bidding: so much per cubic yard of concrete, including forms, reinforcing and finishing, for example. This works fine as long as you're dealing with standard installations. But if you're pouring, say, an 8'' concrete slab instead of a 4'' slab, unit pricing won't work. This is where knowledge and experience pays off. An experienced estimator can spot anything out of the ordinary, and know when something has to be priced separately to yield an accurate result.

Here's another example. You can't usually pour a slab with a raised foundation directly over a sewer line. You have to estimate the cost of running the sewer line to the front of the house and then making the tie-in there. This kind of installation can't be based on your plumber's unit cost. You have to figure in additional material, such as elbows, and labor. This part of your plumbing estimate has to be figured separately using the actual cost of the materials and labor. Plumbing fixtures are also hard to estimate by the unit price method. There are too many types of fixtures and too many possible combinations of fittings and accessories.

Costs will vary widely in concrete work, finish carpentry, masonry, and specialty trades like terrazzo. This is where major differences are most likely to occur. There are too many variables in this type of work. That's why we prefer stick measuring here. Always be extra careful when pricing these trades.

The cost in your price book won't apply on every job, of course. You can't expect a cement contractor to charge the same amount per square foot on a 40' sidewalk as he would charge for a 40' driveway with a turnout. There will be one unit price for standard jobs like sidewalks, patio slabs and straight driveways. If there's a curve or a grade involved, expect to pay more.

Price Variables

Most of your cost on most jobs will be in subcontracts. After that, your biggest expense will be direct labor cost. Unfortunately, direct labor is the most difficult part of most jobs to estimate. How long will it take your crew to install each item? Pricing materials is relatively easy. Just call your dealer for a quote. But figuring the installation time is much more difficult.

Of all the trades, carpentry may be the hardest to estimate. Be careful when listing typical carpentry costs in your price book. For example, the time it takes to frame a 20 x 20 foot room addition on sloping ground is considerably more than doing the same framework on flat ground. A skylight in an existing hallway or room will cost more than it would cost installed in a new hallway or room addition. Raising an existing roof will be much more expensive than putting a new roof on a new addition. All these jobs take the same materials, but the labor cost may be completely different.

Carpentry prices are sometimes quoted by the square foot. This can be very misleading. At $60 per square foot a 400 square foot (20 x 20 feet) room addition would cost $24,000. Included in that price may be three windows, three doors, plumbing fixtures, tile in shower, one heating duct, twelve electrical outlets, roofing, siding, and concrete footings.

If the owners decide to add 5 feet to the length of the room, the additional cost may be only $600 (for 100 extra square feet) because you haven't changed the windows, doors, plumbing, or heating. That 100 square feet cost only $6 per square foot. Even though the base cost is $60 per square foot, adding or subtracting 100 square feet may make very little difference in cost.

The cost per square foot will vary widely with what's included. For example, a closet will cost much less per square foot than a bathroom, even though both measure 5' by 6'. Be sure to keep that in mind if you estimate with unit costs.

The productivity of your tradesmen also has a major influence on cost. Every work crew is different and every crew will work at a different pace. Even the same crew will have good days and bad days. Tradesmen are human beings and are subject to the same faults and shortcomings we all have. Estimating isn't a science. It's an art that takes judgement and experience.

During extremely hot or extremely cold weather, workers are less productive. Especially those who are working outside. So when you're coming into the "dog days" of summer or the bitter cold of winter, you'll need to tack on a few hours extra to your labor costs to compensate. That may not sound like much, but anything that reduces productivity will cut into your profit.

Updating Code Work

It's common for the building department that will inspect your work to insist that parts of the building be brought up to existing code standards. This is particularly true of plumbing and electrical work. You won't know what extra work will be required until demolition begins. Even if the building appears to meet existing code requirements, the contract should specifically exclude all code-mandated changes to the existing building. Be sure you explain to the homeowner that if his home needs this work, it *must* be done. It's required by law.

Unless you include upgrading to code as part of your initial bid, advise the homeowners that there will be a separate charge for this work based on time and materials. Be sure you do this *before* the homeowner approves the contract.

Be aware that contractors who fail to bring older buildings up to current codes may be held liable for breach of contract.

Update Your Prices

Your estimating price book should be revised as often as time permits. Stay current with changes in labor and material costs. In any case, review your prices at least twice a year. Using stale prices will cost you money.

Material prices change constantly. Some items change between the time you estimate the job and the time you actually buy materials. The price of plywood, for example, can change daily. It's a commodity item that changes like the price of gold or silver. Usually price increases or decreases at the mill take about a month to reach materials outlets. Prices for common lumber like fir or pine 2 x 4s and 2 x 6s are a little more stable. But all lumber prices should be reviewed at least every six months. When estimating, it's good practice to include a small cushion to cover price inflation.

Labor costs change too. But movement is more like a glacier, except up instead of down. Sometimes movement is faster, sometimes slower, but the direction is nearly always the same. And remember that changes in labor rates affect both your labor costs and the labor costs of your subcontractors.

When updating your price book, note that improved tools, equipment and materials can reduce labor costs. When you or your subcontractors find more labor-efficient ways to do the work, part of the savings should be passed on to your customers in the form of lower prices.

A good job superintendent or foreman *should* always be able to tell you how many manhours a sub took to do a particular job. It's his responsibility to monitor progress on every job every day. This is essential for management control. By making notes of daily progress, he can verify the accuracy of your installation rates.

Estimate From the Ground Up

Nearly all estimators estimate the job in the order in which the work is to be done. Some say they close their eyes and visualize each step of the process. Others make lists of the trades in the order they'll be needed at the site, then figure labor, installation, and material costs under each trade. We estimate jobs in the order the work will be done because it helps us remember every cost item in the job. That should be the focus of every estimate.

Estimate and Cost Breakdown Sheets

If you don't have an estimating sheet like the kind we've been using in our examples, by all means take the one in Figure 5-5 to a local copy shop and have several hundred copies run off. We discussed using this cost breakdown sheet in Chapter 2. Now you'll see why it's organized the way it is.

Notice that it begins with preparation and ends with closeout, covering each step of the remodeling project in sequence by trade. As you go through and figure your costs for each item, you'll also be compiling your labor figures. By the time you complete each trade, you'll have a good start on a job schedule. You'll know fairly accurately how much time to plan for each trade, and when to schedule the next trade on the job so you won't waste time.

If you're new at estimating, some of these steps may seem a little complicated or time consuming. But after you've gone through this several times, you'll find the procedure becomes automatic. By following a regular sequence, you have less chance of error. If something is out of the ordinary, you'll probably notice it right away.

There's one heading that's not in Figure 5-5 that should be. It's fasteners . . . nails, screws, straps, and other small items that everyone needs and uses every day in construction. It's easy to overlook them if they aren't listed separately or included as an added cost to each material to be installed. To get an idea of how much money you might lose by forgetting this category, price 100 pounds of nails or screws and multiply it by the total number of jobs you expect to complete in the next twelve months. You'll be surprised!

Contingency Fund

Note the last item on Figure 5-5, Contingency Fund. No matter how well you plan or how conscientious you are, there'll usually be problems and delays that you didn't count on. A worker can get sick, a material delivery may be short or late, an electrical tool may malfunction — any number of things can happen which can add to your costs.

ESTIMATE AND COST BREAKDOWN

Office _____ S.M. _____

Salesman

Owner _____ Date _____

Address _____ City _____ Phone _____

PREPARATION			ELECTRICAL		
1. Plans	$		55. Service Change & Relocate	$	
2. Engineering	$		56. Circuits, Panels, Raceway, Home Runs	$	
3. Building Permits, Plan Checks, City Fees	$		57. Electrical Units #	$	
4. Survey — Variance	$		58. Electric Heaters, Fans, Smoke Detectors	$	
5. Control Fee					
6. Lot Book & Blueprints	$		**PLUMBING**		
7. Scaffolding & Staging	$		59. Plumbing Units & Fixtures #	$	
8. Temp Power	$		60. Plumbing — Sewer ft.	$	
9. Temp Toilet	$		61. Plumbing — Other	$	
			62. Cesspools — Septic	$	
ALLOWANCES					
10. Appliances	$		**HEATING & A/C**		
11. Bath Accessories	$		63. Unit E-G	$	
12. Flooring sq. yds	$		64. Thermostat	$	
13. Hardware Finish	$		65. Duct Work	$	
14. Electrical Fixtures	$				
15. Paneling & Trim shts.	$		**ROOFING**		
16. Other	$		66. Roofing L & M sqs.	$	
			67. Roofing Extras	$	
DEMOLITION			68. Patio Roof ft.	$	
17. Interior MD	$				
18. Exterior MD	$		**WALLS & CEILINGS**		
19. Tree Removal S M L	$		69. Drywall ft	$	
20. Equipment Rental	$		70. Plaster yds.	$	
			71. Stucco yds.	$	
FOUNDATIONS — CONCRETE & MASONRY			72. Patching	$	
21. Excavate & Grade	$		73. Blown Acoustical ft.	$	
22. Concrete Foundations & Piers ft	$		74. Ceiling Squares & Luminous ft	$	
23. Concrete Slab & Flatwork ft	$				
24. Concrete Steps, Porches P & S	$		**CABINETRY**		
25. Drives, Approaches, Curbs	$		75. Pullmans	$	
26. Concrete Walls	$		76. Kitchen Cabinets	$	
27. Concrete Cutting	$		77. Custom Work	$	
28. Concrete Pumping	$		78. Wardrobes	$	
29. Vapor Barrier, Sand or Fill	$				
30. Reinforcing Steel-Wire Mesh	$		**FINISHING**		
31. Masonry — Fireplaces	$		79. Ceramic Tile	$	
32. Masonry — Walls, Flatwork, Stone ft.	$		80. Laminate — Formica	$	
33. Asphalt Paving ft.	$		81. Marlite — Tile Board	$	
			82. Mirrors	$	
MATERIALS & LUMBER			83. Fencing & Gates	$	
34. Lumber Rough x	$		84. Flooring ft	$	
35. Hardware Rough	$		85. Breakfast Nook	$	
36. Jambs & Frames	$		86. Ornamental Iron & Columns	$	
37. Window — Sash W A S, Skylights	$		87. Sheet Metal & Gutters, Vents	$	
38. Screens & Patio, Enclosures	$		88. Weatherstrip, Waterproofing	$	
39. Doors — Wood	$		89. Clean Up lds. & Trash Dump Fees	$	
40. Doors — Garage	$		90. Other	$	
41. Doors — Closet, Misc.	$		91. Pickup — Contingency	$	
42. Doors — Sliding Glass	$				
43. Doors — Shower & Tub Enclosure	$		**DECORATING**		
44. Insulation	$		92. Sandblast sqs.	$	
45. Lumber Finish	$		93. Patch	$	
46. Hardware Finish	$		94. Labor sqs.	$	
47. Mill Runs — Special	$		95. Trim sqs. extra	$	
48. Siding & Decking Materials	$		96. Materials	$	
49. Stairways W S	$				
50. Structural Steel — HWT Enclosure	$		**CLOSEOUT**		
			97. Overhead	$	
CARPENTRY LABOR			98. Sales Commission	$	
51. Rough MD	$		99. Builders Profit	$	
52. Siding — Decking MD	$		100. Contingency Fund	$	
53. Cabinetry MD	$				
54. Finish MD	$				
	$				
SUBTOTAL $			**COMBINED TOTAL** $		

MD = Man Days (Incl. Tax & Insur.)
Concrete: P = Porch, S = Steps
NIC: Not Included

UP = Unit Price (Installed)
Windows/Stairways: W = wood, A = aluminum, S = steel

Estimate and cost breakdown sheet
Figure 5-5

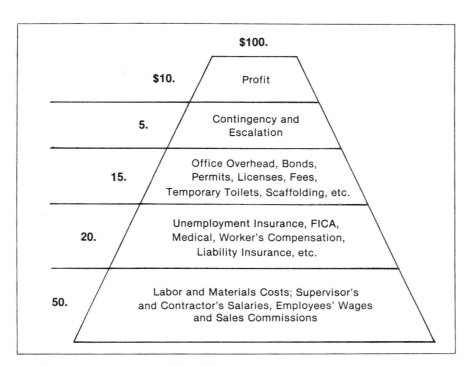

Breakdown of costs per $100 bid
Figure 5-6

Since there's no way to foresee these kind of problems, add a percentage to your labor and material costs to cover additional expenses. There's no established sum for a contingency fund. You might add a maximum of 10 percent to small jobs, decreasing the percentage on larger jobs to a minimum of 5 percent.

So on a $1,500 job, your contingency fund would be 10 percent, or $150. On a $20,000 project it would be $1,000, the minimum of 5 percent. If you make your fund any larger on a big project, you risk losing the job to a lower bidder.

After every job is completed, recheck your labor and material costs. Are they in line with your previous estimates and actual costs on other similar jobs? If they're higher or lower and you know why, no problem. If you can't explain why they're higher or lower, keep looking. There's probably an error somewhere. If you've made an error in your pricing, make sure you know where the problem is and correct it.

Profit
Profit is the money that's left after *all* other costs and expenses of a job have been paid. These include such obvious costs as materials, labor, subcontractors, hardware, delivery fees, vehicles, removal of debris, and supervision.

Less obvious costs are your fixed and variable overhead, union dues, employer's share of social security tax, state unemployment taxes, workers' compensation and other insurance costs, permit fees, licenses, and bonding. Since all jobs vary, so will the costs and expenses.

Figure 5-6 shows a breakdown in costs for a typical remodeling job. The number of dollars in each category may change a little from job to job, but the fact is that for every $100 that comes in, $90 goes back out to cover expenses. Only 10 percent remains for profit, and that's if you're very lucky! Your profit reflects how well you've anticipated *all* your costs. Don't make the mistake of some beginning contractors who fail to figure in a wage for themselves when pricing a job. In Chapter 1 we said that every contractor should include his or her wage as a job cost. That wage should cover each and every function you perform, from sales to supervision.

If you don't include your personal labor costs in your estimate, it will throw your figures off. If someone else covers one of your regular functions for you, their wages will be over and above your estimated costs. Don't plan to pay anyone's wage out of the contingency fund. That's poor planning. Neither should *your* wages come out of the company profits.

Some jobs will take only a few hours to estimate. Large jobs can take 40 to 50 hours over a two or three week period. This can mean night and weekend work. You'll probably supervise work in progress during the day and estimate jobs at night and on the weekends. Keep in mind that supervising a small job takes almost as much time per day as a larger job. But since there's normally more profit on the larger jobs, you earn more per hour for the time spent on them. Consider this when bidding smaller jobs.

Most surprises on a job will reduce your profit, not increase it. Ultimately, profit on any remodeling job depends on the efficiency and skill of your tradesmen, and good management.

Finalizing Your Estimate

Be careful when extending costs on your estimate sheet. We've seen very good estimators work very hard to identify every cost in a job and then make a foolish mistake in arithmetic that turns a good bid into a solid loss. Always check and double check your figures. When you use fractions, convert them to decimal equivalents which are easier to use. To be on the safe side when rounding numbers, always round up, not down.

Figure 5-7 shows the decimal and millimeter equivalents of common fractions from 1/64 of an inch to one inch. Figure 5-8 shows decimal equivalents of fractions from one inch to one foot. Figure 5-9 shows the decimal equivalents of minutes in one hour. Make copies of these tables for your estimating price book. These tables will save you a lot of figuring and prevent costly mistakes.

We have included the millimeters in our equivalents because the metric system of weights and measures is here to stay. Outside of the United States it's the most commonly used standard for weights and measures. Because of the rise of multinational corporations and the increasing number of American firms involved in international trade, there's a growing need for a universal system of mathematical quantities. Worldwide exchange of goods and services is easier if we use a single set of measurements. By the year 2,000, the metric system will be the world standard.

Verifying Pricing

Over a hundred cost items may be included in a small and simple job. With so much detail, it's easy to overlook something. Checking for mistakes yourself may not locate the error. You've probably become "blind" to the mistake. That's why most good estimators always have someone else check their price extensions and transfer of figures from one sheet to the next.

Fraction	Decimal	Millimeter	Fraction	Decimal	Millimeter
1/64	.016	0.397	3/16	.188	4.763
1/32	.031	0.794	13/64	.203	5.159
3/64	.047	1.191	7/32	.219	5.556
1/16	.062	1.588	15/64	.234	5.953
5/64	.078	1.984	1/4	.250	6.350
3/32	.094	2.381	17/64	.266	6.747
7/64	.109	2.778	9/32	.281	7.144
1/8	.125	3.175	19/64	.297	7.541
9/64	.141	3.572	5/16	.312	7.938
5/32	.156	3.969	21/64	.328	8.334
11/64	.172	4.366	11/32	.344	8.731
23/64	.359	9.128	11/16	.688	17.47
3/8	.375	9.525	45/64	.703	17.86
25/64	.391	9.922	23/32	.719	18.26
13/32	.406	10.32	47/64	.734	18.65
27/64	.422	10.72	3/4	.750	19.05
7/16	.438	11.11	49/64	.766	19.45
29/64	.453	11.51	25/32	.781	19.84
15/32	.469	11.91	51/64	.797	20.24
31/64	.484	11.91	13/16	.812	20.64
1/2	.500	12.70	53/64	.828	21.03
33/64	.516	13.10	27/32	.844	21.43
17/32	.531	13.49	55/64	.859	21.83
35/64	.547	13.89	7/8	.875	22.23
9/16	.562	14.29	57/64	.891	22.62
37/64	.578	14.68	29/32	.906	23.02
19/32	.594	15.08	59/64	.922	23.42
39/64	.609	15.48	15/16	.938	23.81
5/8	.625	15.88	61/64	.953	24.21
41/64	.641	16.27	31/32	.969	24.61
21/32	.656	16.67	63/64	.984	25.00
43/64	.672	17.07	1"	1.000	25.40

Decimal and millimeter equivalents
Figure 5-7

Inches		Decimal	Inches		Decimal
1"	=	0.083	7"	=	0.583
1½"	=	0.125	7½"	=	0.0625
2"	=	0.1667	8"	=	0.667
2½"	=	0.2087	8½"	=	0.708
3"	=	0.25	9"	=	0.75
3½"	=	0.2917	9½"	=	0.792
4"	=	0.333	10"	=	0.833
4½"	=	0.375	10½"	=	0.875
5"	=	0.417	11"	=	0.917
5½"	=	0.458	11½"	=	0.958
6"	=	0.50	12"	=	1.00
6½"	=	0.5417			

Decimal equivalents of fractions in one foot
Figure 5-8

Minutes		Decimal Equivalent	Minutes		Decimal Equivalent
1	=	0.0167	31	=	0.5167
2	=	0.0333	32	=	0.5333
3	=	0.05	33	=	0.55
4	=	0.0667	34	=	0.5667
5	=	0.0833	35	=	0.5833
6	=	0.10	36	=	0.60
7	=	0.1167	37	=	0.6167
8	=	0.1333	38	=	0.6333
9	=	0.15	39	=	0.65
10	=	0.1667	40	=	0.6667
11	=	0.1833	41	=	0.6833
12	=	0.20	42	=	0.70
13	=	0.2167	43	=	0.7167
14	=	0.2333	44	=	0.7333
15	=	0.25	45	=	0.75
16	=	0.2667	46	=	0.7667
17	=	0.2833	47	=	0.7833
18	=	0.30	48	=	0.80
19	=	0.3167	49	=	0.8167
20	=	0.333	50	=	0.8333
21	=	0.35	51	=	0.85
22	=	0.3667	52	=	0.8667
23	=	0.3833	53	=	0.8833
24	=	0.40	54	=	0.90
25	=	0.4167	55	=	0.9167
26	=	0.4333	56	=	0.9333
27	=	0.45	57	=	0.95
28	=	0.4667	58	=	0.9667
29	=	0.4833	59	=	0.9833
30	=	0.5	60	=	1.0

Decimal equivalents of minutes in one hour
Figure 5-9

The cost or accounting department in a large construction company usually checks the math on all contracts that come in. In a small operation the checking must be done by the owner or the bookkeeper. Mathematical errors are a big problem, and one of the leading causes of lost profit in the remodeling business.

Your Final Price Quote

Use *price psychology* when you write your bid. You may have wondered why merchants price things at $49.95 or $99.50. It's because our minds don't really grasp that the figure we're really looking at is $50 or $100.

Suppose your estimate comes out $8,136.57. If you have a good profit built in and don't anticipate any significant problems, drop your price to $7,990.57. Always throw in pennies.

It looks like you worked your figures to the bone. Now you can say to your client, "I'm really pleased to tell you that we can do this job, with the quality you want, and still keep the cost under $8,000. So, if you'll approve what we've agreed on, we'll be able to start work next week." (Remember, you never ask people to *sign* anything, always approve or confirm.)

Keep Estimating Records and Files

It's very important, especially for new contractors, to file and keep every estimate you prepare. Some contractors keep these records for as long as three to four years, even for jobs that weren't accepted.

The heading at the top of the first page of every estimate should show the owner's name, address and phone number; the date and time of day the estimate was presented; who was present, including the name of the salesperson; and who verified the estimate.

Each subsequent page should have the homeowner's name at the top. All meetings with the homeowner should be recorded. If the estimate wasn't accepted, include a cover memo with an explanation. You should file these estimates under the job category, such as "Kitchens" or "Baths." That way, when you estimate future jobs, you can review all similar bids, the successful as well as the unsuccessful.

Estimating Is a Continuing Process

We've covered the basic estimating rules in this chapter. But no explanation can teach you how to estimate. You've got to try it yourself, make the mistakes, and sharpen your skills with hard work and experience. Good estimators aren't born. They're made. Don't be discouraged if your first estimates aren't accepted and if your first winning bid isn't a money-maker. Estimating is a very important skill. In time you'll learn all you need to know — if you keep trying.

Keep the following suggestions in mind when you begin any estimate:

- Be selective about the jobs you bid

- Always visit the site before preparing a bid

- Maintain a complete and up-to-date estimating price book

- Verify subcontractor, material, and direct labor costs

- Check your figures and have them verified by someone else

- Keep an eye on your profit margin

And remember, it's the surprises inside the wall that can make or break an estimate. If you're careful in your preparation and meticulous with your figures, you'll be right far more often than you're wrong. Your company will not only get the job, but make a profit as well.

Know Your S's: Supervising and Subcontracting

*N*o matter how large or small your remodeling company, two things are important to your success. One is being able to plan your time so that all parts of your business receive the proper amount of attention. The other is scheduling your projects efficiently. You want your jobs to start on time and finish on schedule, with the fewest possible problems or delays.

If your company is small and you're working on the job as well as running the business, scheduling your own time should be one of your biggest concerns. You have to find time to be an estimator, accountant, salesperson, supervisor, and perhaps a tradesperson as well. Every job must be checked daily, and the small jobs take just as much time to check as large ones. Constant checking is the best way to maintain control. Lose control and you lose your profit, almost as surely as night follows day. Take on more work than you can handle and all jobs will suffer.

"Four-On, Four-Off"
When you're starting out, limit yourself to three or four jobs at a time. Make them as close together as possible so you don't have to spend too much time driving from site to site, especially if you work in a large metropolitan area.

A good rule to follow is "four-on, four-off." Spend four hours of your day working in the field, and the rest in your office. This gives you time for new clients, record keeping, working up estimates, ordering materials, and keeping tabs on your subcontractors. Even though your company is small, you still have the same responsibilities as you would in a large business.

If you're working as your own supervisor or job superintendent, be very careful about scheduling. Try to stagger the completion dates. More supervision is needed at the beginning and end of a project. Plan to be available at those times. Also, starting too many jobs at the same time can deplete your working capital. You need money coming in at regular intervals to avoid a cash crisis. Otherwise, you may have to borrow to stay in business. Loans reduce your profit margin.

Daily Job Records

You or your superintendent should keep daily job records for every job in progress. Make it a habit to keep good written records. And store those business records for a minimum of five years.

It's nearly impossible to remember all the details about every job, especially if you have several going at one time. When questions come up, it's essential to have written records to back you up. Otherwise, it's your word against your customer's or supplier's. No one really wins in verbal disputes. They just take up your time and end only in mistrust or bad feelings.

Job records can be quite simple. Figure 6-1 is an example. Your reports should include the following information:

- Property owner's name and job location

- Type of work being done

- Time of day the site was visited

- Kind of trades and number of men on the job

- Progress made from previous day (Is job on schedule, or is it ahead or behind?)

- Change orders, if needed

- Problems

DAILY CALL REPORT

JOB # _____

HOMEOWNER _____

ADDRESS _____

TYPE OF JOB _____

_____

TRADES ON JOB _____

_____

_____ NO. OF MEN _____

COMMENTS:

MATERIALS NEEDED _____

_____ DATE _____

INSP. (KIND) _____

DUE _____

DATE _____ TIME _____

SUPT. _____

Keep a daily record of each job
Figure 6-1

Hiring a Superintendent _____

As the owner and manager of your own small business, you'll probably do your own supervising for the first year or so. When the business grows to the size that the responsibilities become too much for one person, consider hiring a superintendent to help run your jobs. That person can make or break you quickly, depending on how well he's chosen and motivated. A good superintendent is to a remodeling contractor what a master sergeant is to the commanding officer. He makes sure the job gets done right, and on time!

Besides having experience, good superintendents must be good with people. They need the respect and cooperation of the people they work with. They should be leaders by example, not the type who gets things done by threatening or bullying your crews. If a superintendent is abrasive with customers and overbearing with the work crew, he's of no value to you no matter how talented a worker he is.

Look for these characteristics in your supervisor:

1) He'll take an interest in the success of your business.

2) He'll represent you effectively and honestly, without making any side deals with owners, workers, subcontractors or suppliers.

3) He's aware of your financial position and will help maintain a healthy income.

Your superintendent needs to spot problems and solve them before they affect your business. He should communicate easily, keep you up-to-date on each job, and be able to juggle schedules with subcontractors when necessary. His work standards are as high as yours. And they should certainly be as high as, or higher than, the customer's. After all, happy customers are what make your business profitable.

A good, competent, and confident supervisor welcomes advice, takes criticism well, and admits mistakes and makes corrections. If he does a job well, he won't object to performance evaluations.

Hiring any employee is a risk. But this is especially true when hiring a superintendent, estimator or salesperson. Their performance can have a major impact on both the integrity and financial success of your company.

Keep Your Superintendents Happy

Your supervisors will take much more interest in the progress of their jobs if you offer incentives for meeting job or company goals. One caution regarding profit sharing programs, though. Watch to make sure your supervisors don't take shortcuts after the job has started. If they're in too big a hurry to complete the job and increase their share, they may sacrifice the quality you want and expect on each project.

Remember that your employees' work reflects on the company as a whole. In the end, you're responsible for all the work done in your company's name, good or bad. Keep all new employees under close supervision, even your superintendents, until they have proven themselves. If they're incompetent or guilty of misconduct, it's important that you find out early, before too much damage is done.

Besides profit sharing or bonuses, be sure you *tell* your supervisors when they're doing a good job. Put it in writing from time to time. A "pat on the back" is a great morale booster and costs nothing but a little effort to express your appreciation. But it can pay big dividends in loyalty.

Your Superintendent's Responsibilities

Your superintendent is the eyes and ears of the company. He's usually the first to see or hear about problems, and the first who can respond to the situation. He's the one who deals on a day-to-day basis with tradespeople, suppliers, subcontractors, and your customers.

A superintendent's job includes many responsibilities. One of the most important is scheduling. Scheduling for each project begins as soon as the building permits are received. Materials must be released and deliveries set up. A time sequence for each step of the job has to be arranged, and subcontractors notified so they can make up their schedules as well. The superintendent makes the plan, then works the plan.

Once a job starts, he's responsible for visiting the site daily to check progress, answer questions, and resolve any problems that come up. He must update schedules regularly, show each job's progress, and make sure change orders are followed.

The way you schedule projects depends on how many jobs you're working, how big they are, and the number of trades that will be involved. All these details can be clearly shown on something as simple as a bar chart or as detailed as a CPM diagram (The Critical Path Method is discussed in the next chapter). You can make up your own schedule forms or buy printed forms. Whatever works best for you is the best choice.

Copies of your work schedules should be available to your accounting people or staff since they have to pay for materials, subcontracted work, and meet payroll on each job.

Also, subcontractors and suppliers will be calling your office to get information about each job. Your office personnel should be able to answer most of the questions about schedules and job conditions. The superintendent shouldn't be the only one who has this information. If the people who answer your phone don't have ready answers, material deliveries and subcontractors may be delayed. This can cost you money and cause problems. Other people's schedules may depend on having this information available to them.

Keeping your staff informed about job schedules is an easy way to promote good customer relations. Be sure your clients get prompt answers to their questions when they call your office. Living in a torn-up house is never easy. Frayed nerves and unanswered questions can lead to confrontations, and when you have confrontations with your customers, there are no winners. Keep your clients informed and happy.

Hire Good Tradespeople

To be effective, your superintendent needs the kind of tradespeople who'll minimize, not maximize, his problems. Negligent craftsmen can destroy both your company and your reputation. Incompetent tradesmen also pose a danger to themselves and to co-workers. One thing you don't need on the job is an insurance risk. Good workmen with good supervision ensure consistent, safe, and efficient production.

Of course, no matter how well your crew performs, you'll seldom eliminate all the problems that can happen on the job. The important thing is to have a superintendent who can handle problems quickly and get on with the work.

Daily Scheduling

If you're acting as the company superintendent, your typical day starts the evening before, in your home or office. That's the time to set up the following day's work. Call the tradespeople who'll be on the job and tell them what they need to know about the job. Next, make up your materials list, and arrange for deliveries.

Review the day's work, particularly if there were problems. Were the problems resolved? Are your jobs still on schedule? What adjustments do you need to make? Finally, make out the schedule for tomorrow.

In general remodeling (room additions, kitchens, and baths) you can only *visit and run efficiently* a maximum of 15 to 20 jobs at one time. If you're working in the high end of those figures, you're going to be running pretty hard.

Suppose you spend ten minutes on each job and you allow ten minutes to get from job to job. With 20 jobs, you've got over six and a half hours spoken for, and you still have to eat, make out job reports, and stop by the office.

Even if everything goes well (and we all know how often that is), you've put in a pretty heavy day. By the time you're working 20 jobs, you'll be ready to give serious consideration to hiring a superintendent.

Some contractors claim to have superintendents who run 50 to 75 jobs or more from their office. It may be possible for single-trade construction companies that specialize in roofing or re-siding to run 50 or more jobs by phone. But the title "Remodeling Contractor" is misapplied here.

We know of remodeling companies that claim to have one supervisor running 30 or 40 jobs. But these companies usually have no tradesmen on their payroll. They advertise heavily. When the sale is closed, the superintendent subcontracts the entire job. The subcontractor is responsible for completing the job. The superintendent only checks in occasionally with the sub to make sure the job is on schedule so he can process his work-in-progress invoices. If there are any problems, the subcontractor has to resolve them. If there are extra costs, they come out of the subcontractor's pocket. The homeowner rarely, if ever, sees anyone from the company they hired once the salesman is out the door.

Start/Completion Notices

If your company is large enough to have office help handling payroll and accounting, you need some system for notifying everyone when a job has started and when payments have to be made. Small jobs, taking only a week or so, may have no progress payments. Larger projects will have work-in-progress payments. If you rent equipment for a job, your office staff needs to know when it was delivered and when it was picked up.

The Starting and Completion Ticket shown in Figure 6-2 is a good form for keeping everyone informed of job progress. Your superintendent should fill out and distribute these notices to office personnel.

Make up a Starting and Completion Notice for each job. The top part of the card is perforated. When you begin a job, the top left side of the card (the Starting Ticket) is detached and sent to your accounting office. It shows the actual starting date and the date equipment was delivered to the job site. The ticket is authorization to make payments for labor and materials.

Starting Ticket					Completion Ticket			
Job Checked					Checked Job With Owner			
Matl List		Job Started			All Due Work Complete			
Matl Shipped								
Supt		————						
Foreman		Genl Supt			Supt		Genl Supt	
Equipment Delivered					All Equipment Picked Up			
		Order	Complete			Estimate		Cost
Amount	Bank				Labor			
Down Payment Pd	F H A Appr				Material			
Other Pd	Months				Permits			
Other Pd					Archt			
Job Started					**Sub-Contract**			
Job Complete								
Foreman					Item	Estimate	Company	Cost
Extras								
	Paid In Full							

Courtesy: Ashland Building & Improvement Company
Starting/Completion notice
Figure 6-2

When the job is completed, inspected, and approved by the customer, the top right side of the ticket (the Completion Ticket) goes to your accounting department. It's the authorization to bill for any balance due and make final payment for materials, labor and subcontracts.

Notice the columns for Estimates and Costs in the Subcontract section of the Starting and Completion Notice. If costs exceed the estimate, you'll want to investigate the reason for the difference. File the ticket in the job folder for future reference. It's your reminder that a subcontractor couldn't complete the work for the bid price. You may want to drop subs like that from your bidders' list.

Importance of Daily Inspections
You or your superintendent should check every job daily. There's no substitute for visiting the site, asking questions, and responding to questions from your tradesmen, subcontractors, and the owner. When you check each job, you see for yourself what's happening. Don't take the tradesperson's word for it. Examine everything yourself. Know about all the details. Review the plan with your work crews. Be sure everyone understands exactly what has to be done. If you don't insist that everything is done exactly right, something's going to end up exactly wrong. Count on it.

Good communication between the superintendent and workers is essential. If it's not in the plan, it's not done! If it's not in the contract, it's not done! If it's in the contract *and* in the plan, then do it! Your tradespeople should never deviate from either the

Customer: Mr. & Mrs. John Goodneighbor **Date:** 5/5/88

Address: 1452 Robin Drive **Job. #** 14,286

City: Des Plaines **Phone:** 882-3947

Attention: To the trades: G & B Plumbing

Please follow instructions as listed below, as it is a duplicate of the contract. If the **Owner** requests additional work, other than specified, **Call This Office For Approval** before you start.

Per your bid 4/1/88. Remove existing kitchen sink, laundry tray and water heater. Relocate water heater to new position on rear of house per plan (attached) inside enclosure. Relocate waste and water lines and install 3-part kitchen sink with deck-type faucet (see allowances for plumbing fixtures). Install the plumbing for and connect owner's dishwasher unit.

Install waste and water lines and install owner's washer and dryer. Run gas line for owner's dryer. Vent owner's dryer. Install a water line for owner's refrigerator position. Install gas line and connect range and oven. Relocate a hose bib on the rear of house where the openings are changed. The new water line lines to be installed in kitchen shall be copper (per code). Re-attach owner's garbage disposer.

Courtesy: Ashland Building & Improvement Company
Subcontractors work order
Figure 6-3

contract or the plan, no matter what the homeowner says, asks, begs for, or demands. The plan can be changed, of course — with a change order and a revision of the contract price. But no one has the authority to make changes without a change order, and all change orders must be approved by you — the owner!

On large jobs involving multiple trades and considerable work, it's not a bad idea to issue a work order to each trade spelling out what was agreed on and what you expect. It minimizes the number of questions that might come up if the subcontractor works only from the plans.

A good example of a subcontractor work order is shown in Figure 6-3. It not only clarifies what is to be done, but also reinforces the order that no changes are to be made without the express approval of the home office.

Always take a copy of the job schedule, work orders or a checklist of the work in progress with you on your daily inspection tour. This is especially important if you're running a lot of jobs at once. With a heavy work load, it's easy to miss something if you're rushed or distracted.

A Happy Customer

. . . is an informed customer. Even when things are going wrong, knowing is better than wondering. Don't make your customers guess about what's happening. Keep them informed of progress (or equally important, lack of progress) on the job, and they'll be happy. That's why it's so important to have a supervisor who's sensitive to the wants and needs of your customers. Good customer relations pays off again and again. And customer relations is one of the prime responsibilities of your superintendent. Once a job begins, your superintendent should be available for contact with the owners every day.

As one seasoned contractor notes: "You can stay off the job for days and even weeks, as long as you tell the customer. But if no one is there and the customer wasn't advised, they'll be on the phone immediately and their concerns and comments are seldom complimentary."

Your superintendent should respond quickly to a customer's questions or complaints. He should resolve misunderstandings so both sides are satisfied and can get on with their work.

No matter how well you prepare your customers before work begins, they're never quite ready for what happens after it starts. The dirt, the noise, the inconvenience and delays, are all much more than they expected. Joyous anticipation about the changes can quickly degenerate into irritation and misunderstandings. The person who takes the heat is, as usual, the superintendent. He has to be professional, efficient, pleasant, and above all, available.

Here's how to promote good customer relations:

• Contact your customer on each daily visit. If your customer isn't there, leave a note saying you were there. If they've asked you to take care of any problems, let them know you have. If leaving a note is difficult, make a brief phone call later to keep the customer up to date.

• Advise your customer when materials are due to be delivered, which workers will be on the job, when they're coming and how long they'll be there.

• Notify your customer when inspectors are coming and tell them what's being inspected.

• Be upbeat at all times. If the job is on schedule, tell them it's looking good. If it's behind schedule, tell them why and what you're doing about it. Then add, "Even though we're behind, it's going to be one of our best!"

Homeowners always have questions about the project. Instruct your workers to give enough information to be polite, but to refer all specific questions about the job to you or your superintendent. In particular, make sure your workers never discuss costs, changes, or anything that isn't in the contract or plan.

Change Orders

Your superintendent is responsible for seeing that no changes are made to any job without a written change order (Figure 6-4). If he makes any changes without signed authorization, it's not a question of *if*, but rather *when* you'll run into problems. Changes made on the basis of verbal agreements will boomerang no matter how simple they seem at the time.

Write change orders immediately. Have the customer sign the original, whether or not there is a price change. Attach the original change order to the contract. One copy goes to the customer and one to your office.

Make changes to the job plan and note the date and change order number on the plan. You may want to give a copy of the change order to tradesmen or subcontractors affected by the change. Have them sign and date your copy of the change to show they've received it. Review the changes with the work crew.

Whenever you make a change to the original plan or contract, for your own protection, get it in writing. If you make changes without a formal change order, your customers could later decide they don't like the change and want it changed back. They might forget exactly what was said, or they might deny that they said anything at all. In any case, you need a signed agreement authorizing the additional charges which result from the changes. If you don't have this agreement, guess who's going to end up paying for the change?

One contractor we know learned a hard lesson about change orders early in his career. He was doing a room addition, and the contract called for a window to be placed on the east wall. Early in the project the homeowner decided he wanted it on the west wall instead. Since framing on the west wall hadn't been completed, switching the window wasn't a problem. The contractor didn't get a written authorization or a change order. He simply instructed his crew to make the change.

When the interior *and* exterior walls were complete, the homeowner decided he didn't like the window on the west wall after all. He wanted it put back on the east wall, *as it was shown in the plan.*

The contractor reminded the customer that the change was made at his request. The customer said, "I know I asked you to change it, but now I don't like it. The contract says the window should be on the east wall, and that's where I want it! Nothing in our contract says that moving the window or changing it back would cost me more money, so the expense is yours."

Bong! Unfortunately, the customer had the legal right to make the contractor put the window where the contract said it should be. Morally, it was wrong. The customer should have paid, or at least shared the cost, but he refused.

The point is, you can't depend on a customer's conscience to help right a wrong. Any change, whether it involves an even exchange, an increase in cost, or a decrease in cost, must be formally written up and signed by the customer.

Just about any change in the job increases the overhead and probably *extends the completion date as well.*

You'll avoid most change orders if your customers understand the plan and the contract before they sign. Emphasize that changes made after the work begins can be *very expensive.* That usually works!

Date _____   Job# _____

Order For Additional And/Or Change Of Work

_____, who has entered into a
                            Owner

contract with _____
                        Contractor's name and business address

_____, for work at _____
                                            Job site

orders the following additional and/or change of work:

_____

_____

_____

_____

_____

_____

_____

_____

_____

Contractor agrees to furnish and supply all labor and material necessary to do this work in a neat and workmanlike manner.

The owner (s) agree (s)
   to pay _____ Dollars ($)
as follows:
Cash (herewith) _____ Dollars ($)

Cash (on completion) _____ Dollars ($)

Accepted for _____   _____
                    Contractor   Owner

By:_____   _____
                                             Owner

Change order
Figure 6-4

Other Supervisor Responsibilities

There are several small but important details that your superintendent should take care of personally.

• Place a sign on the job advertising your company name.

• Protect materials from weather and theft.

• Provide temporary closures to protect the building from weather if the project is open to the outdoors.

• See that the job site is kept clean, neat, and safe. All tools, materials, and equipment should be stored and the site swept clean at the end of the day. This will please your customers and may prevent an accident. Don't let safety hazards accumulate on your jobs.

• Arrange for toilet facilities. Most homeowners don't want workmen in their homes, using their bathrooms. Sending tradesmen off to the nearest gas station several times a day will cost considerably more than having a chemical toilet on site.

• Prepare legal papers, such as 20-day lien notices. The law varies from state to state. Your superintendent should be doing whatever your state requires to protect the lien rights provided by law.

• Arrange for inspections and follow up to make sure they've been completed as scheduled.

• Write up a brief status report on each job every day. A short paragraph should be enough to keep you and your office staff informed about the work in progress. Keep these reports in your files for future reference.

• Meet with company management to discuss problem jobs (not job problems) that require joint decisions.

Subcontracting vs. Going Direct

Some remodeling contractors do most work with tradespeople on their payroll (direct labor). Others use subcontractors whenever possible. There are advantages and disadvantages either way. The bottom line, though, is cost. If you can get attractive bids from qualified subcontractors, why take the risk of doing the work with your own crews? The one thing you can't chance, however, is the quality of work. You can't compromise on quality.

Direct Labor

The biggest benefit you get from having a direct labor force is that you have control of your workers' time. You know exactly where they're going to be, and how long they'll be there. You know how fast they work and the kind of tools and skills they bring to the job. You learn what performance and work quality to expect. This makes scheduling easier and more accurate. And, you have a team that wants to complete every job on time.

If you want a direct labor force but also want guaranteed prices per installed unit, consider paying tradesmen on a unit price basis — so much for each square foot of framing installed, for each cabinet hung, for each sink set, and so on. When your tradesmen work on piecework, installed costs are simply the cost of installation plus the cost of materials and supplies. Many highly skilled, highly productive tradesman are happy to work on a piecework basis. They make more money that way.

A word of caution: Paying tradesmen per unit installed makes it harder to control quality and may cause resentment among employees who work on a straight hourly basis.

If you're fair with employees, they'll always try to find a way to accommodate company needs. They know that their future is only as good as the future of the company.

Subcontracting

The major advantage to using subcontractors is that they usually give you a guaranteed price. You know what your costs are going to be. They carry their own overhead, which keeps your indirect costs down. If there's a problem or a delay, they fix it, and they pay.

Another advantage is that subcontractors are specialists. They're usually faster and more skilled than direct labor.

The disadvantage to using subcontractors is that you don't have control over their time. Most will try to work within your schedule. But sometimes another job will have a higher priority. It isn't just that *some* subcontractors show up late *some of the time,* it's that *most* subcontractors show up late *most of the time.* A direct labor force is very appealing when an irate homeowner is threatening to sue because the job's behind schedule.

This may sound like a pretty big disadvantage, and it can be at times. You have to be flexible when working with subs. Everything shouldn't come to a halt if a sub doesn't show up some morning. Very few remodeling jobs run exactly according to schedule. Sometimes you'll schedule a subcontractor and it's *you* who won't be ready for him.

There needs to be a lot of "give and take" in relationships with subcontractors. Be as understanding of their problems as you want them to be of yours. And avoid subcontractors who aren't a little accommodating. If you choose your subcontractors carefully and if you're fair with them, they'll try to be dependable.

Have at least three qualified subcontractors for each trade you use regularly. Some subcontractors may not have the manpower you need on particular jobs. Others may be too busy to take on more work just when you need them. So even if you have one subcontractor whose work you prefer, always have several others you can call on to keep your jobs running. Friendly competition between your subs will help keep their work efficient and professional.

Subcontractor Agreements

Protect yourself from poor workmanship and delays with adequate bonding and insurance. These items are covered in detail in Chapter 9. No insurance program can prevent careless, negligent workers from sabotaging your jobs.

Be sure that any subcontractor who works for you carries liability and workers' compensation insurance. Don't hire a subcontractor who can't show you a certificate of insurance. It's standard practice in the industry to provide this information on request.

Never subcontract any work without a written agreement. Too much can go wrong. You can get a good subcontract agreement form from the American Building Contractors Association. Their address is:

American Building Contractors Association
11100 Valley Blvd.,
Suite 120
El Monte, CA 91731

A well written contract should describe the type of work to be done, the price and terms of payment, and when the work is to begin and be completed. Other items you should include in your terms and conditions are:

1) Permits and licenses
2) Extra work
3) Labor and materials releases
4) Extra time
5) Property damage or injury
6) Insurance
7) Work stoppages
8) Guarantee
9) Arbitration

Figure 6-5 is a subcontract agreement developed by a contractor. It's tailored specifically to his needs. Some of the terms and conditions covered in this contract are especially important and should be included in any agreement, whether it's a standard form or one you've designed yourself.

• Section (4) states that the subcontractor is held responsible for all federal, state and local taxes.

• Section (5) specifies that the agreement does not constitute an employer-employee relationship. This protects you from certain workers' compensation and payroll tax liability.

• Section (6) has a breach of contract clause by which the contractor can complete the job and bill the subcontractor for completion if he doesn't show up for three working days without prior written agreement.

Subcontract Agreement

This Agreement, made this _____ day of _____, 1988, by and between **Ashland Building &
Improvement Company,** 5065 North Lincoln Avenue, Chicago, Illinois 60625, hereinafter called the
Contractor, and_____, whose address is _____
_____, and phone number is _____, hereinafter called the
subcontractor.
Property involved:_____
Owned by: _____ Phone # _____ Job # _____
It is agreed between the parties as follows:

1. Subcontactor will furnish all materials to be installed, unless otherwise specified.

2. The Subcontractor will furnish at his own risk, cost and expense all scaffolding, equipment and labor
necessary to complete the installation on the above mentioned property in accordance with the sales
contract, a copy of which is attached hereto, except as expressly noted in work order attached hereto.

3. The Subcontractor will furnish to Contractor a certificate evidencing both public liability insurance and
Worker's Compensation Insurance covering the Subcontractor and all his employees, and further, in any
event, the Subcontractor guarantees to hold harmless from all claims by reason of injuries or any other loss
arising out of this Subcontractors agreement.

4. The Subcontractor is an independent business entity, and as such, expressly declares that the
Subcontractor is solely responsible for the payment of all federal, state and local taxes which any other
separate and independent business is liable to pay.

5. The parties hereto expressly declare that they do not intend this agreement to be construed as an
employer-employee relationship and that all the terms and conditions of this agreement are contained
herein - no other terms or conditions are included.

6. The Subcontractor agrees to do all work promptly and in a good workmanlike fashion, and to promptly
repair or replace any item of work found defective due to any breach of this Agreement. In the event the
Subcontractor shall be absent from the installation, once work is initiated for a period of three (3) working
days without prior written consent of Contractor then it shall be presumed that the Subcontractor has
breached this agreement, and Contractor may at its option have the work completed by some other
contractor. Any additional monies paid to complete the installation will be charged to the Subcontractor.

7. Contractor agrees that the Subcontractor will supervise his workmen, make his own work schedule, follow
his own work procedures and methods and make all other decisions regarding the installation, herein agreed
to, except as specified in paragraph six of this Agreement.

8. You, the Subcontractor (supplier), by execution (acceptance) of this contract (order) agree to defend,
indemnify, reimburse and save harmless the owner _____
and the Contractor of and from all loss and damages to person or property and from all claims, suits,
demands arising from damages or injuries, including death, to you and your employees, to the owner and his
employees, to the Contractor or other Subcontractors and their employees, and to the general public or
members thereof, due to, arising from, or connected with operations, employment or work on this job (order)
performed by you, your agents or employees, or your Subcontractors or materialmen and their agents or
employees. The obligations set forth in this Article shall, but not by way of limitation, specifically extend to
and include all claims, demands, suits and/or judgements arising or alleged to arise under the Illinois
Structural Work Law, Safe Place to Work Statutes and the Subcontractor is responsible for his own
worker's compensation and liability insurance. In consideration whereof, the Contractor agrees that he will
pay the Subcontractor, the sum of

_____

_____.

The undersigned having read all the terms and conditions and in full agreement set their signatures hereto.

_____   **Ashland Building & Improvement Company**

By: _____   By: _____

Courtesy: Ashland Building & Improvement Company

Contractor/Subcontractor agreement
Figure 6-5

• The work to be carried out by the subcontractor is detailed in a separate work order which is attached to the agreement as noted in Section (2).

Of course, you can always draft your own contract. But be sure to have a lawyer review the contract before using it on your jobs. Every contract has to comply with the law.

Appearance and Penalty Clauses

An appearance clause implies that you'll be ready to have the subcontractor begin work on a job at a particular date and time. This may seem a handy clause to have, but it's a two-edged sword. What if *you're* the one not ready?

Penalty clauses are seldom used in remodeling for several reasons. First, most remodeling jobs are too small in dollar value to warrant a financial penalty for a delay. Second, even when a job is delayed, the delay is usually just a few days. Remodeling jobs are rarely delayed weeks or months, as can happen on large construction projects.

If you do agree to a penalty clause, be realistic about your completion date. Set the date based on the actual manhours you figured the job would take in your estimate. Being too optimistic on this figure is asking for trouble.

There are times when you can turn a penalty clause to your advantage. Let's say your customer wants a $50 per day penalty for every day the job goes over the contracted completion date. Fair enough, as long as you're going to get the same amount for each day the job is completed *ahead* of schedule. Be careful how much of a penalty you want to agree to though. Strike a balance between a maximum penalty which won't break you and a maximum bonus which is acceptable to the customer. Some contractors set a limit at about five percent of the total contract price.

Selecting Subcontractors

Be as selective in hiring subcontractors as you are in hiring employees. Ask for references and check on the quality of their work. You want subcontractors whose quality standards are in keeping with yours.

Price and delivery are your primary concerns when selecting tradespeople and subcontractors. But you're entitled to a little more. Choose subcontractors who are:

• Efficient with their time and careful not to waste yours.

• Well prepared. They bring the right tools to the job, and do the job right the first time.

• Considerate of your customers. They should protect the homeowner's property and furniture; protect exposed areas not being worked in; close up the property at the end of each workday to protect it from the elements; clean up their work area; and last, only use the owner's phone or toilet with permission.

• Safety conscious. They should keep dangerous materials and tools out of the reach of children; disconnect all power tools when away from the job and store them properly at night, and install covers or barricades on access openings and ditches.

• Conscientious. They study the plans and specifications; work with a minimum of supervision and take pride in the job they do; set a good example for apprentices.

Until you get to know a subcontractor well, watch his work carefully. That's another important reason to check every job every day. Substandard or defective materials can be concealed if you're away from the job too long. There are some unscrupulous subcontractors or tradespeople who bid a job based on one brand name of materials then install a cheaper grade. Watch for this. Subcontractors who think you won't notice or believe you don't understand their trade may try to take advantage of you. If you don't discover the problem until work is completed and paid for, you'll be richer in wisdom but not in pocket.

Please don't misunderstand. Most subcontractors are very good at what they do and very professional in their relations with builders and remodelers. But as in any field, there are some bad apples, and they hurt us all. The important thing is that *you* select competent subcontractors and use their skills to best advantage.

Look for Experience

When you select your subcontractors, consider the experience they've had in remodeling. There's a definite distinction between new construction contractors and remodeling contractors. Remodeling is like making a custom-tailored suit — everything has to be cut to fit a special size and shape. New construction can be compared to buying a ready-made suit off the rack. All it takes is a little alteration and you have a fit.

The remodeling contractor is working with a custom-designed product. And like tailoring the suit to the man, no two jobs are the same.

Your subcontractors have to know if the existing building violates current codes and what upgrades the building department will require. Will you have to replace the service panel and all wiring to pass the final inspection? Or can you bring the job up to code easily and at little cost with a simple modification?

These problems don't come up in new construction. But they *always* come up in remodeling. An inexperienced subcontractor can waste time, money, and materials dealing with them. And his mistakes reflect on your job performance.

Which is Best, Direct or Subcontract? _____

Most remodelers use both employed tradesmen and subcontractors on most jobs. The mix depends on the type of work and who is available. A balance between direct labor and subcontracting is usually the most efficient and cost-effective.

You may ask "Which do I use, when?" The answer depends on the type of remodeling work you do. If you do nothing but kitchens and baths, there's probably room for a plumber and rough and finish carpenters on your payroll. If you specialize in room additions, you won't need a full-time plumber. But having an electrician would be cost-effective. But you'll need 15 to 20 jobs working continuously to justify a full-time journeyman electrician or plumber.

The same is true for a drywaller. Drywall work can go pretty fast. Even if you're working on several large jobs at one time, you probably won't generate enough work to keep a drywaller and helper busy 5 days a week.

Concrete and carpentry tradesmen can be hired. You can easily keep these trades busy if you have a fair-sized business. Many contractors prefer to have their own carpenters, especially finish carpenters. A good finish carpenter can cover up most of the mistakes a rough carpenter makes. Your finish carpenter needs to be someone you can rely on to solve problems. That's hard to find in a subcontractor.

If you're asked to do work that involves custom designs or requires highly specialized skills, you'll want to have an expert do the job. On high-class, custom projects, even the largest contractors have to subcontract portions to specialists. Using a less-skilled tradesman on a job like this just because he or she is on the payroll can be a big mistake.

Multi-Skilled Crews

The ideal remodeling operation is the small contractor who has an all-purpose, multi-skilled crew. He can finish a job in 40 percent less time than the contractor who has to subcontract half or more of the work.

With a multi-skilled crew, you have total control of the job. You can coordinate your crew, materials, work, and inspections straight through until the job is completed. When you rely on subcontractors, you'll almost always have delays during the transition from one sub to another.

Trade Unions

Trade unions can be a good source for workers, especially in large cities and metropolitan areas. Most union tradespeople have good skills. They bring both experience and the right tools to the job. If they don't perform their work properly, your complaints will be heard back at the union hall.

Remodeling contractors using union tradesmen don't always have to negotiate a union agreement. Many times the jobs are too small. However you should respect the union policies governing the trades in your area when hiring union workers. If a contract is required, sign it and abide by its provisions.

Let Your Size and Specialty Determine Your Workforce

The type of work you do will usually determine whether you hire tradespeople or subcontract the work. It's usually best to subcontract mechanical trades (HVAC and plumbing) and electrical work. Most remodelers also subcontract shingle roofing jobs, siding, and drywall installation.

Electrical work, mechanical, shingle work, siding and drywall installation require special skills. If you're a general remodeling contractor, putting these trades on your payroll will add substantially to your overhead and payroll expense. You'll need a lot of volume to keep them busy all the time. It's not practical to pay a worker for 40 hours if you can only keep him busy for 26!

The remodeling business is cyclical — downs always follow the ups. But if you can get and keep good people . . . good supervisors, tradespeople, and subcontractors . . . you'll have less slack time and your peak periods will get longer. The difficult jobs get easier and the ordinary jobs become showplaces. All you need is the right help.

seven

Planning and Scheduling

A well-managed remodeling business does consistently good work on time and within
budget. That's not just wishful thinking. It can be done. We've seen it. You may
have too. But it doesn't happen by accident. You need efficient planning and scheduling,
careful project monitoring, and tight control. First among these, in our opinion, is
planning and scheduling. And that's the subject of this chapter.

There's no scheduling magic that works on all jobs. At least, we haven't found any.
Contractors seldom agree on the type of schedule that works best. The schedule that
works best for you will depend on the kind of work you do. The more complicated the
job, the more sophisticated the planning and scheduling must be.

Types of Schedules

Scheduling can be no more than some notes and lines connecting boxes — a job diagram
using the Critical Path Method (CPM). Other methods include printed schedule
calendars, bar charts, and pegboard systems.

We don't recommend writing out a schedule like Figure 7-1 unless your business is
very small and most of your jobs are single-trade. They simply don't provide enough

Job Schedule

Job # *4-2187*

Date *4/21*

For *BRUCE BROOKS*
1901 LYNBROOK
FLINT, MICHIGAN

Job description *INSTALL GUEST*
BATH + CLOSET OFF
GUEST BEDROOM

Permit(s) Rec'd (dates) *CITY 3/17,*
PLUMBING + ELECTRICAL 3/18

Starting date *3/31*

Materials ordered *3/22*

3/31 DEMOLITION + CLEANUP   (1½ DAYS)
4/1 ROUGH CARPENTRY   (2 DAYS)
4/2 ROUGH ELECTRIC   (½ DAY)
4/3 ROUGH PLUMBING   (1 DAY) INSP. ELECT
4/6 INSTALL DRYWALL   (2 DAYS)
4/8 INSTALL COMMODE, LAVATORY
PULLMAN, + SHOWER STALL   (1½ DAYS) INSP. PLUMB.
4/9 FINISH ELECTRIC   (½ DAY)
4/10 FINISH CARPENTRY   (1 DAY)
4/11 PAINT   (1 DAY)
4/14 INSTALL FLOORING   (1 DAY)
4/15 INSPECT + SIGN OFF

Superintendent *L. Streich*

Simple handwritten schedule
Figure 7-1

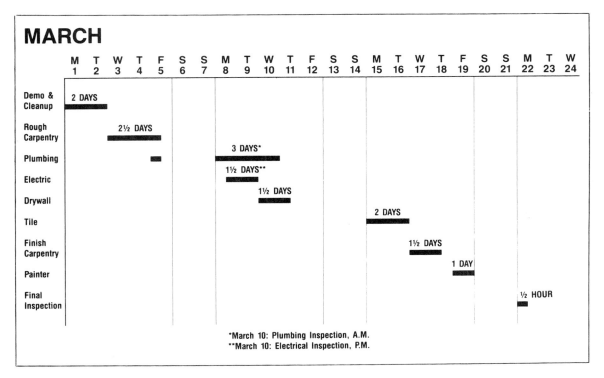

Scheduling chart
Figure 7-2

information. If something goes wrong on the job, a schedule like this won't help you visualize the effect on each trade and what it will do to your completion date.

When something major goes wrong and you have several jobs going at once, watch out! Things can get out of hand very quickly. Generally, there's a domino effect. When something goes wrong on a remodeling project, it can slow down or stop not only that project, but your other jobs as well. You or your superintendent can put out only one fire at a time. If one job falls off track, you have to leave the others to deal with it. And if you can't provide a "fix" that gets work back on track quickly, you may be playing catch-up indefinitely. That's a bad position to be in!

Although the job in Figure 7-1 is fairly simple, note that several trades are on the job at the same time. You can't *see* that at a glance.

The bar chart in Figure 7-2 offers a little more information about when each trade is scheduled and when they'll overlap. Bar charts help you see when several tasks are to be done at the same time and have to be coordinated.

Figure 7-3 shows a unique way one company handles scheduling. It was developed by the general manager of a medium-sized midwest remodeling company.

He wanted to keep the schedule simple, but still be able to track all the key elements necessary for starting and completing a project on time. The advantage of this particular system is that it works just as well for a small contractor with four or five jobs as it does for a larger contractor with twenty jobs or more.

Job no. 221

Job no.	Job	Plans to owner	Revisions	Owner approval	Permit In	Permit Rec'd	Ready	Concrete	Lumber	Carpenter	Notes
221	S. Streich 1705 Laurel Elmhurst	3/19	✓	4/4	4/6	4/10	4/15		H&G 4/15	BOYD 4/6	Job Sign 4/16
In 3/3 Out 3/19 /21	KITCHEN BROOKS WISOM	Heat	Electric EZ	Plumbing DOOBY	Masonry	Taping W.G.H			Solar room		

Job no. 222

Job no.	Job	Plans to owner	Revisions	Owner approval	Permit In	Permit Rec'd	Ready	Concrete	Lumber	Carpenter	Notes
222	D. Buck 3162 Flushing Palatine	3/31	change inv. to double	4/5	4/6	4/21	5/3		CONS. SPEC 4/22	D. BROWN 5/16	Job Sign 5/16
In 3/4 Out 3/25 /26	BATH BROOKS J.A.S.	Heat	Electric 5/3	Plumbing 5/10	Masonry	Taping			Solar room		

Job no. 223

Job no.	Job	Plans to owner	Revisions	Owner approval	Permit In	Permit Rec'd	Ready	Concrete	Lumber	Carpenter	Notes
223	A. Kirka 666 Chelmsford Elkgrove	6/10	✓	6/15	6/19	7/3	7/7		B&B 7/5	D. BROWN 7/6	Job Sign 7/5
In 5/5 Out 5/25 /29	FAMILY ROOM BROOKS WISOM	Heat	Electric	Plumbing	Masonry	Taping			Solar room		

Courtesy: Drew Builders, Inc.

Sample work schedules for small remodeling company
Figure 7-3

Each job schedule is made up individually on heavy paper stock and tacked on a bulletin board. The actual size of the schedules are 2 by 16 inches.

As soon as a project is sold, it's assigned a job number. The owner's name and the job location go in the next column. The name of the salesperson and the superintendent go in the boxes underneath. At Drew Builders, the superintendent is responsible for the job measurements. The *Out* and *In* boxes are for the dates he goes out to measure the job, and when he finishes.

The next three boxes cover plans. They tell when the plans are released to the owner, if the owner made any revisions, and the date he or she gave final approval for the plans.

The permit section shows when permits were applied for, when they were received, and the assigned start date of the job.

The names of the subcontractors go in the blanks under the various trades. The start date for the trade is shown on the top left side of the box, and the completion date on the bottom right side. Blank boxes are included for specialty trades required for particular jobs.

The *Notes* section allows space for listing special items such as the date the job sign was put up, if scaffolding is needed, or when portable toilets were ordered.

With a system like this, a superintendent can tell at a glance what's happening on the job and what he needs to do next.

Another common scheduling method is the pegboard system. Each trade is identified by colored pegs. The pegs are moved each day on a pegboard to show job progress.

Many successful remodeling contractors use varying forms of charts and pegboards for their schedules. Most of these systems, with the possible exception of the example in Figure 7-3, have a major drawback. They don't pinpoint the critical parts of the project. In every project there are tasks that are time-critical. A one-day delay in a critical task will delay the project by one day. Other tasks are not critical to on-time completion. There may be several days available to finish a one-day task. In that case, a delay of a day or two doesn't affect the completion date at all.

Any task is critical if it affects the next task to be done, or the overall completion date. For example, pouring a foundation is critical because nothing else can be done until the concrete is in and set. The same can be said of rough carpentry and framing, since the other trades are held up until the joists and studs are in.

When there's a delay in a critical area, you should be able to see at a glance where adjustments can be made. You have to correct the problem quickly to keep the project on schedule. A bar chart or pegboard doesn't show what can be set aside or where to "press" if a problem occurs and your completion date is threatened. A diagram of the project, using the Critical Path Method (CPM), is a great tool in helping you make just this kind of decision. A CPM network, like the one shown in Figure 7-4, becomes a master plan that shows time relationships between all tasks. It combines planning, scheduling, monitoring, and control, in one system.

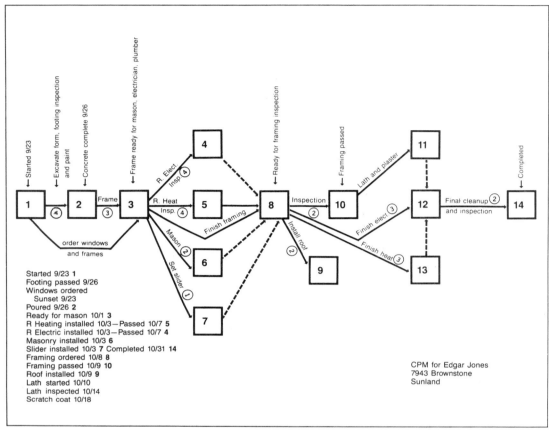

Courtesy: Charles Trim Construction Company
CPM diagram
Figure 7-4

Planning Comes First

On every job, planning should come first. It's the most important phase of the project. If you fail to plan, you've planned to fail. Some planners simply develop a list of activities and arrange them in chronological order. That may or may not work. If you've handled many jobs like this before, you've probably made all the mistakes already and will muddle through O.K. But if you're dealing with more complexity or more trades than you've handled previously, lack of a good plan can cost you dearly.

Planning includes scheduling trades and ordering materials. You have to order materials so they're available on the job when needed — not too soon and certainly not too late. On smaller jobs, it's enough to make a list of materials and order everything at once. That way, when it's needed, it's there. But what about larger jobs? What happens if you don't need all the materials for 60 days? You've tied up cash for two months and need a place to store everything. The job site isn't a good storage area. Materials left exposed and unguarded tend to get damaged or simply disappear.

Other contractors order materials for one trade when the previous one is finishing up. If this is your habit, what happens if you need custom-designed materials, or if deliveries run late? Your job is held up while you wait. This costs you and your subcontractors time and money.

The best way to order materials is to determine when they're needed. Then determine how much lead-time is needed by the supplier to guarantee delivery by the date needed. Lead-time determines order time. Good planning begins at the end and works back to the present day.

Managing project details can be a complex task. You or your superintendent have to work with subcontractors and suppliers who have many other responsibilities. You have to cooperate with architects, designers, inspectors, tradespeople, and suppliers, to get the job done. They, in turn, must also be able to rely on you.

The Critical Path Method (CPM)

If you're handling projects that involve several trades and last for more than a week or two, consider trying the Critical Path Method (CPM). Many contractors use it (or a variation) and have found that a few minutes of planning can yield big dividends. The CPM is used on nearly every large construction project. But it can be just as useful on smaller projects.

CPM came out of the aerospace program as a production planning system. It was devised to reduce the time needed to manufacture aerospace hardware. It's also used by the Navy as part of their Program Evaluation Review Technique (PERT). It's useful any time the manpower, materials, and time needed to complete a job are known or can be estimated. That makes CPM ideal for use in the construction industry.

CPM doesn't have to be complicated. You'll need to invest a little time to master the techniques and apply it skillfully, but it should be worth the efforts. By the time you finish reading this chapter, you'll know all that's needed to schedule a small bathroom or kitchen job.

Of course, CPM helps you identify the critical items in your jobs. But it also helps you find "dead time" on a job — the time you have to wait for concrete to set or paint to dry. Identifying critical items, non-critical items, and dead time, can make your jobs go much quicker and smoother.

CPM can help you decide if it's economical to add more men or other resources to the work force. If you can shorten the time it takes to complete certain jobs and it's critical to the completion of others, the extra money is well spent. If it's a non-critical area and won't speed up completion of the project, then any money spent on extra manpower is wasted.

Those who use it estimate that the Critical Path Method can cut construction time 10 to 20 percent. Other benefits include:

• Improved communication

• Reduced working capital requirements

- Exposed bottlenecks and errors

- An accurate job history

- A better-informed customer

- Fewer foul-ups by subcontractors

- More completions as scheduled

Everyone who needs to follow the status of the project should get a copy of your CPM schedule. That way they have the same job information that you have and can see the same problems that you see. If the schedule's done properly, even your customers can follow job progress on the CPM schedule. Its simplicity means fewer phone calls and fewer unanswered questions. Also, if for any reason you must change supervisors, the new one should be able to carry on without delay.

How CPM Works

CPM is a diagram of the entire job operation. Figure 7-4 is a completed CPM chart. Each job is broken down into individual events. Each event is represented by a square with a number in it. The events are numbered in the order they must be performed.

The first event is connected to the second event with an arrow. Next to the arrow are listed the job activities or tasks that must be completed before you can go on to the next major step or event in the project. If more than one event follows the completion of a previous event, separate arrows are drawn to each subsequent event. Looking at Figure 7-4, you can see that events (1), (2), and (3) follow one after the other in sequence. Events (4), (5), (6), and (7) occur simultaneously and must all be completed before you go on to event (8).

You have to figure the time required to perform each event, including the activities required between the events. The circled numbers under the arrows show the total number of days scheduled between events. As you can see, there are four days scheduled between events (1) and (2), and three days between events (2) and (3).

All the events and activities in a project are laid out in a structured flow-chart or *path*. The longest sequence of connected events and activities becomes the *critical path*. These determine when the job is started and when it will be completed. The events and activities along the critical path *must* be completed in the time you allow for them.

Those jobs not along your critical path may have some slack time. Rearranging the workers or their schedules probably won't affect the completion date or the total cost of the job. For example, in Figure 7-5, event (7), "set slider," isn't along the critical path. It's a one day job, but other events also leading up to event (8) involve as much as four days. You can see that event (7) can be planned for any one of the four days scheduled between events (3) and (8) without affecting the overall time sequence of the project.

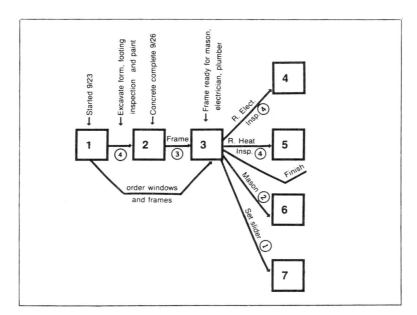

Event 7 is not on critical path
Figure 7-5

The CPM shows how laborers should be used so that no one has to wait to begin work. If slack time is shown, arrange your crew time accordingly. Divert labor to another area, or another job.

Although CPM can be used for almost any size job, its value increases with the size of the job. The more complicated the job, the more complicated and technical the diagram or network becomes, but the easier it is for you to track your project. On larger construction projects, the diagram can be set up and monitored with a computer. We've never seen a remodeling project complex enough to warrant this. But you may.

Diagraming Your Project

To draw an accurate and useful CPM network requires an understanding of CPM planning, full knowledge of the project, good judgment, and some plain common sense. Let's review some of the common terms used in building a CPM network.

CPM Terminology

Event— An event is any separate and distinct step in the project. It's the beginning point and ending point for activities. Events represent a point in time when all activities leading up to that point have been completed and all activities to follow can begin. Events, designated by large squares or circles with numbers, are the milestones in a project.

Every event is assigned a different number, but always in a progressive sequence. That is, events can be sequentially numbered (1) (2) (3) (4) (5), (5) (10) (15) (20), or (10) (20) (30) (40), whichever number grouping works best for you.

If an event along the critical path is not completed by the assigned date, it's a signal that something is wrong. You've got a problem and should be trying to solve it.

Activity— An activity is any work that has a set beginning and end. It's a task or job that has to be done. Activities include getting the building permits, carpentry, or installing electrical wiring and plumbing. Activities, as we have noted, are indicated on a CPM diagram by a solid arrow.

The ground rules for scheduling activities in a CPM network are:

• Each activity is a mandatory task.

• Arrows must indicate, as nearly as possible or practical, the relationships among activities.

• No new activity can start until its originating event is completed. Each activity must be completed before the event to which it leads can begin.

• Arrows generally flow from left to right, but to save space or eliminate redrawing, they can be drawn in other directions as long as the progression of the critical path remains clear. The job sequences must move forward at all times. In this chapter we'll give you examples of networks progressing from left to right (horizontally) and from top to bottom (vertically).

Dummy arrow— There's another kind of arrow used in drawing a CPM network. It's called a *dummy,* and it's designated by a broken-line. A dummy is used when an event to be completed has no direct bearing on the next event. It needs to be completed before the next event, but doesn't necessarily have anything to do with that event.

Dummy arrows represent zero-time, zero-cost activity. In Figure 7-4, events (4), (5), (6), and (7) all must be completed in the time schedule between events (3) and (8). But the framing inspection ordered for event (8) depends only on the completion of event (5) and the framing. Those are the only solid arrows leading to (8). All the other arrows are dummy arrows. They're simply a means of connecting events and progressing along your path.

Designating Events

As explained, numbers are assigned to the events sequentially to show their order in the completion of the project. Let's look at another CPM network, Figure 7-6. Although this figure resembles Figure 7-4, there are a few major differences. Figure 7-6 uses a different numbering system. Here the steps begin with 10, then progress in multiples of

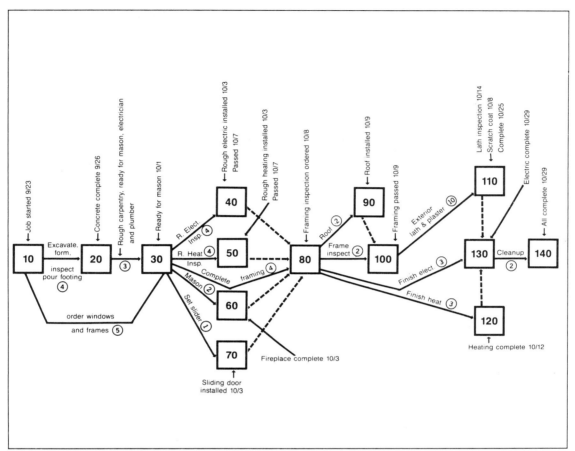

Courtesy: Charles Trim Construction Company

CPM numbering systems may vary
Figure 7-6

10. The advantage of this system is that you can easily insert an additional step without having to renumber your whole diagram. So if you need to add an event between 20 and 30, you can label it 25, and the rest of your diagram remains the same. You can add as many as nine additional events if needed. Use whichever numbering system you think will work best for you.

Another difference in these diagrams is the list of completion dates shown on the left hand side of Figure 7-4. They're shown above the event numbers in Figure 7-6. This is a good way of verifying that your CPM plan is on schedule. You can *see* by the dates where you are at any time.

The Diagram

There are three major steps involved in creating your CPM diagram or network. They are:

1) Project planning

2) Time estimating

3) Scheduling

Project planning— Begin your diagram by analyzing the project and deciding which steps come first and which follow in succession. Lay each step out in a consecutive time sequence and connect them with arrows. If more than one job in the project can be started at the same time, draw arrows for each event that can be carried out simultaneously. As each new activity is drawn into the diagram, you must decide:

• What has to be completed before the next one can be started?

• Can other activities or operations be done at the same time as this one?

• What activities or operations can't be started until this one is complete?

Estimating activity time— Now figure the time needed to complete each event and related activities and show it on your diagram. Your *critical path* is along the longest path, or the path of events and arrows involving the greatest amount of time. This represents the maximum total time needed to complete your project. The only way to speed up construction or move up the completion date is to speed up the jobs along your critical path. If extra time is needed on non-critical jobs, it can be absorbed over the total time of the project.

Estimating your activity times is one of the most critical elements of diagraming a CPM. According to the developers of CPM, you can estimate your time in three ways.

Optimistic time— Your estimate in working days of the best or shortest time an activity could take, if everything went better than expected.

Most likely time— The estimate in working days that you would give if only one time estimate was requested.

Pessimistic time— Your estimate in working days of the time that would be required if practically everything went wrong (barring major disasters such as strikes, fire, floods, hurricanes, or tornados).

How do you come up with these estimates? You or your estimator should have the skills and knowledge to estimate each of the above time frames. You can also use estimates made by your subcontractors. It's really very helpful to expose your subs to CPM. When everyone working on the job is on the same wavelength, there are fewer chances for errors and delays.

You can describe activity duration in hours, days, weeks, or shifts, as long as you're consistent throughout the CPM network. The most common error in scheduling time is forgetting that there are only 22 or 23 working days per month.

If you prefer using days when working out your schedule, don't forget that there are activities which can take place on weekends and holidays which make good use of dead-time. For example, concrete can cure and paint can dry over non-working days. When activities of this type are expected to take longer than five calendar days, be careful not to overestimate the time needed. In this case, a seven-day curing requirement can be estimated as five working days.

It's a mistake to estimate that you'll have good weather throughout the project. Of course, you can't schedule a blizzard. But you can estimate the number of days that will be lost due to bad weather during the course of the job. Include a safety factor for bad weather in your time estimates. But don't overdo it. It's better to add a little time to the total project than to try to guess where you might be held up by weather. A good place to add time is to a key segment, such as pouring concrete or enclosing a room addition.

When estimating the time for a given activity, look at the activity as totally independent of what comes before or after it. Don't assume that it will take longer because the materials needed are usually delivered late. Ordering materials should be considered a separate activity. If materials from a specific supplier are always delivered late, order earlier, so you'll receive your deliveries on schedule.

When you've figured your time estimates for each event and activity, the critical path should be clear. Now your project plan is complete. Events and activities have been defined and the normal performance time for each activity estimated.

Scheduling— At this point, you can begin scheduling. Once you apply days and dates to the network diagram, your superintendent will have a clearly defined, realistic schedule to work with. He can manage the project better.

It should be emphasized that it's *you,* not CPM, that makes the decisions. The CPM merely helps you make better, more informed decisions.

It isn't hard to learn CPM. Some study is required. But like many things that seem difficult at first, the more you do them, the easier they become. Once you've mastered CPM, you'll find yourself looking back and saying, "What was so hard about that?"

A word of caution: Don't try to set up a CPM master network that you can adapt to every job. It won't work. Every project is different. Every new project requires a new CPM network. Besides that, it isn't necessary to have a master. Once you grasp the technique, you'll find you can draw a new network in an hour or two.

Using CPM

Some contractors use CPM for every remodeling job. Others use it only for large or complicated jobs requiring several trades, a variety of materials, and staggering of the work schedule. Still others, usually those who've been in business for many years, prefer a bar chart, pegboard or some type of construction calendar. But everyone can agree, some kind of written schedule is always needed.

Let's look at how one Southern California contractor we know uses CPM in his business:

Charlie was introduced to CPM at a seminar given by a large aircraft manufacturer over 20 years ago. He recognized that the principles could also apply to small businesses, such as remodeling. He tried adapting the basic principles of CPM to his remodeling jobs and liked the results he got. For him, the big advantage of CPM is that it provides a precise, orderly schedule for each project. CPM lets him find and concentrate on the parts of the job that need the most attention.

Laying out a CPM diagram forces Charlie to anticipate what is required for each part of a project. For example, when ordering customized doors or cabinets, he must plan carefully so the order arrives when the carpenter is ready for it. Or, if his customers want to select certain items, he must have them make their choices in enough time to avoid delaying installation.

He feels that CPM helps him organize his subcontracted work more efficiently as well. If the plumber can't put the finish plumbing in until the cabinet installer has put the pullman cabinet in, and the tile installer can't complete his work until the plumber finishes, the system lets him know that the cabinet installation is critical to the completion of the project.

The CPM diagram shows him the degree of urgency for each step in a project. If there are problems, he knows how and where to adjust the work so the overall schedule isn't delayed.

Preparing a Sample CPM Schedule

The procedure Charlie uses for his CPM diagrams is shown in Figure 7-7. He uses a circle to show each event (you can use any symbol: circle, square, triangle). The activity required to complete that event is written out along the arrow leading to the next event. Each arrow and circle represents a single task. Following the path of circles and arrows provides you with a simple graphic picture of the total job, showing when each step begins and ends and what happens in between.

Before he draws the network, Charlie goes over the contract with the customer to be certain every item has been included. This is also an opportunity to clarify any unanswered questions.

Once the contract has been reviewed, he sets up his CPM network. When the network is completed, he doesn't have to check the contract again. All his information is on the CPM diagram.

For Charlie, making a CPM diagram reflects the three phases of working a project. The first is planning; the client's needs are determined, the design drawn, the contract is written out, and all details are reviewed and approved. In the second phase, he converts this information to a visual picture by drawing the CPM diagram. He uses the diagram to schedule his crews and order equipment and materials. The third phase is following the diagram through to completion. The CPM gives him control all along the way.

Before he began using CPM, Charlie had trouble laying out a schedule that everyone could understand. He wanted a chart that could provide a clear, simple picture of a project. It had to show what was important, what was critical, and what could be safely delayed. He wanted his workmen to be able to look at it and have that information immediately. CPM gives him all that, and more. It's an information network and a framework for the efficient scheduling of materials, manpower, and equipment.

Using The CPM Network

Figure 7-7 is Charlie's network for a simple room addition with a shower, which can be used as a den or guest room. The events are numbered beginning with (10).

He drew this particular network vertically rather than horizontally in order to get it all on one page. As we said before, CPM networks can be drawn either way depending on which is most convenient for you.

The first activity is "excavate and pour." While this is being done, Charlie has the homeowners select the pullman cabinet, marble top, paneling, and wardrobe doors. These items can take several weeks for delivery. He has to make sure that their delivery doesn't delay the project.

Figure 7-7 shows 51 working days from event (10) to event (120), which is the "earliest possible completion date." If he can't make this date work, Charlie will have to reevaluate each event to see if something can be done to speed up one of the items along the critical path between (10) and (120).

The key dates which make up the critical path for this project (excluding July 4, and weekends) are:

- Start June 1.

- Event (10) to event (20), 6 days — excavate, form, pour and inspection — complete June 8.

- Event (20) to event (30), 7 days — rough carpentry, ready for rough electric and plumbing — complete June 17.

- Event (30) to event (40), 4 days — finish rough carpentry and electric — complete June 23.

- Events (40), (50), (60), and (70), 5 days — install roof and flashing, ready for rough inspection — complete June 28.

- Event (70) to event (80), 2 days — install insulation — complete July 1.

- Event (80) to event (90), 4 days — install exterior lath and interior drywall — complete July 8.

- Event (90) to event (100), 2 days — ready for inspection — complete July 12.

- Event (100) to event (110), 7 days — finish drywall — complete July 21.

- Event (110) to event (120), 2 days — install shower tile — complete July 25.

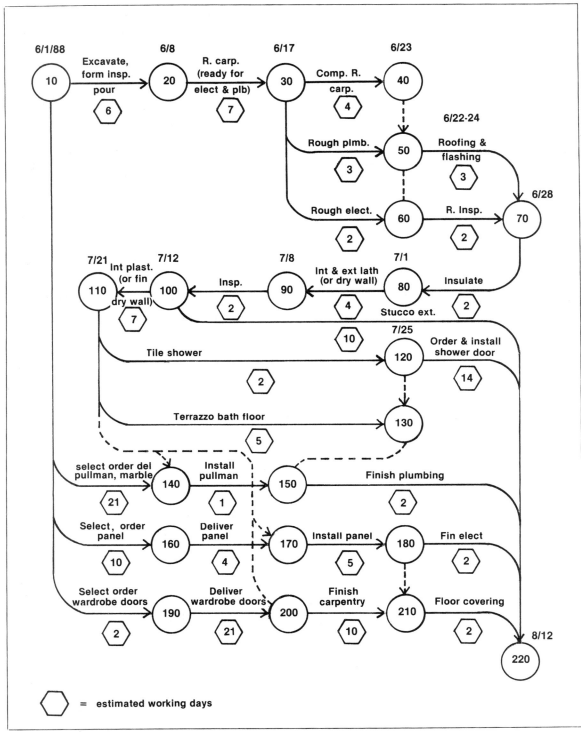

Courtesy: Charles Trim Construction Company

Vertical CPM diagram
Figure 7-7

(There are 35 work days leading up to event (110). It's now critical for the pullman, paneling and wardrobe doors to be on the job. Charlie can't have them delivered earlier because there isn't a place to store them safely. They could be ruined if they sat around during the plastering and drywall.)

• Event (120) to event (220), 14 days — order and install shower door; finish plumbing, electric, and carpentry; finish interior installations — complete August 12.

These last two weeks involve a great deal of interior work, all of which is dependent on the events leading up to item (120) being completed. Charlie can make up time on this project by having his crews work extra hours on Saturdays or a couple of extra days over the 4th of July holiday weekend, if time is critical.

Charlie estimates the number of days it will take to complete the events that aren't on the critical path. These times are figured as accurately as possible. However, if there were a high degree of urgency to speed up their completion, the project manager could consult with the supplier, mechanic, or subcontractor for more specific times before charting the labor.

To show how certain events can become critical, let's look at some of the key events not along the critical path. Remember, any event can become critical if its completion date threatens to delay the total project. For example, the job can't be completed if:

• the pullman and marble lavatory aren't ordered early enough. They can hold up final inspection if they aren't delivered in time to be installed and the plumbing completed.

• the panel installation isn't completed on schedule. If it's to be done by the finish carpenter and he isn't available for the full 15 days required to complete the paneling and other carpentry work, someone else must work on the paneling so the job can progress.

• the shower door doesn't arrive on schedule. It could possibly either be purchased elsewhere, (providing he can find one that fits or have one custom-made quickly) or Charlie can provide a shower curtain for temporary use. This isn't a good practice, however. It's better to "press" for the shower door delivery.

• the wardrobe doors aren't delivered on time. They could probably be installed the last days of carpentry, but if the cabinets can't be built or installed until the doors are fitted in place, they too become critical.

Charlie knows that most of the finish carpentry could be completed before the wardrobe doors are delivered. However, in order to simplify his project networks he likes to emphasize those items that take time to be fabricated. This calls attention to possible or probable problem areas before they become critical.

Look again at the location of events (140), (160) and (190) on the network. Charlie places them in this particular position so they'll be noticed every time the project is evaluated. There's no excuse for them to hold up completion. "These are the types of items which in actual practice *do* delay a project," he says. "We wouldn't forget to order and deliver concrete or rough lumber! But if we don't schedule items like pullmans and doors properly, you can almost guarantee they won't be there when we need them."

Notice there aren't any dates given for the events that aren't located directly along the critical path. Some contractors like to insert dates here. But Charlie doesn't fill in these dates because he thinks that everything should be done as soon as possible, not on the last allowable date. Often, if you allow workers extra time, they'll take it!

Here's another point that underscores the importance of doing everything as soon as possible. Charlie can sometimes create slack time which allows him to pick up a few days along the critical path. This can be a tremendous benefit in meeting the completion date if he gets bogged down elsewhere by unexpected delays.

Charlie figures he has 23 days of slack time built into his schedule between events (10) and (220). Here's where you find them: from (10) to (140) he's allowed 21 days, while from (10) to (110) there are 35 days. This gives him 14 days of available slack time. From (110) to (140) to (220) there are 3 days, and from (110) to (200) to (220) there are 12 days, which gives him another 9 possible days. This adds up to a total of 23 days, if his most optimistic estimates work out. Usually they don't. That's why it's important to build some slack into the schedule.

The dotted lines from (110) to (140), (170) and (200) show him where his pullman, paneling and doors become critical. Event (140) must be completed in 21 days to allow him to continue work from (110). Events (10) to (160) to (170) must be completed in 14 days, and (10) to (190) to (200) in 23 days, or they too will hold up work.

Charlie's network also gives him the last possible date for completion of events not along the critical path. If you add up the number of days required to complete the project after a particular event is scheduled to be ready, you'll see how a delay in that event will affect his overall completion date.

- The latest possible date to install the pullman is 3 days before final inspection.

- The latest possible date to deliver the paneling is 7 days before final inspection.

- The latest possible date to deliver the wardrobe is 12 days before final inspection.

Earlier, we pointed out that one of the reasons for using event numbers (10), (20), (30) or (100), (200), (300) is so you can insert another number in case you forget something or have to change something. It's much easier to insert an additional event between (10) and (20), like (15), than to try to fit something in between (1) and (2).

In Figure 7-7 there is no final inspection date given. Since this generally takes one day, it could easily be added on at the end. So event (220) to (230) would be "final inspection." However, this extends the completion date one day.

Instead, since the floor covering is carpet, the final inspection can take place while the carpet is being laid. To show this, Charlie made the final inspection a separate event, number (215), and modified his network to include this event, as shown in Figure 7-8.

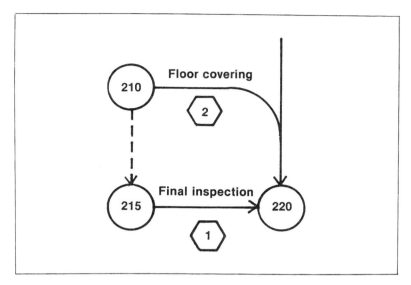

Adding an event is easy
Figure 7-8

Daily Reviews

Using CPM doesn't eliminate the need for daily reviews. It does keep the time involved to a minimum, however. It gives you or your superintendent a quick and accurate record of the progress of each project to report to management.

If the CPM schedule is used properly, you should show current job status every day. As Charlie emphasizes, "We review our projects daily in our superintendents' meetings. That way nothing is overlooked, even on a little project. The meetings are usually pretty routine: Have the proper trades been called? Are they going to be on the job as scheduled? At the end of the meeting, we know where we are for that day. If we have a problem, we know what we're going to do about it, *that day.* We take care of everything on every job before it becomes a problem. You don't want things coming back to haunt you three days later."

CPM also helps you keep track of where you're going. It's a "tickler file" for your superintendent. It tells him what he has to do next.

If the plumber needs three days lead time, your superintendent doesn't have to go to the job to see if it's ready. He should know the job's status from the CPM schedule. If it's three days before the plumber is due, one of the activities on the CPM should be "call plumber." At that time he should also reconfirm the plumber's completion date so that the next trade's schedule can be verified.

Responsibility for keeping your jobs on schedule rests with your superintendent. He needs all the help he can get. A CPM schedule will remind him what has to be done today and what he should do about tomorrow.

This becomes more urgent as the work load gets heavier. If a superintendent is running only one job at a time, he can probably keep all of the scheduling in his head. But if he's running 10 to 20 jobs, you can't expect him to keep track of all the events and activities going on in the course of a day without a pretty detailed schedule on hand.

Job Size

Are there jobs too small to use CPM? Not really. Although for single-trade jobs, a few notes on the type of job and the materials needed on a 3'' x 5'' file card, and a simple handwritten schedule may be enough. However, consider using CPM on any job using two or more trades. Once you understand the power of CPM, you'll probably want a CPM schedule for every job, regardless of size. It's a definite aid in coordinating your work load. If you don't have some kind of schedule for every job, it's easy to overlook something and get behind.

Your Client and the CPM

Should you give CPM diagrams to your clients? Some contractors say "yes" and some say "no." There are good arguments for both sides.

On the "no" side, many contractors feel that when the job is off schedule (which is frequently the case), it's better that the homeowner not know how much or where. They should know that a schedule exists, but not necessarily have a copy of it. As long as you know you can finish the job on time, why worry clients about delays within the job? Also, if homeowners have a copy of the schedule, they tend to become "second-party superintendents." They don't usually understand the accordion effect of remodeling. When the job is three days behind, they think there should be extra workers there all day long. You have to assure them that the time can be made up along the way. Otherwise they'll have trouble with the idea that certain tradespeople will be there only one or two hours, and no one else will come that day at all. Of course, if someone is supposed to be there and isn't, the homeowners have a legitimate complaint. And they don't usually hesitate to keep you informed of what is and *isn't* happening on the job.

On the positive side, a copy of the CPM schedule can help you keep your clients informed and eliminate unnecessary phone calls. They should know what to expect each day. This is one of the biggest advantages of using CPM. If you're running eighty jobs with four superintendents, you don't need your clients calling to say that nothing is being done on his or her room addition.

But if they do call, or there's a misunderstanding, you can review the situation and make a decision in a moment. The CPM schedule can give you an immediate and detailed picture of the activity on that job, even if you've never been to the site. If a homeowner is confused about the lack of activity on their project, you might need to point out the fact that the plumber had been there one day, the electrician the next, and the city inspector is due any moment. You can quickly assure them that the work is proceeding according to their schedule.

There will be occasional misunderstandings. That's natural — and probably unavoidable. But make it clear that you're in touch with the problem. Don't let a client feel that their project isn't your most important job.

Planning Is Always Required

The CPM isn't a magic wand. You still have to plan. You still need experience to draw a CPM diagram. Its accuracy and effectiveness is only as good as the planner.

The CPM is different and helpful because it's a picture of reality — the way each project should happen. The technique is consistent regardless of who is doing it. Anyone familiar with the system can review a CPM network and understand what's happening and when it has to be done. This makes CPM a valuable management tool.

CPM brings planning, scheduling, directing, and monitoring into a single unit. One of the ground rules of the CPM is that it deals with each item as a distinct and separate operation. This is especially helpful in eliminating the confusion which often results when planning and scheduling are treated as the same thing.

Of course, it's possible to complete any remodeling project on time and within budget even if you don't have a plan. But it isn't very likely. Our advice is simple. If you aren't satisfied with the planning that goes into your jobs, use the information in this chapter to develop a CPM diagram for your next job. See if CPM doesn't eliminate some of the problems you've been having and put a little extra cash in your pocket. It has for many remodelers and it could for you too.

eight

Financing: Keeping the Till Full

*I*f you have trouble keeping enough cash in the company checking account, don't think you're the only one. That's a common problem for many remodeling contractors. Suppliers, subcontractors, tradesmen and supervisors have to be paid — whether it's your busy season, or during slack times when you're having trouble collecting from a client, or even when you're way over budget on a job.

Most remodelers are at least a little short of cash much of the time. Consider cash shortages a part of the remodeling business. Fortunately, it's fairly easy to avoid most cash problems and plan around shortages before they happen. This chapter will explain a way to help keep the company's till full — at least most of the time.

Here's a common problem for many remodelers. You've sold the job and finished most or all of it. It's time to get paid. Your client apologizes, but insists that the money isn't available, promising a payment by month end or next month or later. Whose fault is that? In our mind, it's yours. You should have taken steps to ensure that the money owed you would be there in time to pay *your* bills. Fortunately, there's a fairly easy way to handle this kind of problem. We'll explain how in this chapter.

Most of us want more than we can afford. People who want their home improved certainly aren't exceptions. There's really no way for the average homeowner to judge the cost of improving a home until they get a bid. And when their budget was $10,000 and your bid is $25,000, they don't know what to do. They had their hearts set on the improvements — surely you can figure a way to do it for $10,000. But remodeling isn't like buying a car. Estimates aren't sticker prices that can be bargained down.

Some customers simply aren't realistic about what they can pay for or finance. Usually the improvements you make are genuinely needed. They're not a luxury. There's little room for compromise, either in your price or in what your customer needs.

Most customers don't realize that remodeling carries three costs. First, there's the cost to tear out the existing construction. Then there's the cost of the new materials and the labor to install them. And finally, in older homes, there's the additional cost of bringing the building up to current code standards. This last expense is for the good of your customers, but it doesn't make them feel like they're getting anything new for their money. This is one cost that very few owners consider when planning to remodel.

For whatever reason, let's say your customers budgeted $10,000 for a remodeling job that's going to cost $25,000. Their needs are legitimate, not extravagant. From your conversation with the owners, you can tell that there's some uncertainty about where the extra $15,000 is going to come from. What should you do? You've got the job at your price and you're anxious to begin work. Should you keep your fingers crossed and hope the owners can come up with the cash when you present the bill? We don't recommend it. Instead, be very candid. Ask the owners if they need financing. If the answer is anything but a flat "no," offer to help them get a loan.

Arrange Bank Financing

No one in the remodeling business wants to pass up a good job just because the clients are short of cash. If a homeowner wants the improvement, with your design and at your price, it's to your advantage to help them get financing. Over 80 percent of remodeling work is financed at least partly with proceeds from a loan. Many remodelers work closely with a bank or savings and loan. Having some type of financing available helps close the deal. And getting the loan approved in advance usually guarantees that you'll be paid on time.

If you can help customers get bank financing, it's good for them *and* good for you. They get their home improvements and you're able to increase your business base. Offer financing to attract the customers with the larger jobs. Forty jobs a year at $10,000 is $400,000. But 40 jobs a year at $25,000 and you're running a million-dollar-a-year business. That's a nice place to be.

Even high income customers with lots of assets can have cash problems. Don't get drawn into their crisis. Don't be surprised with, "I have to pay a few other bills first . . . I'll pay *you* next month." If your remodeling business is like most, you pay this month's bills out of this month's income. If just one or two of your 40 customers are slowpaying, you've got a serious cash problem.

Set up a financing program with a local lender to avoid this kind of crisis. Of course, every lender decides who they will loan money to and who they won't. But their judgment is at least as good as yours — probably better. If anyone's going to lose money, it usually won't be the lender. And if you're riding on their wagon, you'll be safe too.

When a lender refuses a loan to one of your prospects, chances are they know something that you don't. Be glad you didn't take the job. There are enough problems in the remodeling business without adding collection problems.

But if the lender says "yes," and you brought that borrower to the bank or savings and loan, you've won twice: with your customer, of course, and also with the financial institution for bringing them more business.

Financing Promotes Good Relations

Helping arrange customer financing promotes good will. More often than not, when a customer tells a friend or neighbor about their beautiful new kitchen, they're also likely to add that you helped them get financing. Since referrals represent a large portion of all new remodeling business, any extra service you provide helps *you* in the long run.

When your customers finance the job, you'll be paid promptly and in full, provided the work is completed on schedule and the customers are satisfied. Cash flow is important no matter what size business you have. The larger your business, the more obligations you have to suppliers and tradesmen, and the more critical your cash flow can be.

Develop Credit Sources to Improve Your Cash Flow

Cash-short remodelers are very resourceful in finding ways to meet their obligations and keep their projects going. One way to make your cash last longer is to use your credit cards. For example, most building material dealers offer a 30-day credit term to their contractor customers. When the 30 days are up, you can pay the bill with your credit card. This will help you conserve your cash to meet more pressing needs, like the payroll.

One Illinois dealer we know spends about $10,000 a month on building materials. Nothing unusual about that — except that he charges the whole thing on his Visa. He says, "Try borrowing from a bank. You get all dressed up, drive downtown, and then beg for the money. It takes a lot of time and trouble. Visa, on the other hand, sends me junk mail begging me to use their money." He admits the interest charges are steep if he's slow to pay his bills, but he feels the convenience is worth the cost.

If you don't think you can pay your credit cards off monthly, and you don't want to worry about the high interest rates, your best bet is a short term loan. With the deregulation of the banking industry, contractors are finding a friendly welcome at many savings and loan associations . . . and at lower interest rates than banks, too.

If you can't connect with a bank or savings and loan, you might want to consider working with a finance company. Finance companies have less rigid lending policies than banks. To get a loan, however, you may be required to take extra services. But the extra burden may be insignificant. Some finance companies will want to become your credit department, your collection agency, your accounts receivable and bookkeeping department. But long-term customers have been known to qualify for loans up to a million dollars — or even more. If you can repay quickly, these loans aren't prohibitively expensive.

Qualifying Your Business

When you go to a financial institution to set up a credit program for your clients, their initial concern is *you*. This is true even though the finance contracts will be between the lender and your clients. The length of time you've been in business or your dollar volume of business isn't the lender's first concern. They'll be most interested in your company's *reputation*.

Your Reputation Is Your Biggest Asset

The lender will want to know about the *quality* of your work *and* your list of satisfied customers. It's hard to collect from dissatisfied customers. When you've addressed these issues, the lender will decide if more information is needed to qualify you as an acceptable contractor. If you pass that critical first step, you'll be well on your way to becoming an approved contractor.

Of course the bank or savings and loan will require business and personal financial statements, including a statement of your net worth. But no matter how healthy your financial records look, they will still look closely at your relationships with your clients and associates. Your chances for setting up a home-improvement financing program are pretty slim if you haven't built a sound management team and you don't have a list of satisfied customers.

Your Stability Counts Too

Most lenders prefer that you've been in business for a minimum of five years before they'll work with you on a financing program. Some, however, will consider contractors who have as little as three years of experience if their net worth is good and there's a pre-existing business relationship. You may need to talk to several lenders in your area before you find one that you feel will work well for both you and your clients.

You'll also need to provide:

1) A list of trade references, including suppliers and subcontractors, you've been doing business with for some time.

2) A statement showing the types of remodeling work you do and the geographical area in which you operate.

3) A list of recent clients and their project descriptions.

4) A list of employees showing, in particular, the number of building tradespeople and sales personnel you have on your direct payroll.

The Evaluation Process

Besides checking your references and credit rating, the lender will make a background check to be sure that you're not on any list disqualifying you for FHA or HUD projects. They'll also check your client list to make sure there haven't been any complaints about the quality or workmanship of your jobs.

Some lenders prefer that you have your own work crew. They feel you have better control over the quality of your work than if you rely on subcontractors. However, if you do use subcontractors, explain why. Good reasons will probably satisfy the lender.

Assessing Your Net Worth

A lending institution will be interested in your net worth. The assets you need depend on the type of work you do and how much you're handling. The key is to have enough working capital to meet your current needs.

One banker we know told us how he evaluates the financial condition of a remodeling contractor:

"Most of a remodeling contractor's income goes back out for expenses, and that doesn't leave much money in the business. So, we look at his personal financial statements as well. In the case of a small contractor whose gross sales are under $500,000, we look for a liquid cash net worth of $30,000 to $75,000.

We might feel that as little as $30,000 in net worth is enough for a contractor who does exterior work such as porches, siding, and windows. His material costs and job turnaround times are low. And his expenses are predictable — they don't vary much from job to job. He doesn't need a lot of working capital to pay for his labor and materials costs.

A contractor with $2 million annual sales needs much more working capital, so we look for a higher liquid net worth to support his operations."

Figures 8-1 and 8-2 show jobs completed by two different contractors. Both jobs required skill and knowledge, but one is clearly more complicated and expensive than the other. The bay window shown in Figure 8-1 was installed by a single trade contractor who specializes in jobs where material costs are modest. He doesn't need a lot of capital or assets to impress his banker. He does need a good reputation, however. He'll have to be able to show his banker that his suppliers and workers are paid promptly, that he does quality work, and that he completes his jobs on schedule.

A lender will require a higher net worth for a contractor who does remodeling jobs like the kitchen shown in Figure 8-2. There's greater risk because of the higher cost of materials. Although there were few structural changes in this project, it required installation of new counters, appliances, wrap-around cabinets, and the addition of an island in the middle of the room.

Courtesy: Pella/Rolscreen Co.

Bay window added to sunroom
Figure 8-1

Courtesy: Armstrong World Industries, Inc.

Customized kitchen
Figure 8-2

A contractor who specializes in customized kitchens needs skilled workers and expensive materials. Custom grade cabinets can be very expensive and superior workmanship is needed for installation. Because of the higher cost, the finished job will be judged much more critically.

Let's assume the average cost per job for the contractor who installed the window is $5,000, and half his cost is materials. The contractor doing the custom kitchens will average $20,000 per job, with about two-thirds for materials. If each has 15 jobs on the books, the first contractor owes $37,500 for materials, while the second owes $200,000. If each has four customers holding back their payments, the first contractor will have to cover about $10,000 out of his working capital. But the second contractor is going to be dragging over $50,000!

Chances are the first contractor can weather the storm. But the second contractor may very well go under. A lender is concerned with issues like this when deciding which contractors they want to work with. If you regularly take risks with customers or take on more business than your cash flow can comfortably handle, the lender's going to think twice before doing business with you.

Our banker friend pointed out that on larger projects, such as room additions, there's another dimension to look at, and that's timing. He says, "A project may take 60 to 90 days or more and require many kinds of work. Each phase of the job, whether it's laying the foundation, electrical wiring, plumbing or finishing, requires supervision. The contractor needs a large capital base to meet the payroll and pay for materials. For these kind of jobs, we look for substantial assets.''

Assessing Your Business Skills

Never assume your lender knows nothing about home improvements or the kind of improvements required in a given market. He or she is going to look at the product you're selling and where you're selling it to see if they match up. You may be surprised at how much your lender knows about carpentry and plumbing. They're very careful about protecting their interests.

Lenders recognize that older communities need home improvements the most. They know that the roofs begin to wear out in suburban neighborhoods about 20 years after construction. People will replace the roofs, gutters and downspouts. Then they'll add new siding. Eventually they'll also want to improve their kitchens and baths, and finally add a room. Lenders know how much improvement is justified, and whether the proposed project offers a safe return on their money.

But just because a lender seems knowledgeable about construction, doesn't mean he or she knows about *your* business. Many financial consultants suggest that you prepare a brief two or three page summary of your business, even if you've been associated with a particular bank or savings and loan for some time. Describe how your business has grown from its beginning to the present. Tell what you do and how you do it. Explain how you get new business. List the qualifications and experience of your employees. If your business has had problems, don't try to hide them. Tell briefly what they were and show how you resolved them. Outline your future business plans.

Many lenders will ask that you submit a business plan summarizing how you do business. If you're new to planning, there's a book titled *Contractor's Growth and Profit Guide* listed on an order form at the back of this book. It explains what your lender wants to see and includes a complete sample plan designed to impress any loan officer.

If there's more than one principal in your firm, prepare a separate resume with a paragraph or two about each of you. Stress your special talents and experience, and describe how you each contribute to the operation.

Bank and savings and loans are in the business of lending money for profit. They need more than verbal promises to guarantee their loans. They want written assurances backed by facts they can verify. If they make bad agreements, they lose money. And if the lending institution loses money, the loan officers lose their jobs. That makes them *very* conservative. They shy away from risk. Convince your lender that working with you *isn't* risky, it's profitable.

Some criteria used by lenders in deciding to accept you as an approved contractor aren't flexible. Others can be a matter of judgment. A flawless reputation in the remodeling business isn't easy to maintain, especially considering the number of problems you face in dealing with customers. It's something you have to be aware of and work at all the time. On the whole, you'll find most loan officers who deal in your area of business are pretty astute and fair. Of course, there are always exceptions. If you go to a lender who can't explain their program so you can understand it, or who confuses you with the number of deals they have to offer, go elsewhere. You need to feel as satisfied with your lender as they are with you.

Lenders are looking for good business managers. Good managers don't have bad reputations. They either head off problems or solve them to everyone's satisfaction. A good manager always keeps problems from repeating.

Getting on a financial institution's approved contractor list can be an important asset to your business. Make every customer aware of your approved status. It shows that you're a valued member of the business community. Once you've met the strict business, financial, and personal requirements needed for approval, you're also an asset to the remodeling industry as a whole. By imposing high standards, lenders help weed out the disreputable and inferior tradespeople who give our industry a bad name.

Who Should You Deal With?

As with anything else, it pays to shop around when you're looking for the right bank or savings and loan. If the loan officers are overly demanding or overly cautious with you, they're going to be the same with your customers. This can cost you business. You want to work through an institution that will be friendly and cooperative with both you and your customers.

Find several banks or savings and loans that have working arrangements with contractors. Then choose the ones that offer the best home-improvement loans and terms for your customers. The requirements and programs can vary from institution to institution, city to city, and state to state. Ask other contractors in your city which lenders offer such loans. Ask for a referral from your regular bank if they don't offer the service themselves.

Don't feel limited to dealing with banks or savings and loans in your immediate community. In some states, financial institutions must publish a Community Service Agreement describing the geographical area or community in which they provide services. The Agreement also lists the kinds of services they provide.

The community service area for a bank may include several counties. You or your customers could live 60 miles or more from a bank and still participate in their home-improvement financing program. Unless they offer you a special deal, however, it's more convenient to have a bank closer to home.

Program Approval

In a number of states, home improvement loans are offered by both banks and savings and loans. However, each individual institution determines whether or not it wishes to extend this service. Some institutions promote their loan programs actively and solicit contractors to send them their business. They may even offer special loan application packets to your customers. Others don't promote them, but make the loan programs available to contractors through word-of-mouth. Still others make them available only to preferred contractors. In some states, banking regulations prohibit this type of loan arrangement. In that case, the customer must find his own financing without the aid of the remodeling contractor.

The type of programs offered by banks and savings and loans vary greatly. It's been our experience that there are about as many different deals available as there are lenders offering them. Each institution sets its own loan fees and interest rates, although they are generally competitive. Many experienced contractors feel that it's wise to be approved by two or three different institutions. Lenders can be very selective and turn down loan applications for obscure reasons. Often, if one institution turns down a customer, another will grant them the loan.

Home improvement loans are made at both fixed and adjustable rates. The rates can change almost daily. To give you an idea of how they vary from institution to institution, here are the fixed Annual Percentage Rates (APR) charged by several different banks and saving and loans on the same day.

Banks	(APR)	Savings and Loans	(APR)
A	10.62	A	10.759
B	10.748	B	10.894
C	11.05	C	10.80

Adjustable Rate Mortgages (ARMs) carry a lower APR to begin with. The low introductory rate is temporary. It's designed to give borrowers time to adjust financially to their new obligation. After a certain period of time, every six to 12 months for example, it is adjusted upward. It may start at 7.25 percent and rise to an annual rate of 10.78 percent over a set period of time. Generally the lender will have a "cap" on an ARM, such as a maximum 4 percent increase.

Figure 8-3 is an example of how some savings and loans promote their home improvement loan program. They send out letters like these to remodeling contractors one or more times a year to show what they have to offer customers. Of course, the rates change, depending on how much the prime rate fluctuates. The terms and conditions used here are for illustration only. To get current figures, contact a local institution which offers home improvement loans or has a program with remodeling contractors.

The Trial Period

Your lender will probably limit the number of jobs they'll finance for you at first. They'll watch you very closely to see that you meet the standards for quality and workmanship they require for the type of work you do.

This trial period has nothing to do with your customer's credit rating or their ability to pay. These items are considered separately, and have no bearing on your position as an approved contractor.

WILMONT *Savings & Loan Association*

1321 Dell Street, Wilmont Il 60076 Phone 439-3873

Fixed Rate Loan Programs

September, 1988

Term	A.P.R.*	Fees	Points	Cost per $1,000 per Month
3 Years	10.00%	Title & Appraisal	3	$31.98
5 Years	10.00%	Title & Appraisal	3	$21.00
7 Years	10.00%	Title & Appraisal	3	$16.39
10 Years	10.75%	Title & Appraisal	3	$13.21
15 Years	11.00%	Title & Appraisal	3	$11.01
20 Years	12.00%	Title & Appraisal	3	$10.72

There is *no* application fee up front. The borrower may add the appraisal, title and point closing costs to their loan, or we can deduct them from the proceeds so they will incur no out-of-pocket expense.

Prime Advantage Line Of Credit

The borrower may establish a line of credit account up to 80% of the value of their home, less their mortgage balance. They draw funds against their line whenever they need funds simply by writing a check. Interest will be charged only on the checks drawn, and not the line of credit amount. We are charging *prime* percent on this loan from now through January 1, 1989 at which time the rate will go to *prime* plus 2% for the balance of the ten-year loan term. Prime is currently 7%. Please refer to the enclosed brochure and ad copy for ideas in explaining and promoting this program.

If you need new loan application packets for either of these programs, or any additional information, please contact the Main Office and ask for "HILPs."

Determining Monthly Payments

Example: Borrowing $10,000 for 15 years.
10 x 11.01 = $110.10 per month.

* This is only on a set amount for a specified period.
All rates and terms subject to change without notice.

Savings Insured up to $100,000.00 by the Federal Savings & Loan Insurance Corporation

Your lender will outline finance terms
Figure 8-3

The lender will check with your customers to make sure they're satisfied. They know that happy customers are less likely to contest their contracts or default on payments. If you can't produce happy customers, the bank will be reluctant to continue their relationship with you.

Your lender could check on your salespeople as well. Who are they and what kind of deals do they make? If the lender finds them overselling or overpricing, they'll probably refuse to issue further credit on your projects.

At first, your jobs may be inspected by a representative of the bank or savings and loan. More often though, this inspection will be made by an outside service. They'll look for quality craftsmanship and whether the job was finished on schedule. They'll also require the customer to sign a *completion certificate* similar to the one shown in Figure 8-4.

This form says that the work has been completed to the customer's satisfaction and gives their OK to release payment to the contractor. Both the borrower and the contractor have to sign the form. In doing so, you're both stating that there was no collusion either in the form of a cash payment or rebate, or a promise of future business involved in the transaction.

As your lender continues to grant loans to your customers, they'll check from time to time to be sure that your work continues to be satisfactory. If they don't find any major problems, you'll have the lender as your partner. That's an important asset for your business. Best of all, you'll have an established cash flow. On every job financed, depending on the arrangement and your location, you can expect to receive final payment within 32 days after the completion certificate has been signed. This doesn't always happen when the customer is the one paying.

Who Gets Turned Down?

There is one kind of contractor who is sure to be turned down by banks and savings and loans. Lenders won't consider setting up a homeowner financing program with a contractor who's operating on a shoestring. There are many tradespeople who become contractors and assume that makes them a businessperson as well. They don't bother to set up an office or to get the necessary insurance. They operate out of a truck and use their home phone for business. This kind of company, with poor record keeping and no organization, isn't an acceptable partner for a bank.

"It's unfortunate," our banker friend says, "that many contractors today are basically just tradesmen. Because they have experience working for a regular remodeling contractor or new home builder as a subcontractor, many think they can be become general contractors and do the whole job themselves. It's a rude awakening when they discover that there's more to being a general contractor than passing the exam and getting a customer."

Your Customer's Credit

The responsibility for establishing your client's credit is the lender's. However, you can do a little pre-screening when making a sale. While you're closing the sale, ask your

---

COMPLETION CERTIFICATE

(Property Improvement Work Done and/or Materials Delivered)

Completion Date: _____

We, the undersigned, being respectively the obligor(s) (Buyer(s) and Co-Buyer(s) or Co-Signer(s), if any) and the contractor (Seller) under a Retail Installment Contract dated _____, 19 ____, do hereby certify that the contractor has satisfactorily completed the performance of labor or the delivery of materials or both to:

(Address of Property) _____, in connection with the abovementioned contract to improve, create an addition to, repair or remodel such property or to supply materials for that purpose or both; and that, as of this date, the value of the labor

performed and materials delivered is $ _____ and there remains no further labor to be performed
(Cash Price)

or materials to be delivered under said contract.

To further induce each future assignee of the contractor's rights under the aforesaid contract to purchase the same from the contractor:

1. The obligor(s) and the contractor further certify and warrant that the abovementioned labor and/or materials constitute the entire consideration for the obligor(s) obligations under said contract; that the obligor(s) have not been given or promised any cash payment or rebate nor has it been represented to the obligor(s) that the obligor(s) will receive a cash bonus or commission on future sales as an inducement for the consummation of the aforesaid transaction; that said contract contains the entire agreement between the obligor(s) and the contractor; and that a fully-completed copy of said contract; as well as two fully-completed copies of a Notice of Right of Rescission, were delivered to and retained by each of the obligor(s) when said contract was signed.

2. The obligor(s) further certify and warrant that they understand that the selection of the contractor and the inspection and acceptance of the materials supplied or used and the work performed by the contractor is the obligor(s) responsibility, and that the assignee(s) of the contractor's rights under said contract do not inspect or guarantee either the materials or the work performed.

3. The contractor further certifies and warrants that all signatures hereon and on said contract are genuine; that this Certificate was signed by the obligor(s) after the satisfactory completion of the work and/or delivery of the materials; that the improvements have not been misrepresented to the obligor(s); and that all bills for labor and/or materials payable by the contractor in connection with the performance of said contract have been paid or will be paid within 30 days.

NOTICE TO THE OBLIGOR(S): DO NOT SIGN THIS CERTIFICATE UNTIL YOU ARE SATISFIED THAT ALL WORK HAS BEEN COMPLETED AND/OR ALL MATERIALS HAVE BEEN DELIVERED IN ACCORDANCE WITH THE TERMS OF YOUR CONTRACT. *READ BEFORE SIGNING.*

This Certificate is signed this _____ day of _____, 19 ____.

_____   _____
          Obligor   Contractor

_____ By _____
          Obligor

_____   _____
          Obligor   Title

White — Lender's Copy,   Canary — Purchaser's Copy,   Pink — Dealer/Contractor Copy

Your client will sign a Completion Certificate
Figure 8-4

customer how much of the job cost they want to finance. Also, find out what their income is and how much equity they have in their home. A few properly phrased questions can save you a lot of time. If you have serious doubts about their ability to qualify for a loan, chances are your lender will turn them down as well.

Always be prepared to answer the financial questions that most customers ask. "How much can I borrow?" "What are the interest rates, and what is the maximum term of the loan?"

How Much Can a Client Borrow?

There's a limit to the amount a bank or savings and loan will lend. The formula is pretty simple.

Let's say a homeowner has a home appraised at $150,000 and wants to finance a $25,000 remodeling job with a home equity loan. The improvement is included when considering the loan. However, the value added to the home is only 50 percent of the improvement cost. If the improvement totals $25,000, it will only add $12,500 to the appraised value of the home. Most financial institutions will lend up to 80 percent of the appraised value of a home, less the mortgage balance currently owed.

In this particular case, the home plus the improvement has an appraised loan value of $162,500. Eighty percent of this amount is $130,000. Let's assume that they have a single $30,000 mortgage outstanding. (Many banks and savings and loans won't grant a home improvement loan if the homeowner is carrying both a first *and* second mortgage.) Subtract that amount from the total the bank will loan. That leaves $100,000 available for a home-improvement loan.

Of course, the bank must decide whether the homeowner's income is enough to cover the payments on their loan and whatever else they owe. In this instance, we'll say that the homeowner qualified for the $25,000.

Figure 8-5 shows another example and the formula used by most lending institutions to determine a homeowner's equity.

Determining Equity Factors

Example: A customer's house is currently appraised at $175,000. Their existing mortgage has a balance of $75,000. They want to remodel the kitchen which will cost $30,000.

House Appraisal	$175,000
50% of new kitchen	15,000
Improved appraisal	190,000
	x 80%
Maximum borrowing power	152,000
Less first mortgage	75,000
Actual borrowing power	**$77,000**

---

*Some institutions will not grant a home improvement loan if the homeowner is carrying a second mortgage.

Determining homeowner's equity
Figure 8-5

Lenders aren't really concerned with the kind of improvement or the cost. The red flag will go up, though, if other homes in the neighborhood are valued way below the home in question. The lender will *always* make sure they can recover the loan if a homeowner is unable to meet his obligation.

Finance Charges and Loan Terms

The rates for a home-improvement loan will normally be higher than a regular home mortgage. Generally they run two to three percent more. Check with your bank regularly so you can give your clients accurate information when they ask about finance charges.

The usual payback period on home-improvement loans is 10 years. Occasionally loans can be extended to 15 or 20 years, but then the interest rate will be higher. It may be better for your client to refinance their property than pay the higher rates for a longer term loan.

When setting up a repayment schedule, the banks look into the borrower's income and expenses. They'll set the monthly payment as high as possible without creating financial difficulties for the borrower. One banker describes the way he sets up payments for borrowers by saying that he "always makes sure the shoe fits, but pinches just a little bit."

Know the lending policies in your area so you can answer customer questions. Make sure they understand, however, that it's the lender who approves the loan and decides how much can be borrowed.

Insured Loan Programs — FHA

Another good source of financing for your clients is an FHA- (Federal Housing Administration) insured loan. These loans are made by lending institutions approved by FHA and HUD (Department of Housing and Urban Development). The government insures the lender against loss due to default by either the contractor or the borrower. Because these loans are insured, financial institutions are more willing to make loans for home improvements. The government helps keep money available for homeowners this way.

The FHA doesn't lend the money; it only insures the amount loaned by the bank or savings and loan. The program is administered through the financial institutions. Although the FHA doesn't deal directly with contractors, it won't secure a loan to a contractor they've had problems with before.

To be eligible for an FHA-insured loan, the homeowner must meet specific financial requirements. They must also have a satisfactory credit rating and be able to show that they can repay the loan. The requirements and the dollar limits for the loans vary from region to region. Banks and savings and loans have information that applies in your region.

Your clients can apply for loans by filling out a special loan application. It requires documentation by the contractor in the form of a written estimate or itemized cost breakdown. This means you'll have to prepare a formal bid, have it approved by the homeowner, and make copies for the lender. You won't be able to recover these costs if your customer doesn't qualify for the loan.

Government insured loans can also be subject to government inspection after completion. Your customer will have to sign a consent statement authorizing the bank or insuring agent to inspect the property and determine that the improvements specified in the loan application have been made.

Some contractors prefer to stay away from guaranteed loan programs because of the red tape. It takes longer for their customers to qualify and there's more paperwork involved. However, if you're going to provide full service to your clients, you need to know how these programs work. When other means of financing fail, the FHA may offer your clients an acceptable alternative. Conditions change with the times. If your clients can't get loans from conventional sources, have alternatives available.

Keep the "Till" Full, But Minimize the Risk

Any significant remodeling project will cost $20,000 or more. If you have 10 to 15 jobs in the works, that's several hundred thousand dollars committed to labor and material costs. Few contractors can afford to carry that kind of overhead. To keep your business growing, take advantage of the opportunities available.

Most opportunities come with at least some problems. If they didn't, someone else would have seen the opportunity and capitalized on it before you came into the picture. Some contractors prefer not to work with banks and government agencies. We think these contractors could be missing out. All you need to become an "approved contractor" is an established business and a good reputation. It doesn't cost *you* a cent, but it can be a big advantage.

Lenders don't go door to door soliciting business from contractors. But they do want to make arrangements with qualified contractors. They recognize that there's a real need for remodeling contractors. Every community needs quality housing. You provide that service. It's good business for them, and good business for you too.

Insurance, Bonds, and Liens

*E*very remodeling contractor is exposed to risk from accidents, lawsuits and liens on the job. And, unfortunately, you have very little control over many of these risks. To make matters even worse, many remodeling contractors know far less about insurance, bonds, and liens than they do about any other important part of their business. That's the reason for this chapter.

Our purpose here is to create an "information bank" for your use. You may just want to skim through the pages of this chapter for now. Don't worry about all the details. You'll soon discover that insurance, bonds, and liens are very complex subjects. But because of the effect they can have on your business, you should be aware of where and how they apply to your daily activities. It's unlikely you'll get far in the building business without encountering them. And when you need to know something, we hope the information in this chapter gives you some help you need.

However, when you purchase insurance and bonds, or if you need to file a lien, it's still best to seek professional advice. This chapter is meant to assist you, not to take the place of people trained and qualified in the laws of your state. A good insurance agent or lawyer with experience in the remodeling and/or construction industry is an invaluable asset to your business.

The main topic of this chapter is insurance. Here's why. Every business, especially every small business, is vulnerable to suit today. People sue (or threaten suit) whenever they feel they've been harmed. And there's no shortage of lawyers willing to take their case. You're betting your financial future if you don't have adequate insurance protection. Insurance coverage includes the cost of defense in court. Your carrier will provide the legal talent needed to defend and will pay (up to the policy limits) if they lose. You can go on building and remodeling while the suit drags on through the courts.

Insurance isn't the only coverage you need. You'll also need bonds for some types of work on some jobs. Insurance protects you. Bonds may also protect you, but more likely will protect those you work for. We'll cover both bonds and insurance in this chapter.

The cost of most insurance and bonds is included in your overhead as a cost of doing business. There's usually some overlap between insurance costs which fall under general overhead and insurance related to direct job costs. Some jobs require extra insurance, and that's directly chargeable to the customer. Keep the two types of insurance costs separate for your records where you can.

Overcoming Insurance Woes

People in the insurance or bonding business say that very few remodeling contractors carry adequate coverage. This is particularly true of small- to medium-sized contracting businesses.

Why? The reason is simple enough. Insurance is complicated and expensive. And you may not need it. Why buy what you may not need?

Even before insurance premiums began to soar in the mid-1980's, the cost of insurance was high. Today, it's a major expense for contractors. Premiums that were once hundreds of dollars are now thousands of dollars — if you can get an insurer to take you.

In today's litigation-happy world, without proper insurance protection the room addition shown in Figure 9-1 could be a lawyer's dream and a contractor's nightmare. Look at the opportunities for accidents:

- The construction debris on the left should have been removed or contained.

- Only half of the patio door has been installed. The glass should have been "x'd" with masking tape and the open section barricaded. The entrance door on the right should also be closed off.

- The wheelbarrow could easily become a child's plaything.

- Because it's close to the work area, the pool should be barricaded in some manner to prevent workers from falling in.

- The pile of stakes by the pool could trip a worker. He could crack his head on the concrete and slide unconscious into the pool.

Avoid unnecessary hazards
Figure 9-1

There are probably several other less obvious hazards shown here as well. The point we're making is that in the remodeling business there's continuous opportunity for all kinds of accidents or injuries. Without insurance a single job like this could bankrupt a contractor.

Every remodeling contractor has to decide how much insurance to carry. It's possible to buy too much coverage — and be insurance poor as a result. You need to select both the right mix of coverages and the correct liability limit. The information that follows will help you do just that.

How Much Insurance Do You Need?

How much insurance you need is hard to say. The reason for having insurance is to protect the major assets you've accumulated — such as your home, your business, your bank account, and expensive equipment, such as your truck. It's not practical to insure every hammer and saw. But you're wise to cover equipment or tools that represent a major investment for you.

Choosing an Insurance Advisor

When you buy insurance, you may want to use the services of a broker rather than an agent. Brokers deal with many insurance companies. Agents represent only one company — the one that pays their salary. Because brokers have access to many companies, they can offer you a wide variety of options and get you the best policy at the best rates.

Give your insurance advisor or broker the essential information about your company. The following information will help him or her determine what coverage you need:

• A description of your type of business (sole proprietorship, partnership, etc.), including a financial statement.

• A description of the types of work you do. Each trade faces different hazards. You'll need to be specific. Do you do earthwork; work with explosives or hot tar; use scaffolding to reach heights?

• How much is your total payroll? How many employees do you have? What are their job descriptions?

• What kind of equipment do you own or use? How much is it worth? Are you responsible for the property of others?

• What is the value of your work in progress? How much is your material inventory worth and where is it stored? How much of your property is on the job site at a given time?

With this information, your advisor or broker can determine the most economical types of bonding and insurance suitable for your business.

Risk Management

Every remodeling business is unique. That's why every remodeling business needs an insurance and bonding program tailored to meet its particular needs. *Risk management* weighs the potential hazards to eliminate unnecessary coverage and increase coverage where you have the greatest exposure. That should give you the best protection for the lowest cost.

Here are the types of losses you'll want to consider when managing the risks in your business:

First there are the small losses you have on nearly every job. For example, pilferage of tools and materials by employees, customers, and neighbors is common. This is exasperating, but the losses aren't really enough to bother insuring against. Because the losses are small, it isn't practical to file a claim. Unless you find you're losing a great deal of money from this kind of theft, you're better off absorbing the losses as part of the cost of doing business. The cost of insuring against losses like these might be more than the losses themselves.

The second category of losses shouldn't be as frequent, but you stand to lose a lot more. These are accidents which damage a client's property. Examples might be paint sprayed on landscaping, or floorcovering ruined by water leaking from a broken pipe. The replacement cost for these items can run from a few hundred dollars to several thousand. Consider buying coverage against damage like this.

The question here becomes one of deductibles — how much of the loss you have to pay before insurance coverage applies. How much of the loss can you afford to absorb? Decide what kind of potential property damage you face and how much you're willing to pay before the insurance company takes over. Of course, the higher the deductible, the lower your cost of insurance.

The final type of risk you need to insure against is the catastrophic loss. We can all agree that coverage is needed for major losses. Fortunately, they don't happen often. But when they do, they can be devastating. If a worker is seriously injured or killed on the job, or if a wall collapses and brings down your whole project, all of your personal and business assets may be placed in jeopardy.

Examine the risks in your business. What claims have been filed against you or against contractors you know in similar work? What kinds of settlements have been made? Are some accidents more common in your specialty? Is the kind of equipment you use more dangerous than that used in other trades? Use your own experience and the experience of others to identify your risks.

Once you know the risks, discuss them with your insurance advisor. Find the most effective and economical coverage for your company. Consider how much of the loss your company can afford to cover. That establishes the deductible. A well-rounded risk management program insures you for good times *and bad.*

Insurance Protection That's a Must

Good insurance protection can be an advantage to your sales program. Customers take risks when they deal with uninsured or underinsured contractors. Your sales force has a major selling point when they can assure customers of full coverage against damage or loss.

Some types of insurance are mandatory; others just make good sense. Let's review the types of insurance you'll need.

Workers' Compensation

Today, all states and U.S. territories have workers' compensation laws. If an employee is injured or killed on the job, the law requires coverage which pays for medical expenses, lost wages, and rehabilitation. All businesses must carry workers' compensation insurance, although in some areas you may be exempt if you have fewer than five employees. To the employer, the advantage of workers' comp insurance is that it relieves him of most liability for injury to employees. Regardless of fault, employees' recovery for accidents or injury is limited to the amounts provided by workers' compensation schedules.

Payments under workers' comp coverage are intended to make up for the worker's lost or reduced earning ability. The amount provided by laws varies from state to state and depends on the extent of the injury. You may want to consider carrying additional medical insurance if benefits are severely limited in your state.

Most standard workers' compensation policies contain some provisions specifying benefits for common occupational diseases. Claims can also be filed for diseases which have developed over a period of time, even if the worker is no longer involved in the job which caused the disease. Most states have extended periods in which claims can be filed for latent diseases. This would include diseases such as asbestos lung disease, hearing loss, or illnesses due to radiation exposure. Even stress-related disorders are being considered in a few states.

Many states limit benefits to specific diseases related to specific occupations. However, policies can be broadened to voluntarily pay compensation to other occupations as well. In all cases, however, coverage extends to all diseases which are shown to be arising out of and in the course of employment.

If you work or hire employees in more than one state, check with your insurance advisor to be sure your coverage is complete. Your insurance should be written to specifically include coverage for each state in which you do business. (Doing business includes recruiting employees from one state to work in another.) A number of states impose stiff penalties on employers who fail to get the coverage required by law.

An out-of-state employee who suffers an employment-related accident or illness can select benefits either in the state where the incident occurred or the state where he was hired. That's why you should be covered in both states.

Workers' compensation laws, benefits, and administration vary widely from state to state. Figure 9-2 is an excerpt from "Analysis of Workers' Compensation Laws 1988" prepared by the U.S. Chamber of Commerce. Compare the difference in penalties for

CHART I — TYPE OF LAW AND INSURANCE REQUIREMENTS — January 1, 1988

JURISDICTION	TYPE OF LAW	INSURANCE	SELF-INSURANCE	PENALTIES ON FAILURE TO INSURE
ALABAMA	Compulsory	Required	Individual and group	Fine of not less than $25 nor more than $1,000. Employer may be enjoined from doing business and liable to suit with defenses abrogated and double amount of compensation.
ALASKA	Compulsory	Required	Permitted	Class B or C felony (up to 10 years' imprisonment, $50,000 fine, or both). Board may enjoin use of labor. Employer liable to suit with defenses abrogated, and employer negligence presumed proximate cause of injury. Individuals in charge of corporation personally liable for compensation.
AMERICAN SAMOA	Compulsory	Required	Permitted	Misdemeanor; fine up to $1,000 or imprisonment up to 1 year, or both. Employer liable to suit with defenses abrogated.
ARIZONA	Compulsory	Required	Permitted*	Employer liable to suit with defenses abrogated; 10% penalty of award, expenses, and attorney's fees, or $500 (whichever is greater) plus 10% interest on amount paid from fund and penalty; award paid from Special Fund; injunction against doing business in state.
ARKANSAS	Compulsory	Required	Individual and group*	$500 fine or 1 year imprisonment, or both; employer liable to suit with defenses abrogated.
CALIFORNIA	Compulsory	Required	Permitted	Employer may be enjoined from doing business. Mandatory penalty upon issuance of stop order is $100 per employee, raised to $500 per employee if case is compensable (maximum $10,000). Failure to obey stop order is misdemeanor; penalty is fine up to $1,000, imprisonment up to 60 days, or both. $50 penalty for failure to respond to Director's inquiry. Penalties are paid into Uninsured Employers Fund and constitute lien on employer's assets. Employee may sue for damages with employer's defenses abrogated *and* file for compensation. Intentional failure to insure is misdemeanor.
COLORADO	Compulsory	Required	Individual and group	Compensation increased 50% or employer liable to suit with defenses abrogated (at option of employee). Employer may also be enjoined from doing business.
CONNECTICUT	Compulsory	Required	Permitted	Fine of not more than $1,000 for failure to insure. Employer may be enjoined from entering into any contracts of employment.
DELAWARE	Compulsory	Required	Individual and group	Fine of 10 cents per day per employee (maximum $50, minimum $1 per day); if default continues for 30 days employer may be enjoined from doing business. Employer liable to suit with defenses abrogated.
DISTRICT OF COLUMBIA	Compulsory	Required	Permitted	Fine of not more than $1,000 or 1 year imprisonment or both.
FLORIDA	Compulsory	Required	Individual and group	Fine of not more than $500 or not more than 1 year imprisonment, or both; employer liable to suit with defenses abrogated, and may be enjoined from doing business.
GEORGIA	Compulsory	Required	Individual and group	Misdemeanor. Compensation may be increased 10% plus attorney's fees. Penalty up to $50 per day.
GUAM	Compulsory	Required	Not permitted	Misdemeanor—fine up to $1,000, imprisonment up to 1 year, or both. Employer liable to suit with defenses abrogated and must reimburse carrier for compensation paid. Corporate officers are personally liable for compensation.
HAWAII	Compulsory	Required	Individual and group	$25 or $1 per employee per day during default, whichever is greater. Injunction against business in the state.
IDAHO	Compulsory	Required	Permitted	Misdemeanor. Employer also liable to penalty of $1 per day per employee, and may be enjoined from doing business after 30 days default. For default in premiums to state fund, penalty is $1 per day per employee, and policy may be canceled after 30 days default.
ILLINOIS	Compulsory	Required	Individual and group	Fine of $100 to $500 for each day's default.
INDIANA	Compulsory	Required	Permitted*	Class A infraction—maximum fine $10,000. Uninsured employer may be liable for medical and legal expenses plus double compensation and may be enjoined from doing business.
IOWA	Compulsory	Required	Individual and group	Employer liable to suit with defenses abrogated and presumption of negligence of employer. In coal mining, employer is liable to penalty of $10 to $100 per day and may be enjoined from further noncompliance.
KANSAS	Compulsory	Required	Individual and group	Employer liable to suit with defenses abrogated.
KENTUCKY	Compulsory	Required	Individual and group	Failure to secure payment of compensation—claimant may claim compensation and bring action at law or in admiralty with employer's common law defenses abrogated. Employer may be enjoined from doing business.
LOUISIANA	Compulsory	Required	Individual and group	12% penalty and reasonable attorney's fees for collection of claim.
MAINE	Compulsory	Required	Individual and group	Employer liable for civil penalty of up to $10,000 payable to Second Injury Fund. Corporate employers subject to revocation or suspension of its authority to do business. Class D crime. Employer liable to suit with defenses abrogated.
MARYLAND	Compulsory	Required	Individual and group*	Fine of $500 to $5,000 and/or imprisonment for not more than 1 year. Additional penalty for failure to comply with Commission's orders amounting to 6 months insurance premiums. Employer also liable to suit with defenses abrogated. Other insurers assessed to pay unpaid claims of insolvent insurer. Fine of $150 and 15% penalty on award payable to Uninsured Employers Fund.
MASSACHUSETTS	Compulsory	Required	Individual and group	Fine of not more than $500 or imprisonment for not more than 1 year, or both; employer liable to suit with defenses abrogated.
MICHIGAN	Compulsory	Required	Individual and group	Fine of $1,000 or imprisonment for 30 days to 6 months, or both; employer liable for damages.
MINNESOTA	Compulsory	Required	Individual and group	Penalty of $750 if under 5 employees; otherwise $1,500.* Additional penalty 5 times lawful premiums for continued noncompliance. Employer may be enjoined from further employment. Employer to reimburse compensation paid plus 50% penalty. Intentional noncompliance is gross misdemeanor. Employer liable to suit with some defenses abrogated.
MISSISSIPPI				Fine up to $1,000 or one year imprisonment or both. Employer also liable to suit with defenses abrogated.
MISSOURI				...able to suit with defenses abrogated. Worker may receive medical and/or death benefits out of Second Injury ...er is liable for amounts paid plus fine of $100 per day of noncompliance after date of injury (up to $5,0... ...from doing business. Double amount of unpaid premiums assessed as penalty... ...tion payable up to $50,000. Employer automatically negligent if no ... ...Fund.

Courtesy: U.S. Chamber of Commerce

Note variations in penalties from state to state
Figure 9-2

failure to insure in Alaska, California, and Delaware. Don't assume that the laws or penalties will be similar when you're doing business in several states. Some states are as lenient as others are tough.

This U.S. Chamber of Commerce booklet is very useful if you do business in several states. It summarizes workers' compensation programs for all states. The booklet has three sections. Part I summarizes coverage of the law. Part II discusses the benefits provided. Part III describes how the laws are administered in each state. It could save you time, money, and even legal advice if you have problems or questions about workers' compensation laws. This booklet is revised annually and is available for a small charge from:

> Chamber of Commerce of the United States
> 1615 H Street NW.
> Washington, DC 20062
> Telephone: (202) 463-5512

Although workers' compensation programs vary, they generally include the following provisions:

1)   Employees are automatically eligible and they are entitled to benefits whenever they suffer an accidental personal injury in the course of employment.

2)   They are eligible for benefits regardless of the cause of the injury. An employee can collect even if the accident was caused by his or her own negligence. Benefits are not determined by fault.

3)   Coverage is limited to those who are "employees" as defined under the Workers' Compensation Statute. Independent contractors aren't covered.

4)   Benefits include cash payments (generally based on wages), payment of hospital and medical expenses, compensatory damages for permanent injuries, and in the event of death, dependent benefits.

Generally, workers' compensation laws protect employers by abolishing the right of covered employees to sue their employers for damages under any covered incident. This prevented the possibility of a large settlement being awarded by a jury in the case of a trial. In some states this principle is being challenged. For example, in an Illinois case, an injured worker didn't sue his employer, a construction contractor. Instead, he brought suit against the owner of the building where the accident occurred. The building owner then sued the contractor. The contractor moved for dismissal, claiming the injured worker had already received workers' compensation benefits. The court denied the motion and the jury returned a verdict in favor of the injured worker.

This and similar cases in other states will probably open the door for claims by many injured employees. The result is sure to be higher liability premiums.

In nearly every state you can either set up a self-insurance program or buy insurance through a private carrier or from a state fund. In practice, only the largest contracting businesses set up self-insurance programs. Most contractors buy insurance, either from the state fund or a private insurance company.

The type of insurance you carry is, at the time of this writing, still elective in only three states: New Jersey, South Carolina, and Texas. Contractors in those states should check with their state licensing boards or insurance department to determine which type of policy gives them the best coverage under the local laws. All other states have specific program requirements.

Statutes affecting workers' compensation change frequently. Review your own state's program annually to determine if there have been any changes.

Contractor's Liability Insurance

Many construction contracts require that you provide proof of insurance before work begins. Your insurance company can provide a Certificate of Insurance for your client's file. The certificate will show the name of the carrier, the policy limits and the expiration date.

Most comprehensive general liability policies can be written to cover incidents that occur during and after the work is completed. For example, insurance could cover windows broken during installation; falling ceilings or warped floors which occur after the work has been completed; even faulty materials and workmanship. You can't insure against incompetence or totally defective workmanship, though. Your supervisors and tradesmen have to protect you against risks like these.

If you can get Certificates of Insurance from your subcontractors, your own coverage can be reduced. That just makes sense. If your plumbing subcontractor's liability carrier is liable for the plumber's negligence, your liability carrier is off the hook. That saves you insurance dollars. That's why you'll probably request certificates of insurance from subcontractors any time you have to provide a certificate of insurance on a job.

Premiums for liability coverage are based on the type of work you handle and your loss experience. The more claims you've had, the higher the rate. After enough losses, it may be impossible to get any liability coverage at all. Most new contractors pay higher rates until they've established good loss records. The rate itself will be a percentage of payroll for the trades covered and will be higher for higher policy limits.

Insurance experts recommend that you place all liability policies with the same carrier if possible. If your automobile insurance is with one company and your general liability insurance is with another, each carrier could deny responsibility for a particular claim. If both policies are with the same company, it becomes simply a matter of which department will pay the claim.

Vehicle Insurance

A comprehensive liability insurance policy will cover vehicles owned and operated by your company. A basic policy provides coverage against all possible claims involving the use of your vehicles in your construction work. Additional coverages can be included in your policy for additional cost. These coverages are called *riders*.

Each rider covers a special risk you or your company may have. For example, you can cover employee vehicles and those of your subcontractors while they're conducting business for you. You can even cover vehicles that are not owned by anyone connected to your company, if they are being driven by company employees. Here are a few of the extra coverages you might want to consider:

Automobile Liability Insurance— Protects you against loss or damage claims for bodily injury or property damage resulting from the operation of vehicles you own.

Employers' Non-Ownership Liability Insurance— Protects your business against claims resulting from the use of vehicles owned by others, especially employees or business associates.

Partnership Non-Ownership Liability Insurance— Protects a partnership for any liability arising from business use by one partner of another partner's automobile.

Hired Vehicles Insurance— Provides bodily injury and property damage coverage for any rented vehicles.

Building Property Damage Insurance
Many types of policies are available to protect you and your clients against hazards during construction. Your insurance representative can help you put together a good package.

Fire Insurance— If you're a general contractor engaged in heavy construction, you need to have adequate fire insurance for building structures as well as your own property and equipment. This type of insurance is sometimes hard to get in a single policy. A broker with a wide variety of policies can be helpful here. Fire insurance is essential to protect the contractor, the owner, and any lenders on the project.

General Property Insurance— This insurance covers structures and permanent fixtures that are a part of a building you might remodel. Machinery used in building services such as air-conditioning, boilers, and elevators which are permanent parts of the building are also covered. Other items included would be yard fixtures and personal property used to maintain buildings and services. You may need this type of insurance if you do remodeling work in a condominium or apartment complex.

Builders' Risk Insurance— This kind of policy is written for a definite amount to cover specified perils. It's limited to the time a building is under construction. A *Loss Payable* clause may be inserted in favor of a party with a financial interest in the building. Coverage can apply to fire as well as any other hazard except earthquake and flood. Earthquakes and flood can be included only with an additional premium.

Builders' Risk/Completed Value Insurance— This type of insurance protects you and the owner of a building during the course of construction against loss caused by fire. The policy is written for a provisional amount of insurance at a fixed premium. The anticipated completed value of the building is the basis for the insurance.

Contractor's Automatic Builders' Risk Insurance— If you're handling several projects at a time, this coverage is essential. It gives you automatic temporary protection on new projects until you can arrange for permanent coverage.

Builders' Risk Reporting Form— This insurance provides coverage on property under construction to the extent of the actual value at risk at any given time. You'll have to make monthly reports on the value insured under this type of coverage.

Permission To Complete Insurance— After the foundation is laid, the building owner can get this kind of policy. It covers all lumber and materials on a construction site, and eliminates the need for a Builders' Risk policy.

Extended Coverage Endorsement— You can add this endorsement to your policy to cover any direct loss or damage caused by windstorm, hail, explosions, riots, civil commotion, aircraft, vehicles, and smoke. For an additional premium, this endorsement can be expanded to include coverage for vandalism and malicious mischief.

Glass Insurance— Glass insurance provides for replacement of windows and structural interior glass broken or damaged regardless of cause. It includes coverage for supporting frames and bars. You have to specify whether you want to include the cost of lettering and ornamentation which was on the glass. If your projects include a lot of glass, this policy is essential.

Sprinkler Leakage Insurance— This policy covers any direct loss to a building as a result of leakage, freezing, or breaking of sprinkler systems. It may be applied to sections of a building already completed.

Flood Insurance— Flood Insurance protects owners against damage to buildings and contents by catastrophic floods, including inundation from mudslides. This insurance is written in areas specified as eligible by the Federal Insurance Administrator.

Earthquake Insurance— You can include earthquake coverage as a part of fire policies in areas where earthquakes are a potential threat.

Crime Insurance

Crime is a major risk for most construction contractors. Today all businesses should consider crime insurance.

Blanket Crime Policy— This is the broadest crime protection available on a package basis. It protects against employee dishonesty, loss inside and outside the premises, money orders, counterfeit paper currency, and depositor's forgery.

Comprehensive Dishonesty, Destruction, and Disappearance Policy— This policy protects you from loss of money and securities on and off your premises. The loss may be caused by theft, mysterious disappearance, or destruction. It protects against loss due to dishonest employees, disappearance of money and securities inside or outside your offices, damage done to premises and equipment, loss of securities in safety deposit, or forgery.

Mercantile Open Stock Policy— You need this kind of coverage if you keep a large inventory of materials on hand. It covers any burglary on your premises. It also covers damage to stock. All furniture, fixtures, and equipment on the premises are included. Visible marks of forced entry are required to collect payment on a claim.

Bad Debt Coverage

Bad debt insurance has been around for years. But it's only recently that insurance companies have started to push it as part of a well-rounded insurance program. Bankruptcies are more common in an unstable economy, when businesses and individuals have a hard time paying their bills on time. If you do business with undercapitalized developers, for example, consider this type of coverage.

When you add bad debt coverage to your total insurance program, you should get more than just a policy for your premiums. One company's policy includes counseling on how to set up credit policies or credit limits with your customers. It also offers collection services.

Bad debt insurance gives you another advantage. Banks and finance companies are more willing to lend money against your receivables if they know you have this kind of protection.

Despite the cost, or regardless of the cost, insurance is one of the most important obligations you'll have. If you don't protect yourself, you're inviting financial disaster. You're also obligated to protect your customers, and required by law to protect your employees. The cost of going without insurance can be much greater than the premiums you have to pay.

Understanding Bonds _____

Surety bonds are different from insurance. They involve three parties: the *principal* who promises performance (you); a *surety* who guarantees your performance (the bonding agent who puts up the money); and the *obligee* (your customer) to whom the promises are made.

A bond is really two contracts, and you're responsible in both of them. The first contract is between you and the surety. The second contract is between you and your customer. If you fail to live up to your contract with your customer and legal action is taken, your surety (the insurance company) will complete the obligation you had with your customer. Usually this means that the insurance company will see that the project is completed according to plan and for the contract price. If the insurance company (the surety) has to do this, they'll use their contract with you (the contractor) to recover their loss on the job.

Bonds are issued by surety companies. These are usually insurance companies or divisions of insurance companies. But the risk in a bond is different from the risk in insurance. Getting a bond is more like getting a loan. The more assets you have and the more money you have in the bank, the easier it will be to get the bond you need. Bond underwriters aren't dumb. They know that the more you have to lose, the less likely you are to walk away from a project before it's completed.

Before any bond is issued, the surety will investigate your financial condition, the same as a prospective lender would. They'll check your work history and talk to your subcontractors before issuing the bond.

In the past, small businesses and minority companies had difficulty getting bonds. If you fall into either of these categories, you may apply to the Small Business Administration for a Surety Bond Guarantee. The SBA guarantee may help you get the bonds you need.

Bonds are usually issued to cover a single job. The cost is passed on to the customer because it's included with other construction costs in your bid. Some bonds cover only a single trade within a job, such as warranties or roofing bonds.

An insurance broker or surety company can quote bond costs to you once they have specific information about the job being bonded.

Bonds vs. *Insurance*
There are several distinct differences between bonding and insurance.

- Bonding always involves three parties; insurance involves only two.

- When you are bonded, you (the principal) make a promise to perform a job, and your promise is backed up by a surety. You have control over the ability of your company to perform. With insurance, you (the insured) are insuring against *unanticipated* losses which you seldom have control over.

- In bonding, the principal (the contractor) is liable to the surety for losses incurred; with insurance, the insured (the contractor) does not agree to reimburse the insurer.

Essential Bonds

There are two types of bonds that you, as a contractor, should always have. One is fidelity insurance. The other is a performance bond. The first insures you against theft of money or materials. The second verifies that you have a contract which you agree to fulfill.

Fidelity Bonds

Fidelity bonds are used to bond employees who handle money or materials. These bonds are also used to protect contractors against loss of money due to embezzlement or wrongful acquisition of money, securities or other property by employees. Four kinds of fidelity bonds are used to protect a business owner from employee dishonesty. These are:

1) individual
2) commercial blanket
3) blanket position
4) name and position.

Blanket bonds are the most popular. They offer broad coverage and don't require a listing of individual employee names or positions. Blanket bonds cover all employees (except directors and trustees) uniformly. An employee is defined as anyone on your payroll who is paid to perform a service under your direction. In the event of a loss, blanket coverage provides compensation up to the amount of the loss regardless of how many employees were involved.

Fidelity bonds are a complex subject. Your insurance advisor will explain the advantages and disadvantages of each type of bond and help you select coverage appropriate for your risk.

Construction Contract Bonds

Performance and payment bonds guarantee that you'll finish what the contract requires. These bonds benefit your customers and will usually be required only on government or larger private jobs. They cover everything you've agreed to in your contract, including the plans and specifications. Performance bonds are issued after bid bonds have been posted and the lowest or most qualified bidder has been selected. They don't provide any protection to creditors.

Bonds Required Before Work Begins

The following surety bonds are usually issued before work begins on a project.

Bid Bonds

Sometimes you may be required to accompany a bid with a "good faith" payment. This guarantees that if you're awarded the job, you'll sign a contract to complete the work. If you don't, you forfeit the money as a penalty. The required payment is usually five percent of the bid. Instead of a cash deposit, you can usually provide a bid bond. Bid bonds are generally issued for ten percent of the bid price. Obviously, requiring a bid bond makes it unlikely that anyone except qualified contractors will submit bids. It also discourages bids from contractors who might not be able to get the performance bonds and payment bonds that are required for the job.

The bonding company that issues your performance bonds will usually provide bid bond coverage. Bid bonds are usually issued for a year. You simply pay one annual fee and request a bid bond each time you need one. Once the bid is accepted, the performance bond will be issued. Naturally, there's a charge for each performance bond issued.

Labor and Materials Payment Bonds

These bonds guarantee that you'll pay all legitimate bills for labor and materials on a particular job. They may be written as a separate bond or as part of a performance bond. If you can't pay your labor and material bills, the surety will pay (and then try to collect from you). This type of bond guarantees that your client's project isn't burdened with labor and material liens.

Completion Bonds

If you borrow money for a remodeling project, you'll need a completion bond. It guarantees that the project will be completed and that there won't be any mechanic's liens or other claims left outstanding. Lenders usually require both a completion bond and a performance bond when financing a project.

The cost of a completion bond depends on the value of the contract and length of coverage. Your completion record and reputation are important issues in setting the rate for the bond. The bonds are usually issued for a 24-month period. The monthly charge is based on a set amount for each thousand dollars of contract price. If you need to extend the bond beyond two years, the additional cost is figured at a percentage of the regular premium per month. The coverage can be for all or just part of a job.

Maintenance Bonds

A maintenance bond guarantees that you will correct all defects in workmanship or materials on a project. It's issued for a specified length of time following completion of the job, usually from one to three years. Maintenance bonds are often included as part of a performance bond.

License or Permit Bonds

Licence and permit bonds are required in some states to guarantee your compliance with local codes and ordinances. If you work in an area requiring these bonds, they should be charged to office overhead as a normal cost of doing business. If you need one only for a specific job, it's then considered a job expense and charged to your customer.

Subdivision Bonds

Subdivision bonds are issued to guarantee that all site improvements, utilities, and buildings will comply with governing codes and ordinances. These regulations have become quite strict. In many areas they have been broadened to apply to the use of water and natural gas resources, sewers, and to guarantee compliance with air quality standards. Subdivision bonds are filed by the property owner, who in turn is protected by your performance bond.

Your bond guarantees that the project's plans and specifications comply with the local ordinances, so you'd better be sure that they do. Claims are being made against subdivision bonds because a contractor's projects didn't pass final inspection — usually because the contractor didn't comply with some local ordinance.

License Bonds

Most cities and counties require license bonds for plumbers, electricians and some other trades. Some states and counties require additional bonds for those working within their boundaries.

Subcontractor Bonds

As a general contractor, you can require bonds from your subcontractors — guaranteeing that they'll perform their work according to the terms and conditions of the contract. It also assures that they will pay all the bills for labor and materials related to their work.

Supply and Subcontractor Bonds

These bonds are required from manufacturers and installers for specified items. Each subcontractor pays the cost of the bond and adds that amount to the bid submitted.

Filing a Bond Claim

Claims under a bond must be made within a certain time and must follow set procedures. For example, if you file a claim for payment, the other two parties named in the bond must receive notice of the claim. The notice may also have to include the following information:

- The amount owed

- A description of the project

- A description of the work performed or the materials used

- The date materials were supplied or date the work was started and completed

The claim notice isn't a legal action. It's simply a notice that you've billed someone for materials or labor, and your bill hasn't been paid. Bonds stipulate when payments are due and how long you must wait for payment before making a claim.

If you don't get paid, the next step is to take legal action under the bond. Again, you must follow the procedures outlined in the bond. Check the time limits in the bond. It's generally two years.

However, most states have a statute of limitations that requires legal action within a specified time. This period may be different from the limitation stated in the bond. Be sure you know which limit applies, the one in the bond or the one in the law. If you don't follow the right procedure, you can lose your right to collect.

Be sure to keep accurate and complete records to back up your claims. These should include signed receipts for any materials received or delivered and time logs for labor performed. You'll need to furnish copies of these records to substantiate a claim.

Liens

If you've been in construction for very long, you've had disputes with owners, designers, subcontractors and tradesmen. Disputes come with the territory — especially in the repair and remodeling business. Many of these disputes will result in a mechanic's lien being filed by tradesmen, laborers, suppliers, or subcontractors who claim they're owed money for labor or materials. As the prime contractor on a job, you have the most to lose when a lien is filed.

A Mechanic's Lien

A mechanic's lien is defined as "a legal claim created to secure payment for work performed and materials furnished in constructing, repairing, or remodeling a building or other structure; or making other improvements on a parcel of land; the claim being made against the land and the buildings thereon."

Contractors, subcontractors, laborers, tradespeople, and material suppliers can all file a mechanic's lien. It's the most common and most complicated type of lien involving the remodeling industry, but it's not the only one.

In Michigan, for example, the mechanic's lien was replaced by the Construction Lien Act of 1982. This act determines the type and manner of filing liens in Michigan, as well as limiting the liability involved. Other states may follow suit, so it's important to check the lien laws annually in every state where you do business.

Mechanic's liens can be filed only on land and buildings. They're a legal claim for payment of labor and materials filed against the owner's property. If payment isn't made, the property owner can't transfer clear title to the property. That makes it nearly impossible to sell or borrow against the property. A lien applies only against the property. It doesn't create any liability on the part of the owner. But liens can create enormous headaches for property owners, which is why they are very effective.

Laws governing liens vary from state to state. Nearly anything you say about liens won't apply in some states. That's why you *must* know the major provisions of the lien laws in the states where you do business.

Filing a Lien

The procedures for filing liens aren't the same in every state either. Usually, filing procedures must be followed to the letter. Although some states say that *substantial* compliance to the procedure is acceptable, most states hold that strict compliance is required. *Your best protection is to know the statutes in states where you do business.*

If you want to file a lien, it's a good idea to get legal advice, at least the first time. Forms for filing liens are generally available from the city or county clerk's office, building materials suppliers, some stationery stores, or by mail from companies who specialize in printing forms for the construction industry. The forms also vary from state to state, so be sure that the forms you use apply in the state where you're filing.

Protecting Yourself Against Liens

There are several things you can do to prevent a lien from being filed against your jobs.

• Watch your cash flow and make sure you always have enough money to pay your subcontractors and suppliers on time. On large jobs, ask for advances and work-in-progress payments.

• Make certain all change orders are in writing, and that everyone who needs one gets a copy.

• Keep notes on any disputes you have with subs or vendors. Note especially how the disputes were settled.

• Bid, schedule, and manage all your jobs carefully. Cutthroat, slipshod contractors are lien-prone. Don't fall into that category. If you figure your jobs too close, you won't have enough cushion to cover yourself when things go wrong. And they will.

We've covered some complex subjects in this chapter — as promised. Little of it will be of much interest to you until there's a problem. Then it can become the most interesting and essential subject you can think of. Your best protection is to be insurance-, bond- and lien-wise. Anticipate problems before they arise. Do what's prudent to stay out of trouble. Hopefully, this chapter has helped you take several long strides in that direction.

Computers for Remodelers

*T*he word *computer* stirs up mixed emotions in the minds of many people. This stems from the many horror stories circulated about the early use of computers, when large corporations were using them for billing and accounting. Who doesn't know someone who was caught up in the futility of trying to correct a computerized error! Even something as simple as a change of address on a department store charge account could take months to straighten out.

What we didn't know then, but know now, is that a computer is only as good as its operator. Computers were big, expensive, technical, and *intimidating*. Early computer operators blamed the computers for problems which stemmed from their own lack of training. The result was a bad reputation for the computer. Computers were accused of creating more problems than they solved.

Enter the PC's . . .

By the late '70's the computer industry had experienced a dramatic and significant change. Instead of getting bigger and more complicated, computers began to get smaller and simpler. Not only did the new computers perform pretty much the same function as their older counterparts, in many cases they could do more, and do it faster! And, as the computer systems became smaller and more compact, they also became less expensive.

Today, this new generation of personal computers, called PC's, are within the budget range of most small businesses, including remodeling businesses. All the equipment needed for the average business will fit on a desktop or table. Like it or not, computers are here to stay. They have made an enormous impact on business in the last ten years, and by the mid-90's will be as commonplace as copiers and calculators.

Should You Buy a Computer?

Can a computer benefit your business today? If you think so, what area of your business should you computerize? These are the questions you must ask yourself before you invest your time and money in a computer system. On the pages that follow we will offer the pros and cons of using computers in operating a small remodeling business. Hopefully, we can clarify what a computer can and cannot do for you, and help you decide whether this is the right time to put one to work for your company.

In the examples we have for you, you'll see that some contractors use their systems primarily for accounting, while others use computer programs as estimating aids. Nearly every contractor, however, utilizes the word processing feature of their computer systems for letters, contracts, and proposals. Information processing is one of the four main areas that have proven highly cost effective in computerizing construction businesses. The other areas are accounting, cash flow, and business control. Consider how any of these, as well as estimating, might benefit your business as you read this chapter.

Accounting
Traditionally, accounting is the most common area that businesses computerize. Not only can computers make record keeping faster, they can do it more efficiently. You can make multiple postings to various accounts with a single entry. For example, you can summarize your accounts payable, and determine which accounts require immediate payment. You can pay those accounts, print out the checks, and automatically post the payments to the general ledger with a single transaction.

Improved Business Control
A computer can make key financial data on your business available on a daily basis. Computers are very good at storing and retrieving information. That can be a big help when you need to have lots of information available on short notice. For example, making a trial balance using manual accounting procedures can take several days. With a computer that work can be done in minutes, and every day if necessary. Figure 10-1 shows an example.

Cash Flow
Job cost tracking, as shown in Figures 10-2 and 10-3, is an ideal application for a

```
                                    GENERAL LEDGER TRIAL BALANCE FOR ENTIRE COMPANY
          Printing Date:07-01-88            For the Period Ending 03-31-88
```

Asset Accounts

Acc#	Account Name	Beginning Balance	Debits	Credits	Ending Balance
100	Checking Account - Albank	0.00	232,975.56	228,536.54	4,439.02
101	Payroll Account	0.00	5,270.19	0.00	5,270.19
102	Money Market Account	0.00	6,090.86	0.00	6,090.86
103	Dealer Account - Madison	0.00	14,162.62	0.00	14,162.62
104	Petty Cash	0.00	203.22	0.00	203.22
105	Allow. for Doubtful Accts	0.00	0.00	1,831.00	-1,831.00
106	Prepaid Insurance	0.00	7,846.01	0.00	7,846.01
107	Prepaid Commissions	0.00	265.00	0.00	265.00
109	Prepaid Interest	0.00	690.13	0.00	690.13
112	Equipment - Office	0.00	4,095.29	0.00	4,095.29
116	Vehicles	0.00	9,299.79	0.00	9,299.79
121	Exchanges	0.00	9,458.77	4,341.28	5,117.49
122	Stock Inventory	0.00	3,739.31	0.00	3,739.31
123	Miscellaneous Investments	0.00	250.00	0.00	250.00
124	Labor in Process	0.00	23,828.30	0.00	23,828.30
125	Materials in Process	0.00	2,428.24	0.00	2,428.24
126	Subcontract in Process	0.00	5,892.45	0.00	5,892.45
127	Direct Cost in Process	0.00	421.95	0.00	421.95
200	Accounts Receivable	0.00	173,358.00	0.00	173,358.00
205	Note Receivable-Property	0.00	66,829.70	3,177.48	63,652.22
223	Note Receivable-Computer	0.00	0.00	193.00	-193.00
399	Inter-Account Transfers	0.00	502,761.36	541,220.70	-38,459.34
	Total of Asset Accounts	0.00	1,069,866.75	779,300.00	290,566.75

Liability & Equity Accounts

Acc#	Account Name	Beginning Balance	Debits	Credits	Ending Balance
400	Accounts Payable	0.00	30,452.89	37,316.39	6,863.50
401	A/P Lee Lumber	0.00	5,971.85	24,522.03	18,550.18
402	A/P Albert Lumber	0.00	1,706.10	1,706.10	0.00
403	Health Insurance Payable	0.00	0.00	86.52	86.52
406	Note Payable - Dump Truck	0.00	1,201.59	12,610.07	11,408.48
407	Note Payable - Bus. Loan	0.00	0.00	9,000.00	9,000.00
425	Fed Withholding Payable	0.00	8,685.00	8,685.00	0.00
426	FICA Withholding Payable	0.00	4,616.48	4,616.48	0.00
427	Illinois Withholding Tax	0.00	1,261.62	1,720.04	458.42
428	State Unemployment Tax	0.00	1,729.03	1,729.03	0.00
429	Federal Unemployment Tax	0.00	467.30	747.69	280.39
431	Accrued FICA & Fed. W/T	0.00	0.68	0.68	0.00
445	Deferred Income	0.00	0.00	152,980.89	152,980.89
446	Accrued Expenses	0.00	0.00	38,144.38	38,144.38
461	Deferred Gain -Bldg. Sale	0.00	0.00	55,204.10	55,204.10
500	Capital Stock	0.00	0.00	75,000.00	75,000.00
501	Treasury Stock	0.00	22,017.27	0.00	-22,017.27
580	Retained Earnings	0.00	7,414.67	10,102.92	2,688.25
590	Fiscal Year Earnings	0.00	68,184.01	10,102.92	-58,081.09
	Total of Liability & Equity	0.00	153,708.49	444,275.24	290,566.75

Income & Expense Accounts

Acc#	Account Name	Beginning Balance	Debits	Credits	Ending Balance
600	Sales	0.00	1,065.00	163,225.33	162,160.33
601	Miscellaneous Income	0.00	0.00	11,113.15	11,113.15
690	Earned Discounts	0.00	0.00	2.66	2.66
701	Labor	0.00	47,589.15	0.00	47,589.15
702	Materials	0.00	30,146.67	0.00	30,146.67
703	Subcontractors	0.00	77,889.26	0.00	77,889.26
704	Direct Cost	0.00	2,872.90	0.00	2,872.90
706	Small Tools	0.00	752.12	0.00	752.12
750	Advertising Expense	0.00	8,869.12	0.00	8,869.12
751	Vehicle Expense	0.00	4,931.57	0.00	4,931.57
753	Sales Commission Expense	0.00	1,534.65	0.00	1,534.65
755	Selling Expense	0.00	57.00	0.00	57.00
800	Salary - Frank	0.00	6,500.00	0.00	6,500.00
801	Salary - Robert	0.00	6,500.00	0.00	6,500.00
802	Office Salary Expense	0.00	4,420.00	0.00	4,420.00
803	Payroll Tax Expense	0.00	4,616.48	0.00	4,616.48
804	Telephone Expense	0.00	2,291.82	0.00	2,291.82
805	Estimator Salary	0.00	4,600.00	0.00	4,600.00
806	Peoples Gas	0.00	420.15	0.00	420.15
807	Electric	0.00	715.01	0.00	715.01
808	Office Supplies Expense	0.00	1,629.92	0.00	1,629.92
809	Donations Expense	0.00	135.00	0.00	135.00
811	Legal & Professional Fees	0.00	900.00	0.00	900.00
814	Accounting Expense	0.00	4,075.00	0.00	4,075.00
815	Insurance	0.00	4,239.40	0.00	4,239.40
816	Office Cleaning	0.00	175.00	0.00	175.00
817	Repairs & Maintenance	0.00	20.00	0.00	20.00
818	Disposal Service	0.00	105.00	0.00	105.00
821	License Expense	0.00	55.00	0.00	55.00
822	Promotion - Frank	0.00	1,300.00	0.00	1,300.00
823	Rent	0.00	5,392.98	0.00	5,392.98
824	Pagers	0.00	150.73	0.00	150.73
825	Miscellaneous Expenses	0.00	7,981.10	0.00	7,981.10
826	Group Health Insurance	0.00	492.20	0.00	492.20
	Total of Income & Expenses	0.00	232,422.23	174,341.14	-58,081.09

Computer-generated trial balance sheet
Figure 10-1

computer. Figure 10-2 is the first page of a computer printout for a job cost estimate on a small sunroom. Figure 10-3 is the final page of the same estimate. The total cost of the job is summarized for you. The printout for this job shows that the costs are 16.5 percent over par or average. There may be a good reason for this. If there is, the contractor probably knows. But if there isn't, he has been signaled that something in this estimate is wrong. He should go back and recheck the estimate and his figures for errors.

A computer can also help you control your material purchasing. By keeping an exact count on inventory, your superintendent will know what to buy and when to buy it. The same program will also let your accounting personnel know when it's time to pay for the materials ordered.

Information Processing

You can store facts on all your jobs, not only for current control but future reference as well. This makes it easy to compare job costs from job to job — and maybe find cost overruns in time to prevent more serious damage.

With a word processing program and a printer, you can prepare proposals, contracts, letters, and job specs quickly and professionally.

And that's just the beginning.

When Should You Computerize

There are no firm rules here. But we'll suggest some general guidelines.

When your dollar volume reaches $500,000 to $750,000 annually, you should begin thinking about a computer. Or, if you're running over 50 jobs a year, you're probably ready for one. In either case, you're probably generating so much paperwork that your office staff is having trouble processing it manually.

Another area to watch is your staffing. When you think you need to increase your office staff, you may find it's less expensive to add a computer than it is to add someone else to the payroll.

A third test is to ask yourself the following questions: Do you know where your business is today? Do you know if you're making a profit? Are your expenses getting too high? Can you handle more business without adding additional employees? Does it take days or weeks to gather financial data, only to find that by the time you get it, the situation has changed? If you find it difficult and time-consuming to get information or answers to these kinds of questions, it's time to think about using a computer.

What Comes First, the Computer or the Program?

Unfortunately, knowing when it's time to buy a computer and being able to choose the right system are two different things. *A computer is only as good as the programs that are run on it.* So the first thing isn't to buy a computer. The first step is to find the

Job Cost Estimate

(Form date 7/15/88)
Page #1

Date	: 9/11/88	
Job #	: 9740	
Customer	: Rogers	
Street	: 123 Circle Ct.	
City	: Elk Grove Village	
Zip	:	
Phone	: 593-2788	
Lead from	: Show	
Salesman	: Bob	
Date sold	: 8/3/88	

Quote	: $17,600
Bank	: Cash
Financing	:
Months	:
% Sold	:
% Bought	:
Appraisal fee	:
Bank fees	:
T.O.P. Sold	:
T.O.P. Bought	:
Finance	
Manager	:

Prep & Demo

(Turn - in)

001	Fence	Remove	*	Job	25.00	(N/A)
001	Fence	R & R	*	Job	60.00	(N/A)
001	Fence gate	R & R	*	Job	100.00	(N/A)
004	Trees * Stumps * Bushes		*	Job	50.00 C	(N/A)
006	Drier vent	Up to 5 Ft	*	Job	50.00	(N/A)
006	Drier vent	Over 5 Ft	*	L/F	2.00	(N/A)
008	Air cond.	Relocation	*	Job	360.00 H	(N/A)
010	Water spigot	Relocation	*	Job	90.00 P	(N/A)
010	Water spigot	Relocation	*	Job	220.00 P	(N/A)
012	BBQ grill	Remove	*	Job	25.00	(N/A)
012	BBQ grill	Relocate	*	Job	220.00 P	(N/A)
014	Gutter drain tile		*	Lin Ft	3.00 C	(N/A)
016	Gas meter	I/S stubbing	*	Job	90.00 P	(N/A)
016	Gas meter	I/S stubbing	*	Job	220.00 P	(N/A)
016	Gas meter	I/S stubbing	*	Job	350.00 P	(N/A)
018	Chimney Ext	Metal	*	Job	175.00 H	(N/A)
020	Chimney Ext	Brick	*	Min job	450.00 M	(N/A)
020	Chimney Ext	Brick	*	Lin Ft	125.00 M	(N/A)
022	Soil vent	Extension	*	Job	100.00 P	(N/A)
024	T. V. antenna	R & R	*	Job	50.00	(N/A)
026	Awning	Remove	*	Each	20.00	(N/A)
026	Awning	R &R	*	Each	40.00	(N/A)
028	Sewer run		*	Lin Ft	35.00 P	(N/A)
030	Gutters	Existing	*	Lin Ft	2.75 G	(N/A)
032	Demo	Roof	*	Sq Ft	0.80 D	(N/A)
034	Demo misc		*	Job	0.00 D	(N/A)
036	Demo misc		*	Job	0.00 D	(N/A)
038	Misc		*	Job	0.00	(N/A)
040	Misc		*	Job	0.00	(N/A)
042	Misc		*	Job	0.00	(N/A)

Courtesy: Drew Builders, Inc.

Job cost estimate
Figure 10-2

Job Cost Summary		
#9740 123 Circle Ct. Elk Grove Village	Sold by: Bob Job sold on: 8/3/88 Lead from: Show	
% of Job Cost	Turn in	Item
1.5%	$220	Plans
1.4%	$200	Permits
18.0%	$2,665	Concrete
0.0%	$0	Masonry
34.9%	$5,155	Matl & carp labor
41.6%	$6,153	Exterior millwork
1.1%	$165	Gutters
0.0%	$0	Electric
0.0%	$0	Heating & air cond
0.0%	$0	Plumbing
0.0%	$0	Sheet rock
0.0%	$0	Sun room
1.5%	$219	Debris & dumpsters
	$14,777 84.0% (62.5% or less is par)	Estimated direct job cost % of direct job cost

Courtesy: Drew Builders, Inc.

Summary of estimated job costs
Figure 10-3

program that solves your office problems. That's not always easy.

Never buy a computer and then look for the software to program it. Find the software first. Then look for a computer and printer in your price range that can be used with the programs you've selected. A basic computer setup is shown in Figure 10-4. You need the computer, monitor, keyboard, printer, and software (programs).

Supplier Selection

Many of the early computer salesmen were "hackers" or computer hobbyists. They didn't necessarily know anything about running a business. But because they knew computers, they made good salesmen.

Today, computer salespeople are much more knowledgeable about the programs they

IBM Computer system
Figure 10-4

sell. Many specialize in programs for a particular industry — such as construction. If you call a few computer stores, you'll probably find someone who knows something about programs for the construction industry.

In addition to knowledge of your type of business, there are other things to look for in a computer supplier. You need to find out what services they're willing to provide their customers:

• Will they do the installation?

• Do they offer training programs to help you and your employees learn how to operate the equipment you buy?

• If you purchase a software program and it's not effective for your business, can you exchange it or get credit on another one?

• If you have problems with your computer, will they help correct the problem?

• Do they have the peripherals or add-ons that are compatible with your system so you can purchase them at a later date? Do they have both the simple and the more sophisticated equipment that's on the market? If you feel you need a more sophisticated system, can you upgrade your current or planned system without some type of modification?

- If there are improvements in the programs you buy, will they keep you informed?

Get answers to these questions before you buy. Learn all you can about the seller. How long have they been in business? Who are their major customers? Do they specialize in computers and software for other types of businesses as well as yours? Do they intend to keep up all their specialty lines?

Find a company with a good history, one that has been around for awhile, and one you can grow with. Take time to choose both your supplier and your equipment carefully. Never let a high pressure salesman push you into buying a package you're not completely happy with.

The Computer Experience

Let's look at an example of a typical remodeling company going through the process of selecting, setting up, and operating a computerized accounting system.

The boss at Ace Remodeling has decided that a computer is needed to handle the accounting. Bills are going out late and many have mistakes. The manual accounting system is a combination of a "cash" and an "accrual" system. Most accounting programs use an "accrual" accounting — an item becomes an expense as soon as you're billed for it, rather than when you pay for it.

The first thing they learned at Ace Remodeling is that there's relatively little difference between computers of about the same description. Nearly all software, on the other hand, is different. In fact, every accounting program they examined was different. Every package had its own strengths and weaknesses.

They found that many software programs are made up of individual modules, such as single programs for payables, receivables, or a general ledger. These don't necessarily work with other packages offered by the same company. Fortunately, they discovered this before buying the program.

They looked for an integrated system that would tie all their accounting procedures together. With an integrated system, when you receive or make payments, the transactions are automatically posted to both the general ledger and the appropriate job. With a "dual-entry" system, you can't make an unbalanced entry. The computer won't complete the transaction until it's balanced. This is the kind of program they wanted to buy.

They had to talk to several suppliers before they found the right accounting system for their needs. They chose a good company, one that had been in business for several years and had a good reputation in the industry. This was fortunate, because when they had a problem, the company was there to help them. The company they chose sold both software and hardware.

Equipment Selection

Next they had to choose the right computer. The accounting program required 640 K of memory and a hard disk. (A "K" is a kilobyte or 1024 units. A "byte" is the number of bits used to represent characters of information, which for PC's is usually 8 bits). PC's data is stored on either hard disks or soft (floppy) disks. A hard disk stores much more information than a floppy disk. So they bought a computer with a 20 Mb hard disk, thinking it would supply them with enough capacity to last them a long time. (The letters *Mb* stand for megabytes or millions of bytes.) Unfortunately, in six months they found that this wasn't enough! Several people were using the computer for contracts and letters. The hard disk was nearly full. For a while they could unload some files onto floppy disks. But eventually even this became a nuisance. They decided to add a 40 Mb hard disk to double the storage capacity.

This was a good investment for them, in spite of the additional cost. They now have all the storage they need and even the capacity to add on a second business, an architectural firm that they also own.

The new hard disk allows them to keep all of their software programs and data on one drive. If they want to change functions — switch from accounting to word processing for example — there are no disks to change. They simply enter the proper command.

They still use the floppy disks for backup. At the end of the day, everything written to the hard disk that day is also copied to floppy disks. That takes about 10 minutes, but prevents a major loss if the hard disk fails. It's essential that you have backup data, especially for accounting. If the hard disk fails (due to a power failure, for example) all you'll lose is one day's work. All previous data is still safe since it's stored on the floppies. You can recreate one day's information in a day. But restoring all the data in an accounting system might take weeks or longer. That could put a remodeling company out of business — permanently.

Hard disks come in many sizes. When you're deciding what you need, buy enough capacity to meet present as well as future needs. Be realistic, though. Not many remodeling companies need 120 Mb hard disks. Don't buy capacity you'll never use.

Other Hardware Considerations

Once Ace Remodeling decided on the programs to buy, their choice of hardware was easy. But there were still several things they had to consider. Was the hardware reliable? How many expansion slots did it have? Did it have the right keyboard? Would the keyboard be used primarily for word processing, or for accounting and accounting calculations?

They found that although most computer setups were similar, some were easier to operate than others. There were some computer keyboards with "dedicated keys" which would perform an operation in a single step, while others required several strokes to do the same task. They had to consider who would be using the computer, and the kind of work that would ordinarily be done on it.

They also wanted to prepare specifications and contracts with their new computer. So they decided on a laser printer that would produce reports that looked like they had been typeset. Luckily, they discovered in time that the word processing program they wanted to use would only work with certain laser printers. Naturally, not the printer they wanted to buy.

Eventually, they found a word processing program that was compatible with the printer they liked. But that program was relatively complex. It took about a week to master most of the functions built into it. And several employees in the office never did take the time to learn more than the most basic parts of the program.

It took the company about a month before they felt comfortable with their computer system. After about three months the computer was part of the office routine. All payables approved for payment are entered every Thursday. That takes about 45 minutes. On Friday they enter sales and cash receipts, then print their payroll checks. This takes a little over an hour.

The new system saves several hours of clerical time every week. They had been using a part-time bookkeeper to do the accounts payable and weekly journal posting. The checks were typed up and addressed manually by a secretary — a process that took over five hours. On top of that was the bookkeeper's time.

Using the computer, the whole process takes under two hours. Since the computer also prints the name and address of the recipient on the check, they now use window envelopes. All the secretary has to do is put the checks into the envelopes and put on the postage. That takes about 15 minutes. The time savings for bookkeeping and issuing checks is over four hours a week.

The computer is also used for figuring proposals, recording job specs, and preparing work orders.

System Evaluation

Ace Remodeling has now closed their books for the first year on the computer. They kept two sets of books throughout the first year. One set is on the computer and the other was kept up manually, just as it always had been.

There were several reasons for doing this. First, they could compare the two for accuracy. If there was a difference, they could identify the problem. Second, they wanted to compare the two for efficiency. They wanted to be sure they're getting full use of what they paid for.

They no longer need the weekly services of a bookkeeper. They'll now use a bookkeeping service only for quarterly reports. This alone will be a considerable savings for the company.

Another big advantage of using a computer was quick access to information when they needed it. The computer gives them literally unlimited access to financial reports, such as the Budget of Income and Expenses report shown in Figure 10-5. This kind of report can be done daily if necessary. All they have to do is turn on the computer, enter the command, and make sure there's paper in the printer. With the manual system, this would have taken at least a day to prepare. And, if they missed something, the report wouldn't have been accurate.

Budget of Income & Expenses for Fiscal Year Ending 3/31/88				
	Residential	Commercial	Total	%
Sales	200,000.00	700,000.00	900,000.00	100.00
Gross profit %	40.00	27.50		
Prime gross profit	80,000.00	192,500.00	272,500.00	30.27
Salesmen commission %	7.50	0.00		
	11,250.00		11,250.00	1.25
Less : Advertising			24,000.00	2.66
Total advertising & commission			35,250.00	3.91
Profit before overhead			237,250.00	26.36
Less : Overhead			220,580.00	24.50
Net profit (loss)			16,670.00	1.85

Budget of Income and Expenses report
Figure 10-5

They also found that they could do comparative statements quickly once historical information about their company was entered into their system. They could compare this week to the same week last year, or the first quarter of this year to the first quarter of last year. Reports like the one in Figure 10-6 would have taken a day to compile manually. In an active business, finding a day to do something like this might be very difficult.

With current information readily available, they could do more financial planning. They feel that in another year their computer system will have increased company profitability. With a clear and accurate record of their workload by weeks, they could plan use of labor and material better. More important, it has given them a better picture of their cash flow.

Payback

The company, as we mentioned earlier, is actually two separate businesses. One is the remodeling business, and the other is a small architectural business. The architectural business requires many of the same programs as the remodeling business. They found they could use many of the same programs for both. The cost of the computer was split between the two businesses, with the smaller amount being charged to the architectural company.

The owner of the company feels that the computer system will pay for itself in its first two years. It would have had a one-year payback if they hadn't continued to keep two sets of books for the first year, but they didn't want to take any chances. Of course, these dollar savings don't consider the added convenience to employees in both companies.

Their total investment — hardware and software, was a little over $6,000.

Year-To-Date Income Statement
Prepared Without Audit
for the period ending 03-31-88

Operating revenue				
Sales	$	162,160.33		93.58%
Miscellaneous income		11,113.15		6.41%
Total cash sales			$ 173,273.48	100.00%
Earned discounts	$	2.66		0.00%
Total earned discounts			2.66	0.00%
Total gross operating income			$ 173,276.14	100.00%
Labor	$	47,589.15		27.46%
Materials		30,146.67		17.40%
Subcontractors		77,889.26		44.95%
Direct cost		2,872.90		1.66%
Small tools		752.12		0.43%
Total cost of goods sold			159,250.10	91.91%
Gross operating margin			$ 14,126.04	8.09%
Advertising expense	$	8,869.12		5.12%
Vehicle expense		4,931.56		2.85%
Sales commission expense		1,534.65		0.89%
Selling expense		57.00		0.03%
Total direct expenses			15,392.34	8.88%
Gross operating profit			$ -1,366.30	-0.79%
Salary - Frank	$	6,500.00		3.75%
Salary - Robert		6,500.00		3.75%
Office salary expense		4,420.00		2.55%
Payroll tax expense		4,616.48		2.66%
Telephone expense		2,291.82		1.32%
Estimator salary		4,600.00		2.65%
Peoples gas		420.15		0.24%
Electric		715.01		0.41%
Office supplies expense		1,629.92		0.94%
Donations expense		135.00		0.08%
Legal & professional fees		900.00		0.52%
Accounting expense		4,075.00		2.35%
Insurance		4,239.40		2.45%
Office cleaning		175.00		0.10%
Repairs & maintenance		20.00		0.01%
Disposal service		105.00		0.06%
License expense		55.00		0.03%
Promotion - Frank		1,300.00		0.75%
Rent		5,392.98		3.11%
Pagers		150.73		0.09%
Miscellaneous expenses		7,981.10		4.61%
Group health insurance		492.20		0.28%
Total general & admin. exp.			56,714.79	32.73%
Net operating income			$ -58,081.09	-33.52%

Quarterly income statement
Figure 10-6

Computer Costs

When buying a computer and software, how much should you pay? Keep in mind that there are many different manufacturers of computers and computer hardware, and hundreds of software packages to choose from. With so much available, if you don't know what you need, it's pretty easy to spend a lot of money and end up with something you don't need and can't use.

The first thing you must decide is what you want a computer to do. Accounting only? Accounting and payroll? Accounting, estimating, and payroll? Even making these selections for the first-time user can be difficult. Check with other contractors you know who have been in business a while and have been using a computer for several years. They'll probably give you the best advice. Here are some questions you might ask them:

- How are they using their computers?

- What kind of success have they had?

- What kind of problems?

- Who sold them their equipment?

- Would they recommend their dealer?

- What was their initial investment?

- Have they expanded their system?

- If so, what did they add? How much did it cost?

Getting answers to simple questions like these before you buy can save you a lot of money, headaches, and frustration.

If you're doing about $1-million in business annually, your basic system will include the computer with both floppy and hard disks, a monitor, your software package, and a letter-quality printer.

Look for a system that not only meets your immediate needs, but has room for expansion. Keep in mind that having too much capacity is almost as bad as having too little. Computer prices will continue to fall, and better programs will become available. What you buy today will be improved upon in the next three or four years. However, that won't necessarily make your current system obsolete. As long as it works for you, you can use it. *You* decide when it's cost effective to update your system.

It's usually safer to stick with standard systems. For the more popular standard systems there's usually a "migration path" to more powerful computers when they become available. That's important. You don't want to be forced to retype thousands of records when you switch computers. Also, with the more popular computers, you can buy a wider range of "add-ons" and peripherals.

Software

Choosing the right software is never easy. The biggest cost is seldom the purchase price. The cost of learning the program is usually many times what you pay for the program itself. If several people have to learn a complex program, your cost for training may be thousands of dollars. And, in the worst case, after several months of training, you may discover that the program doesn't do what you need!

Nearly all of the more powerful programs take weeks or even months to master. For example, a flexible construction estimating program that sells for about $500 might take several days of instruction and a month or more of practice to master. Even then, you might have to enter the labor and material cost data base before the program can be used. That might take several weeks more. However, once the program is operational you have a new and powerful tool which can help you expand your business.

Word Processing

A truly professional remodeling company should prepare clean, sharp letters, bids, and contracts. Word processing offers this capability. It's one of the more important features of a PC system.

Using a word processer, you can quickly rewrite documents that need editing or slight modification, write formats for repetitious correspondence, and compile data for printouts. You can make changes or correct mistakes on your screen before printing a paper copy. You can adjust the order, wording, type of print, margins, or headings easily to suit the need.

Figures 10-7 and 10-8 show how one contractor effectively uses his word processer. Because he subcontracts all his carpentry work, he found he was spending a lot of time preparing detailed carpentry subcontracts. He eliminated this problem by programing all his carpentry labor costs. Now all he has to do when he has a job contracted is enter the appropriate codes in his computer for the work he needs done. The computer then prints out a detailed description of the labor required and the costs for that particular job (as shown in Figure 10-7). At the end of the labor summary, the computer automatically prints up a formal contract for the job. See Figure 10-8. This saves him many hours of repetitious labor.

Most word processing programs include a spelling checker. If spelling is one of your weak points, this will save you hunting through the dictionary looking for a word you don't know how to spell, or sending out misspelled letters. Some programs even include a thesaurus that helps you find the correct word you need. (This is a great feature if your vocabulary isn't your strong point.) Word processing does two things for you. It cuts the time spent on written communications to a minimum, and it gives your written communications a high-quality professional appearance — no typos, misspelling, erasures, etc.

Many word processing programs are available, from under $100 to over $500. The best way to make a selection is to go to a software store and discuss your needs. Then try out several programs. Make sure that whatever you select is compatible with your hardware. Like any software program, word processing takes a little time to learn, but it's worth the effort.

	**Subcontractor Agreement** **Carpentry Labor**
colspan="3"	**Cust: Jones** **Job # 9825**	colspan="4"	**Date: 8/11/88** **Crew: Pete**
	Item	**Amount**	**Unit**	**Description**	**@**	**Cost**
300 Walls	Base room on slab	400	Sq ft	Shed, hip or gable	1.34	536.00
400 Roof	Base room on slab	400	Sq ft	Shed, hip or gable	0.90	360.00
400 Roof	Base room on slab		Sq ft	If cath add:	0.10	(N/A)
400 Roof	Base room on slab		Sq ft	If open beam add:	0.00	(N/A)
300 Walls	Base if over 400 SF		Sq ft	Deduct :	0.25	(N/A)
400 Roof	Base if over 400 SF		Sq ft	Deduct :	0.25	(N/A)
001 Prep	Fence		Job	Remove	25.00	(N/A)
001 Prep	Fence		Job	Remove & reinstall	50.00	(N/A)
001 Prep	Fence gate	1	Job	Remove & reinstall	25.00	25.00
006 Prep	Dryer vent		Job	Relocate	25.00	(N/A)
018 Prep	Chimney extension	1	Job	Extension	50.00	50.00
022 Prep	Soil vent pipe		Job	Extension	45.00	(N/A)
024 Prep	T.V. antenna		Job	Remove	5.00	(N/A)
024 Prep	T.V. antenna	1	Job	Remove & reinstall	30.00	30.00
024 Prep	T.V. antenna		Job	Relocate	40.00	(N/A)
032 Prep	Demo		Sq ft	Roof	0.50	(N/A)
034 Prep	Demo		Job			(N/A)
036 Prep	Demo		Job			(N/A)
038 Prep	Demo		Job			(N/A)
Prep	Demo		Job			(N/A)
146 Deck	Piers		Each	For :	25.00	(N/A)
506 Deck	Piers		Each	For outside deck	25.00	(N/A)
100 Conc	Stoop		Each		50.00	(N/A)
250 Deck	Knee wall		Lin ft	1 Ft	2.00	(N/A)
250 Deck	Knee wall		Lin ft	2 Ft	3.00	(N/A)
250 Deck	Knee wall		Lin ft	3 Ft	4.00	(N/A)
250 Deck	Knee wall		Lin ft	5 Ft	5.00	(N/A)
250 Deck	Knee wall		Lin ft	5 Ft	6.00	(N/A)

Courtesy: Drew Builders, Inc.
Labor summary
Figure 10-7

Printers

The choice is between dot-matrix, "letter quality," and laser printers. Since they don't come with the computer, you can buy any type of printer that works with the word processing program you've selected.

Dot-matrix printers make characters by creating a series of interlocking dots. The more dots per character, the more perfect the character. Nine-pin printers are suitable for

Subcontract Agreement

We at Drew Builders, Inc. welcome your association with our company. This agreement lists our subcontracting policies. Please sign at the bottom to signify that you agree to abide by these policies. We look forward to a pleasant and profitable business relationship with your company.

1. As a subcontractor of our company, you have become part of our team. We look to you to help "debug" our jobs. If you anticipate a problem not addressed in our plans, or find any code violation or technical problem, please notify us promptly. Acceptance of all bids should be based on a job site visit. If you prefer not to make such a visit, any problem caused by conflicting conditions becomes your problem and your responsibility.

2. All your personnel on our job should support our company and speak well of it. You are an integral part of our marketing program. Both of our businesses stand to lose or gain by our job behavior.

3. **Referrals**: If any of our clients request work directly from you, such as extras or future work, you will need Drew Builders' written permission to do the work. According to our original contract with the client, if any neighbor or passerby asks you to do a job, you must refer them to our office. Any subcontractor who takes such a job directly shall be in direct violation of this agreement and shall forfeit any and all moneys due you from this and any other agreements with Drew Builders.

4. **Changes**: All changes must be approved by our superintendent or our office. If time is a problem, you may proceed with our verbal approval, but you must follow up with a written change order. No prices may be given directly to the client.

5. **Insurance**: Drew Builders, Inc. carries a blanket insurance policy. If a copy of your general liability or workers' compensation coverage is not in our hands prior to any and all payouts, we shall deduct 6% from the amount due you for the general liability and 6% for the workers' compensation.

6. **Job schedule**: If for any reason you get to a job and additional work is needed before you can proceed, please call our office immediately. We can often solve the immediate problem and avoid such work stoppages in the future.

Formal contract
Figure 10-8

7. **Trash**: Your work area is to be left broom clean by you at the end of each day. Sweepings may be left neatly on our designated trash pile. We stock dust protection materials on the job. Your mechanics must dust protect any unprotected area they are working in, before starting work.

8. **Materials**: Acceptance of deliveries, their storage and protection is your responsibility.

9. **Warranty**: All labor is to be fully guaranteed by you for one year after substantial completion.

10. **Open accounts**: Drew Builders, Inc. charges materials at many supply companies. The subcontractor shall at no time use these accounts to charge nails, tools or any other items.

11. **Completion of work**: Subcontractor acknowledges that if, for any reason, he does not complete his work in a reasonable length of time, Drew Builders, Inc. may hire others to complete the job and any amount paid to them shall be deducted from the total amount due to the original subcontractor.

12. **Payouts**: Room additions shall have three payouts of 80% of amount due according to the "Carpentry Labor Price List."

Payout #1: "Under Roof" (including felt installed and building totally weathertight).

Payout #2: "Pull Off" when you are as far as you can proceed and now must wait for other trades to come in prior to you completing your job.

Payout #3: "Final" paid upon total (100%) completion of work and approval of job by Building Department, customer and our superintendent.

All payout requests must be approved by our superintendent.

13. **Taxes**: Subcontractor recognizes that as an independent contractor, it is his sole responsibility to promptly pay all taxes for which the subcontractor may be liable.

Dated:_____

Drew Builders, Inc.:_____

Subcontractor:_____

Courtesy: Drew Builders, Inc.
Formal contract
Figure 10-8 (cont.)

rough drafts and address labels. Printers with 24 pins create letters that look almost as good as those a typewriter produces. The number of pins also influences the price of the dot-matrix printer. The more pins and the higher the speed, the higher the price. The advantage of a dot-matrix printer over a letter quality printer is that it's faster and quieter.

The present disadvantage of a dot-matrix printer is that the print still doesn't look as good as typewriter print. For important letters to your clients, you need top quality type.

Letter-quality printers will give you correspondence that looks as though it was done on a good typewriter. The reproduction quality is excellent. A commercial printer should be able to make clear, readable, high-quality reproductions from your original.

But letter-quality printers also have several disadvantages. They cost more than dot-matrix printers, and they're usually a lot slower and noisier. But, you get good quality. When we say slow, that doesn't mean it's as slow as a typewriter. A letter-quality printer can print up to 60 characters per second — about as fast as you can read. On the other hand, most dot-matrix printers can produce several hundred characters per second.

Many contractors feel that a high-speed, dot-matrix printer is best for their needs. If your primary use for a printer will be accounting and estimating, the letter-quality printer's noise and slower speed can be distracting. A near letter-quality dot-matrix printer produces good correspondence and is fast and efficient for your office copies. And as the technology improves, their print quality is becoming more and more like letter quality. So by the time you're ready to buy one, you may be able to get the best of both worlds.

Laser printers produce the best quality type — nearly as good as the type produced by a phototypesetter, the machine used to make book type. That makes them the best choice for correspondence, and applications like producing newsletters or instruction manuals. They are also very quiet. The disadvantage is that most laser printers are expensive, easily several times the cost of the least expensive dot-matrix printers, and they can't make carbons.

Look Ahead

The computer industry is changing very quickly. Like electronic watches, calculators, and cameras, hardly a month goes by without some new feature becoming available. Fortunately, as the sophistication and performance goes up, prices are coming down.

Even so, buying a computer system isn't cheap. If you buy equipment that can't be expanded, you may waste a lot of time and money.

Get Professional Assistance

If you're not sure where to start, start asking questions. Find someone who knows and understands the needs of a remodeling contractor. Ask other remodelers what they are using and get their recommendation on hardware, software and dealers.

When you look for a company to do business with, find out what they know about construction. You'll want to work with a company that specializes in the industry. Or better yet, find a dealer whose *sole* business is computer systems for contractors.

Obviously, you pay more for this kind of service. However, it's one of the best ways to assure that your company will have a system that is cost-effective and compatible with your needs.

If you're one of those people who are biased against computers or intimidated by them, finding a professional you can trust may be a big step in the right direction.

Decision Time

Once you've made up your mind to buy a computer system, take some logical steps:

1) Go to a reputable dealer. If you don't know what computers can do, find out. Take home literature on those that interest you. Study it thoroughly and learn what the computer can and *cannot* do.

2) Know your business and your needs well enough so your dealer will understand what you require. If you don't know what you need or can't explain your business to someone else, you can bet whatever equipment you buy won't do what you hoped it would!

3) Are you going to operate the computer or is someone else in the company going to run it? If the answer is someone else, they should be in on the selection process.

4) Start by selecting the right software. Remember, the more powerful the software package, the more difficult it will be to learn. Some programs adapt easier and quicker to your manual procedures than others. Look for programs which *you* will find manageable.

5) Most contractors will need at least one of these five basic programs: Payroll, Job Cost, General Ledger, Accounts Payable, and Accounts Receivable. Look for additional software to fill your needs, such as Financial Analysis, Contract Status, Inventory, Billing, Purchase Order Control, Sales Analysis, Sales Commission Accounting, Employee Profitability, Equipment Costing, Service Contracts, and Estimating.

6) Choose hardware that's compatible with the software you select. You may want to hire a consultant to analyze your business and help you in the selection of equipment, or find a dealer who offers this service.

7) Buy only what you need, but select hardware that has the capability for expansion. What needs can you foresee?

8)   Your dealer should provide installation, maintenance, and service on the hardware you buy. They should also provide training and assistance as needed, both in operating your computer and your programs. It should be available as part of the contract or at a nominal fee. No system is trouble free.

9)   Rental and maintenance agreements through a dealer should include follow-up information for your software. Either the dealer or the software company should provide bulletins or newsletters to help you master the programs, as well as tips on how to use them effectively and efficiently.

If you want further information on what to look for in choosing a computer system for your company, get a copy of *Computers: The Builder's New Tool.* It explains just about everything that can go wrong, provides actual case histories, and may save you from making a several thousand dollar mistake. You can order one using the order form bound into the back of this book.

Computers *will* be part of our future. If you're scared of them, you should make an effort to get over it. Once you do, you'll find that making the decisions and selections you've been considering while reading this chapter will come a lot easier.

eleven

Collections: Be the Squeaking Wheel

Probably, you're reading this chapter because you can't collect on some of your jobs or because you have progress payments that are past due. Those are exactly the subjects we're going to address.

Some people never pay a bill until they have to. And your daily routine probably doesn't leave much time for making collection calls. But getting money from your clients' bank account into yours is essential if you're going to stay in the remodeling business. Remember, *no job is complete until it's paid for.* Until then, it's just a money sinkhole.

When you let past due balances slide, you've made collection more difficult. You've also increased the bad debt risk. The longer you wait, the harder it is to collect.

Every passing month means less money for you. Read the short article (Figure 11-1) reprinted from a building magazine. You want a reputation as a company no one can stiff. Begin a collection routine that makes paying the bill less trouble than not paying.

Before you launch a collection effort, *be sure it's not your fault that payments are delayed.* Have you turned in all the waivers, assignments, and verified statements? Have you completed all the paperwork? If you have, then begin to phone, and phone, and phone. But don't get nasty. There are laws against harassment.

If you have a customer who's behind in payments on a job that's still in progress, *stop work immediately.* Review your contract to be sure the progressive payment schedule is

The Depreciation of Accounts Receivable

A bean-counter somewhere invented a formula for figuring the depreciation of accounts receivable that are two or more months old.

It's frightening to review the rapidly deteriorating values of accounts receivable. When a contractor or an equipment or supply dealer enters into an agreement with a private party or public agency, he's investing whole dollars at today's rates. If he doesn't collect immediately when he completes his work or delivers his product, he begins to lose his profit.

By the time he collects all his money, it's questionable whether he's working for himself (and his ever-present partner, Uncle Sam), or for his customer. His profit may be all gone.

Contractors need to watch their accounts receivable closely and pursue collections zealously if they hope to come out ahead. The following depreciation rates could very well apply to any contractor's business operations.

- *Current account—* $1 is worth $1

- *Two months delinquent—* $1 is now worth $ .90

- *Six months delinquent—* $1 is now worth $ .67

- *One year delinquent—* $1 is now worth $ .45

- *Two years delinquent—* $1 is now worth $ .23

- *Three years delinquent—* $1 is now worth $ .15

- *Five years delinquent—* Forget it!

But collect it anyway, if you can get it!

This formula makes the profit picture look pretty discouraging. But contractors stay in the field because it's their chosen livelihood. We wonder whether private customers and certain public agency personnel appreciate the beating that contractors, equipment dealers and suppliers take before they finally recover their initial investment of 100% dollars.

Magazine article on accounts receivable
Figure 11-1

clearly stated. If it is, stay off the job until payments are current. Don't fall for the old "the check is in the mail" routine. Request that the money be delivered in person or by messenger. If you don't get paid in 24 to 48 hours, pull your equipment off the job.

Even if your contract provides a penalty for delayed completion, stop work. Give your client *written* notification that you will not continue the work until you receive the past due payments. Failure to make progress payments on time is nearly always a breach of contract, relieving you of the obligation to continue work. And if you're smart, you'll write a new contract more in your favor when work resumes.

One contractor we know uses a "good guy, bad guy" collection scheme. He was the sole owner of his company, but he kept that confidential. His company wasn't called by his name. He let customers believe he was just one of the principals. Because he was likable and easy-going, people tended to take advantage of him.

To balance his mild personality, he hired a thick-skinned, no-nonsense accountant to manage the money. This accountant was definitely more interested in the company's bottom line than in coddling deadbeats. He had a manner that didn't tolerate excuses or delay from anyone.

The accountant would make the first call to demand payment from a delinquent customer. He didn't threaten, but was always intimidating. Most customers reacted to the accountant's call by appealing to the contractor, who assumed the "friendly" role, being understanding and apologetic. He sympathized with the customer's dilemma, but pointed out that the company's financial people made and enforced the rules. Then he'd suggest that if they could come up with some kind of payment arrangement, he would talk with the accountant to see if something could be "worked out." Of course, it almost always could.

This approach doesn't work for every contractor and with every delinquent account. But it can help keep lines of communication open while getting the message delivered in no uncertain terms. If your associate is too forceful or too clumsy, your client's only reaction may be anger. A client who's under financial strain already may feel cornered by too much pressure. The conversation can end with those three little words no contractor wants to hear, "*So sue me.*"

Solve Collection Problems by Avoiding Them

The best collection system is one that's never used. Honestly, that's not impossible. We know remodeling contractors who seldom or never have trouble collecting. Here are a few steps we suggest you take that will practically guarantee payment on time.

Write Tight Contracts With Progressive Payments
If you're having chronic collection problems, your own procedures are probably the cause. If you don't write progressive payment schedules in your contracts, you're asking for collection problems.

What should your progressive payment schedule require? That's easy. Money should come in just slightly faster than it goes out. During the entire course of the job, you should be paid for work just before you have to pay for labor and materials. Get a small down payment when the contract is signed. The next payment is due when materials arrive at the job site. Payments for the remainder of the job depend on when you'll need money to pay bills. By the time work is finished, you should have collected everything except your profit. That final payment is due when the client signs off on your acceptance form.

Collecting just slightly faster than you have to pay requires some planning. Begin with your payment schedule. When do your suppliers expect to get paid: when you order, when the materials are delivered, 30 days after delivery? Be sure your collection schedule and payment schedule match. If a lender is involved, you'll probably have more trouble "front-loading" the job — inflating early payments. But no one should object to paying for work as it's done. After all, your profit isn't collected until all work is completed.

On any job, set up the most favorable payment schedule permitted under the law. If you use a contract prepared by your lawyer or your state or local building association, be sure that it states that final payment is due *promptly on substantial completion of the job,* as long as such a statement is legal in your state.

Law in some states limits your advance on the job to 10 percent of the contract price for remodeling projects. Asking for more than 10 percent in advance is probably unnecessary and may make closing the deal more difficult. The final payment should be from 10 to 25 percent of the contract price — about equal to your estimated profit on the job. Payments after the first and before the last payment should be timed to match the dates your suppliers, subcontractors and tradesmen will be paid.

Try to schedule progress payments that coincide with the completion of one task and the beginning of another. For example, a payment might be due when framing is complete and before siding is installed. People are more willing to pay for what they can see. And they can anticipate when a payment is due by noting the amount of work completed. Get progress payments on completion of:

- Demolition and rough carpentry

- Rough-in of electrical and plumbing

- Fixtures and appliance installation

- Completion of carpentry, electrical and plumbing

Even if the amount of progress payments is small, get them written into the contract and insist on payments when due. It makes your cash flow more predictable, reduces the number of unpleasant surprises, and helps you anticipate problems before they become a major crisis.

If your state enforces limits on progress payments or if you can't collect fast enough to carry labor and material costs for most jobs, you'll have to do what most remodeling contractors do: hug your banker and material suppliers every day. Your bank and your material dealers are your prime sources of operating funds.

Progress payments are most important for multi-trade remodeling contractors. Single-trade remodelers are usually on and off the job in a few days and should get paid in full on job completion.

Follow State Laws Regulating Payment Schedules

In California, for example, initial payments are limited to 10 percent of the contract price unless there are custom components involved. If the job includes custom kitchen cabinets or made-to-measure windows for instance, the remodeling contractor could increase the initial payment by the price of these items.

FHA-guaranteed loans are used to finance many larger residential remodeling projects. Banks making these loans may not disburse funds, either to the homeowner or the contractor, until the entire job is completed. So you have to either find interim financing or have a very deep pocket.

Some states require that progress payments on a job be for the same dollar amount. The state agency that licenses construction contractors may have regulations that are designed to prevent contractors from front-loading or over-drawing a job. These rules may require you to schedule many small payments at inconvenient intervals. This can lead to a lot of confusion over which verified statements, lien waivers or assignments apply to which payments. Only good record keeping can save you here.

If you arrange interim financing from your own lender, you'll have to furnish completion records to qualify for each payment. In every case, if you don't keep your paperwork straight, you'll have a terrible time collecting.

Fund Disbursements Companies

A good way to guarantee payments coming in on time is to work through a fund disbursement company. Although these companies aren't new, they aren't well known, and most operate primarily on the west coast. They offer benefits to both the lender and the property owner. Here is how they work:

The contractor or homeowner applies for financing for a project through a bank or other financial institution. Once the financing has been approved, the contractor submits the plans, specifications, and a copy of the construction contract with an estimated cost breakdown, to the disbursement company. The disbursement company in turn sets up a trust account for that particular job with a bank. When the funds are deposited in the trust account, the contractor can begin work.

The contractor is given a voucher book, lien release forms, and any other necessary legal papers relating to the job. All subcontractor and material bills are paid with vouchers issued by the general contractor. A voucher is a non-negotiable order of disbursement, like a bank check, used to authorize payments against an account. The vouchers, along with the required labor and material releases, are presented to the disbursement company for immediate payment after they are issued.

The final payment to the general contractor is made after all the following conditions have been met:

1) A notice of completion is recorded with the County Recorder.

2)   All outstanding bills have been paid.

3)   A notarized *Final Payment Affidavit* and *Waiver of Lien* have been submitted to the disbursement company.

For additional fees, the disbursement company will also offer other services, such as periodic job inspections.

Utilizing a system like this protects both the contractor and the property owner from bankruptcy, liens, attachments in civil procedures or credit delinquency involving either party. The funds are always available for the completion of the project, and *you*, the contractor, don't have to put up your own cash. The disbursement company is bonded with a Fidelity Bond to insure they don't misuse the funds entrusted to their care.

Making Sales vs. Getting Paid

Some remodeling companies are heavily sales-oriented. You've probably heard about remodeling contractors who use "boiler rooms" — salespeople working at phone banks, making cold calls all day, trying to set up appointments for a commissioned sales staff. Once these *closers* get a signed contract, nearly all the work is turned over to subcontractors.

This type of remodeling contractor is really more of a *selling company* than a construction company. They're very good at finding likely prospects and closing the deal. But many of these companies are much better at selling than they are at getting the work done and satisfying their clients. That gives the whole remodeling industry a bad name. It's O.K. to be a selling expert. But you have to be as good at remodeling as you are at *selling* remodeling jobs.

Most remodeling contractors could learn a lot from these "boiler room" operations. Selling is an art just like designing a modern new kitchen or laying tile. All remodeling contractors should try to be as good at selling as they are at doing the work once the job is sold.

But there's a major danger in putting more emphasis in making sales. And it has to do with the subject of this chapter — collections.

Here's the problem. It's much easier to sell jobs if your sales people offer more generous credit terms, don't insist on a down payment, don't include progress payments in the contract, don't make it clear that full payment is due when the work is finished, and don't qualify their prospects before making the sales pitch.

It's easy to sell remodeling work to people who can't pay for it or have no intention of paying for it. Salespeople who sign up dreamers like that are creating collection nightmares for you. Don't let that happen. Get a good down payment on signing. Have a progressive payment schedule on any job that lasts for more than a few days. Get agreement that the final payment has to be made *the same day* that the job is finished. Qualify your prospects by checking references and bank balances. Before closing the deal, know where the money is coming from and be sure it's going to be there.

Avoiding collection problems is like a balancing act. Put too much emphasis on getting paid on time and you'll scare even good payment risks into the arms of your competition. Put too little emphasis on payment and you'll win lots of jobs — and about as many uncollectable accounts. Strike a balance between the two. It's not easy, and there's no single answer. Just be aware of the tradeoff between sales and collections and make intelligent decisions you can live with.

Take All the Insurance Work You Can Get

Insurance work is a great source of reliable cash. Collection is a sure thing if you process the paperwork correctly. You'll get paid faster if you get the assignment signed and into the hands of the adjuster or claim office right away. That way your name will be on the settlement check and it can't be cashed without your signature.

This will help minimize problems if you're working for the mortgage holder on a claim. The mortgage company may want to hold the entire settlement payment if your name isn't on the check. That's especially likely if the homeowner is delinquent on the loan after a fire or other major damage.

In that case, negotiate with the mortgage company for the best conditions you can get. Point out that paying you will help restore the building to usable condition. It won't be an eyesore and a hazard any more. It won't attract vandals any more. But cooperate with the mortgage holder. If you insist on your rights under a contract to restore the building to its original condition, you can run into trouble. Lenders can harass you with constant inspection delays or even refuse to process paperwork. Do what the mortgage holder will agree to pay for, say "Thank you," and then pull off the job.

You're in a much better position if you're working for the owner on an insurance claim. Your contract isn't subject to the lender's conditions. Your customer is under pressure to get the job done. He's not shopping around for a room addition he may decide to build *some day*. He needs the repairs done *now!*

Insurance policies usually call for repairing structural damage within a limited time. Payment for repairs is assigned to you so the owner can't elect to live with the damage and pocket the cash. The lender's name is on the insurance policy, and also the loss draft. That way the lender knows when money has been paid against a claim. Lenders will insist that repairs be made so the value of the property is restored. In most losses, all the owner stands to collect is the depreciated or replacement value of the building contents.

Solve Collection Problems by Taking Action _____

Don't overlook the importance of collection letters. Naturally, a personal visit or a phone call is more effective. But those take more of your time. A collection letter can be done in a minute or two on your computer. It reminds your debtor that you haven't forgotten about the debt and are still anxious to collect. With some luck, your letter will arrive on payday when some extra cash is available. No one except hardcore deadbeats can get collection letters without feeling uncomfortable. A low-key letter may be enough to shift a few dollars your way.

A client who doesn't pay on time is probably over-extended, "robbing Peter to pay Paul." Usually that's because of unexpected expenses or some loss of income. You probably won't know the details, but there will be clues. If your client doesn't respond to requests for payment, but the house is still standing and occupied, you know that at least some financial obligations are being met. In this case, you want to be Paul and not Peter. To get the debtor's attention and payment, write a stronger collection letter and back it up with a phone call.

Every time you call or write, squeeze a little harder. Remember, the squeaky wheel gets the grease.

Collection Letters

You'll need either company letterhead stationery or a set of collection letters. Both are available from office supply stores and mail order outlets. Many styles of printed, snap-apart carbonless form letters and notices are available. They can be printed with your company name or you can use a rubber stamp or sticky labels. Some forms come with carbon paper, so all you have to type is the account name and amount due only once for each series of collection notices. They progress from "just a friendly reminder" to "FINAL NOTICE" in three or four steps. Most remodeling contractors don't have the time or staff to prepare more formal, personal letters and notices.

Each collection notice you send carries a "guilt factor" of three. Most people will respond when their guilt factor reaches between six and nine. So three or four form notices or letters should bring some kind of payment.

Printed forms are probably least effective. Some people just don't respond to form letters. If there's some logical reason why an account isn't paying, a form letter probably doesn't address that reason. It's likely to be ignored.

Collection letters do have one advantage. Some people are seldom home and can't be reached by phone. But everyone gets their mail. When you're trying to collect what's due, pull out all the stops. Phone first and follow up with a written notice.

Copy All Checks

When your efforts bring in a check, don't rush right off to the bank to deposit it. First, *take a minute to photocopy the check*. It's good business practice to photocopy every check you get. If there's anything written or printed on the back of the check, copy that too. Here's why.

First, you'll have a permanent record of the customer's bank account number, probably the one used regularly for big ticket items like the mortgage, car loan and charge cards. You'll know the bank branch too. That's important information. If you end up getting a judgment against the debtor, enforcing that judgment by attaching a bank account is easy — if you know the branch and account number.

Be sure to notice anything written above the space for endorsement of the check. Some checks have words like "Endorsement indicates full accord and satisfaction of all claims on this account" on the back of the check. Anything your client claims notwithstanding, those words don't relieve him or her from paying the full amount due — unless, of course, you've agreed to compromise on the amount owed.

Legal Action

If you really can't collect, have your attorney send a letter. Many lawyers will write very effective collection letters for a small fee. Their most effective letter is the last one, which arrives *Certified Mail, Return Receipt Requested* and announces that you're suing.

Some lawyers offer their clients several collection letter formats and a small supply of their letterhead and envelopes. Your secretary can adapt one of these letters to the situation and type it on the lawyer's stationery. If your lawyer allows this, send him or her a copy the day before you mail the original to the customer. That way, if the customer calls directly, your lawyer will at least know what all the shouting is about.

Keep your lawyer informed about your business. The more he knows about your business, the better his advice will be. He can assist you in filing a lien, for instance. If all else fails, that's the last step.

If you use an independent accounting firm or do business with a finance company, they might include collection help as part of their service. If not, they may offer it for a reasonable additional fee. Generally, the larger the firm, the better they are at collecting. No one pays much attention to a smudged note from Joe's Bargain Basement Bookkeeping Service.

Some of the largest accounting firms will accept as clients small businesses with as little as $250,000 in gross receipts. If you're in the market for accounting or collection help, don't hesitate to shop among the big companies.

Collection Agencies

If lawyers and accounting firms are the Air Force, then collection agencies are the Marines. You'll get some of your money, but it will cost you dearly — up to 50 percent of the debt.

If you're going to turn an account over to a collection agency, *be sure to tell your customer first.* We know a builder who called a delinquent account to say he had turned the client's file over to an agency two days before. The client said, "Too bad, I just mailed the check yesterday." The collection agency got $3,000 of the $10,000 payment because they had officially taken over the account the day before the payment was made. They didn't have to do a thing except enter the information in their records and take their fee to the bank.

When all else fails, there's no option but to sue. Remember, however, that in most states you can't sue to collect on the contract unless you're a licensed contractor.

Before you go to court, resolve any dispute over some finishing touches that could be holding up final payment. Then do everything possible to get a partial payment that reduces the amount owed to the maximum allowed in small claims court. You're usually money and time ahead if you can sue in small claims court without a lawyer.

Factors

Some lenders will make loans against your accounts receivable. This is called *factoring* and the lender is called a *factor*. If you use a factor, collecting normally becomes the responsibility of the factor. That's one reason they charge so much.

If you can find a factor who will loan on your receivables, check the contract carefully before signing. One contractor thought he had an inexpensive factor. But to his sorrow he found that after 90 days, uncollected accounts reverted back to him. So he didn't solve his financial problems, he just compounded them. Not only did he get his problem accounts returned to him when they were really "cold," he still had to repay the factor.

Minimizing Bad Debts

You put a lot of work into selling and completing a project. When it's done, you don't want collection problems. Avoid slow pay accounts by creating happy customers. Be as professional and businesslike as possible. High prices, poor workmanship, and late completion dates are the primary causes for delayed payments.

Success in collecting on accounts usually depends on the care and attention you give each job. You won't be the cause of your own collection problems if you pay attention to the following:

Good Workmanship
When you go into business as a contractor, soliciting and accepting jobs, there are two implicit promises you make to your customers. The first is that you'll do a competent and professional job. You'll hire only skilled journeymen and use only diligent apprentices because it's much too expensive to have incompetent tradesmen on a job. Slipshod work leads to conflict, confrontation, hold-backs and litigation. That delays collection and erodes your profit.

The second promise is that you'll comply with the building code. You can't afford to get your customers (or yourself) in trouble with the building inspectors.

Good Supervisors
Some tradespeople, even good ones, require more supervision than others. You have to supervise to control quality and efficiency.

Suppose you have a mason who's scheduled to lay fireplace facebrick for two days, then move outside. If the forecast for the third day calls for bad weather, he might drag the job out an extra day. That way he won't have to lose that third day's pay. Good supervision protects you from problems like that. If your workers are paid by the unit completed instead of the hour, good supervision is especially important.

Good Bids and Bad Bids

Do careful take-offs. Figure everything twice. Find all the costs in the job before work begins. Then allow for the unexpected. Don't forget to include a decent profit — enough so your business has the cash needed to grow.

Compare the number of bids you make to the number of jobs you get. That's your *win ratio*. A Wichita contractor we know says that if he gets more than 75 percent of his bids, his prices are too low. If he gets less than that, he figures his competition is doing something he had better find out about.

A painting contractor who's trying to cut back on his volume and increase his prices and profits might be happy with a 33 percent win ratio. Your percentage and your reasons will be different, but it's still a good idea to keep track of how many bids lead to contracts.

Good Business Procedures

Records and procedures should make your job easier, not harder. Organize your office so that progressive and final payments are billed on time and collections are current. Organize your procedures in the field so that change orders are written promptly and correctly. Organize your purchasing and scheduling to take advantage of supplier discounts. *Organize* — and you'll make more money.

Good Contracts

Be specific when you write a contract. If you leave out even one key element, it could cost you your entire profit. A court trial over a contract could put you in bankruptcy court. Don't forget to specify what the contract *does not* cover. Include in the contract a complete description of items or services to be provided by the owner.

Be sure your contract includes a progressive payment schedule and a realistic due date for the final payment.

Include a clause that says you're not responsible for correcting existing building code violations, except as identified in the contract. State clearly that any additional code-mandated changes will be done *at the owner's expense.* Specify that charges for such work will be based on the actual labor and material cost, plus your normal overhead and profit.

Figure 11-2 shows a section of a contract that specifies allowances for various fixtures and accessories to be selected by the customer. Be sure your client realizes that if he picks a gold-plated faucet or a crystal chandelier, he'll pay the difference between the allowed cost and the actual price.

Good Selling

Many customers prefer to do business with a salesman who can "make a deal." Give your salesmen some leeway to negotiate. But stay in control. Otherwise the sales personnel will be the only people in the office making any money. Sell some jobs yourself so you have house accounts on which no commission is paid.

Make sure your salespeople have a current price book, and be sure all jobs are subject to acceptance by yourself or another senior company representative. The price book

---

Allowances: The following items, where specific prices are indicated, are included in the Contract Price as allowances for the purchase price of those items to be selected by Owner. Owner and contractor agree to adjust the Contract Price after verification of actual cost difference (if any) of said items selected by Owner.

Appliances $ _____   Light fixtures $ _____   Bath accessories $ _____

Floor covering $ _____   Hardware
                                          finish $ _____   And "other" $ _____

Finish hardware is interpreted to include all knobs, pulls, hinges, catches, locks, drawer slides, accessories or other items that are normally installed subsequent to final painting. Light fixtures are interpreted to include only those fixtures that are surface mounted. Bath accessories are interpreted to include medicine cabinets, towel bars, paper holders, soap dishes, etc.

Allowances clause
Figure 11-2

should reflect markups to cover overhead, commissions, taxes, profit and assembly of materials.

Here are some sales and commission guidelines to consider:

- Don't accept contracts more than 10 percent below your base price.

- Pay *no* commission on contracts between 5 and 10 percent below the base price.

- Pay half commission on contracts to 5 percent below base price.

- Pay normal commission for contracts at base price.

- For contracts above the base price, pay the normal commission on the base price and divide the excess over base equally between the salesperson and the company.

- Charge your salespeople 5 percent of their commission for jobs sold on leads generated by the company. If they work their own leads, the 5 percent charge is waived.

Good Steady Growth

Be careful how fast you grow. Taking big jobs too soon is dangerous. Be careful about seasonal variations in volume until you learn to plan for them. Cash flow can become a problem and profits can disappear overnight if you're careless. Good organization can break down if you try to satisfy everybody.

It's better to turn down a job that's too big for you. And it's best to turn away customers you can't handle right. Taking more work than you can finish is deadly. Turning someone away because you're too busy is good business. The customers you turn down will interpret that as a sign that you're a real "pro." They'll be back.

Keep your good reputation and you can charge a little more. Keep your business under control and you can deliver a lot more. When you deliver, you'll make money. And that's why you're in the remodeling business.

The Future Is Up to You

As we pointed out earlier, the construction side of the remodeling profession is more an art than a science. There are no two jobs alike. It takes creativity and ingenuity to plan and execute a project that satisfies the individual needs and desires of each homeowner. What you do for one homeowner most certainly won't apply to the next. Your personal construction skills determine how successful you are in the art of remodeling.

The other side of your profession, the business side, is a science. There are set principles and procedures which apply to all jobs. Being a competent manager and applying proven business procedures will make the difference between your success or failure in the remodeling profession.

Right now, the opportunities in remodeling have never been greater. The high cost of land . . . the growing scarcity of natural materials . . . the decreasing desire of families to uproot . . . the planned restructuring of urban and suburban transportation systems . . . are all major factors contributing to the continued growth of the remodeling industry.

New housing is rapidly becoming unaffordable, except to the select few. This means that much of the future shelter needs of this nation will have to be met by upgrading and remodeling existing homes. In order to survive in today's volatile, ever-changing economic climate, remodeling contractors have to expand their business and managerial skills. Hopefully this book has shown you how and where to begin.

Job Survey

PREPARATION

1. ☐ Plans _____
2. ☐ Engineering _____
2. ☐ Soil Test _____
3. ☐ Building Permit/Plan Check _____
4. ☐ Survey _____
4. ☐ Variance _____
5. ☐ Bond Disbursement Escrow _____
6. ☐ Blueprints _____
7. ☐ Scaffolding & Staging _____
7. ☐ Temporary Street Block _____
8. ☐ Temporary Power, Gas, Water _____
9. ☐ Temporary Toilet _____
   ☐ _____

DEMOLITION

17. ☐ Interior Demolition _____
17. ☐ Shoring Required _____
18. ☐ Exterior Demolition _____
18. ☐ Site Clearance _____
18. ☐ Remove Slab – Eaves _____
18. ☐ Strip Stucco _____
18. ☐ Remove Wall Section _____
18. ☐ Tree Removal
20. ☐ Equipment Rental _____
    ☐ _____

RELOCATION

19. ☐ Planting Shrubs & Trees _____
55. ☐ Electric Service _____
57. ☐ Electric Outlets _____
60. ☐ Sewer Lines _____
61. ☐ Gas Meter _____
61. ☐ Water Lines _____
62. ☐ Septic System _____
65. ☐ Heat ducts _____
    ☐ _____

ALLOWANCES

10. ☐ Appliances: By Owner By Contractor _____
10. ☐ Appliance Total Allowance $ _____
    ☐ Cook Tops E   G – Ovens E G _____
      Hood – Dishwasher – Disposal _____
      Compactor – Refrigerator IM _____
      Washer – Dryer E   G – Electronic Oven _____
      Other: _____
11. ☐ Bathroom Accessories _____
12. ☐ Flooring # _____ sq. yds. _____
13. ☐ Hardware Finish _____

14. ☐ Electrical Fixtures # _____
15. ☐ Paneling & Trim # sheets _____
16. ☐ Other: _____
16. ☐ _____
16. ☐ _____
    ☐ _____

FOUNDATIONS – CONCRETE & MASONRY

21. ☐ Excavate and Grade _____
22. ☐ Concrete Foundations _____
22. ☐ Foundation Slab Construction _____
22. ☐ 1 Story Slab _____ 2 Story Slab _____
22. ☐ Foundation Raised Floor – Vents _____
22. ☐ 1 Story Raised _____ 2 Story Raised _____
22. ☐ Concrete Piers _____ Crawl Hole _____
22. ☐ Underpin Foundation _____
22. ☐ Foundation for Fireplace – Steel _____
22. ☐ Concrete Footings – Other _____
23. ☐ Concrete Slab for Room: (Size) _____
23. ☐ Concrete Flatwork: (Size) _____
23. ☐ Flashings _____
24. ☐ Concrete Porch: (Size) _____
24. ☐ Concrete Steps: (Width) _____ (#) _____
25. ☐ Concrete Driveway: _____
25. ☐ Concrete Apron – Sidewalks _____
25. ☐ Concrete Curbs _____ ft. _____
26. ☐ Concrete Walls – Waterproofing _____
26. ☐ Concrete Retaining Walls _____
26. ☐ Concrete Planter _____ ft _____
27. ☐ Concrete Cutting _____
28. ☐ Concrete Pumping _____
28. ☐ Concrete Color: – Texture _____
29. ☐ Vapor Barrier _____
29. ☐ Sand _____ Fill _____
30. ☐ Concrete Reinf.: Steel Rods Wire Mesh _____
31. ☐ Masonry _____
31. ☐ Masonry Fireplace _____
31. ☐ Fireplace: Brick _____ Stone Veneer _____
31. ☐ Fireplace: Half _____ Full Height _____
31. ☐ Fireplace Raised Hearth: _____
31. ☐ Fireplace: Width _____ Ft. Overall _____
31. ☐ Fireplace: Wall _____ Corner _____
31. ☐ Fireplace: Standard 30" Firebox _____
31. ☐ Chimney Height: Standard – Other _____
32. ☐ Masonry Repairs: _____
32. ☐ Veneer Wall: Brick _____ Stone _____ ft. _____
32. ☐ Flatwork: Brick _____ Stone _____

32 ☐ Precast Stone: _____ Slate _____
32 ☐ Concrete Block: _____
32 ☐ Concrete Cap _____ Coping _____
33 ☐ Asphalt Paving _____
33 ☐ Area Size _____
33 ☐ Repairs: _____
   ☐ _____

MATERIALS & LUMBER

34 ☐ Lumber Rough _____
34 ☐ Joist & Girders _____
34 ☐ Sub Floor - Plyscore _____
34 ☐ T & G Floor on Girders _____
34 ☐ Exterior Walls _____
34 ☐ Exterior Walls: (Alterations) _____
34 ☐ Interior Walls _____
34 ☐ Interior Walls: (Alterations) _____
34 ☐ Drop Header _____ Flush Header _____
34 ☐ Wall Sheathing _____
34 ☐ Ceiling Joists _____ Trusses _____
34 ☐ Roof Style: _____ Sheathing _____
34 ☐ Gable _____ Hip _____ Shed _____
34 ☐ Flat _____ Exp. Beams _____
34 ☐ Mansard _____ Parapet _____
34 ☐ Shoring _____ Bracing _____
34 ☐ Furring: _____
34 ☐ Knee Walls _____ Columns _____ft. ____
34 ☐ Closets: _____
34 ☐ Trucking & Delivery _____
34 ☐ Extra Lumber _____
35 ☐ Rough Hardware _____
36 ☐ Jambs: Int. # ____ Ext. # _____
36 ☐ Pocket Sliders: # _____
36 ☐ Closet Jambs & Frames # _____
37 ☐ **WINDOWS: TOTAL #** _____
37 ☐ Wood # ____ Alum. # ____Steel # _____
37 ☐ In Existing Walls: # _____
37 ☐ New Opening _____ Existing Opening _____
37 ☐ In New Walls: # _____
37 ☐ Window Sizes: ____ X _____
37 ☐ _____ X _____
37 ☐ Style: Double Hung _____ Side Slide _____
37 ☐ Casement _____ Louver _____ Transom ___
37 ☐ Obscure Glass: _____
37 ☐ Special Window: _____
37 ☐ Prime Windows # _____
37 ☐ Window Inserts # _____
37 ☐ Relocate Customer's Window # _____
38 ☐ Window Screens on: Old # __ New # _____
38 ☐ Door Screens on: Old # __ New # _____
38 ☐ Screen Wall Enclosure: _____ lin. ft. ___
38 ☐ Full Height _____ Other _____
38 ☐ Glassene (plastic) Wall: _____ lin. ft. ___
39 ☐ **DOORS: WOOD: INT.-EXT. #** _____
39 ☐ HC Slab _____ SC Slab _____ Panel _____
39 ☐ Special Doors: _____
39 ☐ _____
39 ☐ Int. # _____ X _____
39 ☐ Int. # _____ X _____
39 ☐ Ext. # _____ X _____
39 ☐ Ext. # _____ X _____
39 ☐ Relocate Customer's Door: # . _____
40 ☐ **DOORS – GARAGE:** _____
40 ☐ Wood - Aluminum - Other _____
40 ☐ Single _____ Double _____
40 ☐ Overhead 1 pc. – Sectional _____
41 ☐ **DOORS – CLOSET AND MISC. #** _____
41 ☐ Bi-Pass _____ Bi-Fold. _____
41 ☐ Hinged _____ Pocket _____
41 ☐ Special Doors: _____
42 ☐ Doors – Sliding Glass Patio # . _____
42 ☐ _____ X _____
43 ☐ Doors – Shower & Tub Enclosure: _____
43 ☐ Tub: Glass ___ Plastic _____
43 ☐ Shower: Glass _____ Plastic _____
43 ☐ Neo Angle: _____
44 ☐ **INSULATION:** _____
44 ☐ Walls _____ Ceilings _____ Of New ___
44 ☐ Walls _____ Ceilings _____ Of Existing
44 ☐ Roof _____ New _____ Existing _____

44 ☐ Roof _____
44 ☐ Batts _____ Blown _____ Sheet _____
45 ☐ **LUMBER FINISH:** _____
45 ☐ Base _____
45 ☐ Case _____
45 ☐ Ceiling Mouldings _____
45 ☐ Wainscote _____
45 ☐ Closet Shelves and Poles _____
45 ☐ Closet Pole: Wood _____ Metal _____
45 ☐ Repairs: _____
46 ☐ **HARDWARE FINISH: See #13 Allow.** ___
46 ☐ Locksets # _____
46 ☐ Passage Sets # _____
47 ☐ Mill Runs – Special: _____
47 ☐ Railings: Wood _____
48 ☐ **SIDING & DECKING MAT'LS, EXTERIOR** __
48 ☐ Type _____
48 ☐ Area _____
49 ☐ Stairways _____
49 ☐ Wood _____ Steel _____
49 ☐ Open Riser _____ Solid Riser _____
50 ☐ Structural Steel ____ Erection _____
50 ☐ Beams _____ Columns _____ Trusses __
50 ☐ Hot Water Tank Enclosure, Metal _____
   ☐ _____

CARPENTRY LABOR

51 ☐ Rough Carpentry _____
51 ☐ _____
51 ☐ Patching _____ Repairing _____ Relocating _
52 ☐ Carpentry Siding - Decking (Exterior) _____
53 ☐ Cabinetry Installation _____
53 ☐ Custom Work _____
53 ☐ _____
54 ☐ Finish Trim _____
54 ☐ Install Paneling: By Contractor __ By Owner __
   ☐ _____

ELECTRICAL

55 ☐ Standard Wiring to Existing Service _____
55 ☐ Service Change _____
55 ☐ By Contractor _____ By Owner _____
55 ☐ Relocate Service _____
55 ☐ Enlarge Service: _____ AMP _____
55 ☐ Service to Detached Building _____ ft. ___
55 ☐ Above Ground _____ Underground _____
56 ☐ **CIRCUITS: ADDITIONAL** _____
56 ☐ 220 V. Outlets _____
56 ☐ Add # _____ Relocate # _____
56 ☐ Home Run _____ Panel _____
56 ☐ Raceway _____ Pole or Mast _____
56 ☐ Overhead Lines ____ Underground Lines ____
57 ☐ **TOTAL OUTLETS #** _____
57 ☐ Switches: _____ Add # ____Relocate # ___
57 ☐ 3-Way Switches: _____ Add # ____Relocate # _
57 ☐ Dimmer Switches: _____ Add # ____Relocate # _
57 ☐ Light Outlets: _____ Add # ____Relocate # _
57 ☐ Duplex Plugs: _____ Add # ____Relocate # _
57 ☐ Doorbutton: _____ Add # ____Relocate # _
57 ☐ Doorbell _____ Chimes ____Intercom ___
57 ☐ Telephone Jack # _____ TV Outlet # _____
57 ☐ Disposal – Dishwasher Hookup _____
57 ☐ Range Hood – Trash Compactor Hookup ____
57 ☐ Electrical Kills # _____ Repairs # _____
57 ☐ Yard Lights ____ Flush Lights _____
58 ☐ **ELECTRIC HEATERS – ELECTRIC FANS** __
58 ☐ Wall Heater # _____
58 ☐ Ceiling Bath Exhaust Fan _____
58 ☐ Ceiling Bath Heater _____
58 ☐ Ceiling Cable Heat # _____ of Rooms ____
58 ☐ Base Board Heaters _____
   ☐ _____

PLUMBING

59 ☐ **TOTAL FIXTURES #** _____
59 ☐ Fixtures: White _____ Color _____
59 ☐ New Location _____ Replacement _____
59 ☐ Toilet: Standard Two-Piece _____
59 ☐ Toilet: One-Piece _____ Wall-Hung _____
59 ☐ _____
59 ☐ Bidet _____
59 ☐ Urinal: Floor Model _____ Wall Model _____

59 ☐ Lavatory: Wall-Hung   Pedestal _____
59 ☐ Pullman Lav: Oval _____
59 ☐ Tub: Enclosed _____ Open-End _____
59 ☐ Standard Five-Foot   Other _____
59 ☐ Tub: Square _____ Other _____
59 ☐ _____ Steel _____ Cast Iron _____
59 ☐ Shower Over Tub _____
59 ☐ Fibreglass Tub _____
59 ☐ Stall Shower _____
59 ☐ Hot Mop Shower Pan _____
59 ☐ Pre-Cast Shower Pan _____
59 ☐ Fiberglass Stall Shower _____
59 ☐ Pre-Cast Stall Shower _____
59 ☐ Standard Chrome Fittings _____
59 ☐ Standard Two-Handle Control _____
59 ☐ Single-Handle Control _____
59 ☐ Deluxe Fittings: See Allowance #16 _____
59 ☐ Kitchen Sink: One-Part Two-Part Three-Part _____
59 ☐ Bar Sink: One-Part Two-Part _____
59 ☐ Cast Iron ___ W C ___ Stainless Steel _____
59 ☐ Water Heater: E G _____ Gallons _____
59 ☐ Laundry Tray — Washing-Machine Standpipe _____
59 ☐ New Location _____ Same Location _____
59 ☐ Hose Bibb — Sprinklers _____
59 ☐ _____
60 ☐ Sewer Tie-in Under House _____ ft. _____
60 ☐ Sewer Tie-in Outside Foundation _____ ft. _____
60 ☐ Tie-in Waste to Existing Cesspool _____
60 ☐ New Sewer Line Hookup _____ ft. _____
60 ☐ To Front of Lot _____ To Back of Lot _____
60 ☐ Sewer Changed to Cast-Iron _____ ft. _____
60 ☐ Drainage Tile _____
60 ☐ Plumbing Service to Detached Building _____
60 ☐ _____

PLUMBING — OTHER
61 ☐ New Water Service _____
61 ☐ New Gas Line: _____
61 ☐ Heating ___ Cooking ___ Dryer _____
61 ☐ Barb-Que ___ Fireplace ___ HWT _____
61 ☐ Change to Deck Type Faucets _____
61 ☐ Sink Replacement: Lower Waters _____
61 ☐ Garbage Disposal Hookup _____
61 ☐ Sink Replacement: Lower Wastes _____
61 ☐ Install Shower Over Existing Tub _____
61 ☐ Water Line to Refrigerator-Ice Maker _____
61 ☐ Dishwasher Hookup _____
61 ☐ For New Sink _____ For Existing Sink _____
61 ☐ Floor Drain: New   Existing _____
61 ☐ RELOCATE: _____
61 ☐ Hose Bibb _____ Softener _____
61 ☐ Sprinkler _____ Water Meter _____
61 ☐ Gas Meter _____ Pool Equipment _____
61 ☐ New Sprinkler Heads # _____ Cap Heads # _____
61 ☐ Repairs _____
61 ☐ Sewer-Water Lines _____
61 ☐ Fire Hose _____
61 ☐ Fire Sprinkler Heads _____
62 ☐ Cesspools — Septic Tank _____
62 ☐ Remove — Cap and Fill _____
☐ _____

HEATING AND AIR CONDITIONING
63 ☐ Gas Wall Furnace: Single _____ Dual _____
63 ☐ Existing Wall _____ New Wall _____
63 ☐ Forced Air Furnace _____ BTU's _____
63 ☐ Gravity _____
63 ☐ Air Conditioner: E _____ G _____ Tons _____
63 ☐ Central Unit _____ Window/Wall Unit _____
63 ☐ Heat Pump: _____
64 ☐ Thermostat: Manual   Wall   Unitrol _____
65 ☐ Duct Work: Relocate # _____ Extend # _____
65 ☐ New Ducts: # _____
☐ _____

ROOFING
66 ☐ New Work Only _____
66 ☐ Re-Roof Entire Building _____
66 ☐ Composition: _____
66 ☐ Hot Mop: Cap Sheet;   Rock ___ S ___ L _____
66 ☐ Wood Shingles _____

66 ☐ Wood Shakes: Medium _____ Heavy _____
66 ☐ Regular Zone _____ Fire Zone _____
66 ☐ Tile _____
66 ☐ Slate _____
66 ☐ Other: _____
66 ☐ Roof Tie-in _____
67 ☐ Flashing _____
67 ☐ Coping: _____
67 ☐ _____
68 ☐ Patio Roof: Metal _____
68 ☐ Posts # _____
68 ☐ _____

WALLS AND CEILINGS
69 ☐ INTERIOR FINISH _____
69 ☐ Drywall: New Walls _____
69 ☐   New Ceiling _____
69 ☐   Drywall: Existing Walls _____
69 ☐   Existing Ceiling _____
69 ☐ Taped _____ Untaped _____
69 ☐ Ceiling Squares _____
70 ☐ Lath & Plaster: Int. Walls _____ sq. yds. _____
70 ☐ Lath & Plaster: Int. Ceilings _____ sq. yds. _____
70 ☐ Acoustic Plaster _____
71 ☐ EXTERIOR FINISH _____
71 ☐ Stucco: Walls _____ sq. yds. _____
71 ☐ Stucco Overhang — 2nd Story — Hillside _____
71 ☐ Aluminums _____
71 ☐ Firewall _____
71 ☐ Colorcote Only: _____
72 ☐ PATCHING: Drywall ___ Plaster ___ Stucco _____
72 ☐ _____
73 ☐ Blown Acoustical Ceiling _____ sq. yds. _____
73 ☐ Area: _____
74 ☐ Ceiling Squares: _____ sq. ft. _____
74 ☐ Luminous Ceiling _____ sq. ft. _____
74 ☐ _____
☐ _____

CABINETRY
Measurement is in linear feet of wall coverage
75 ☐ Pullmans (Vanity) _____ lin. ft. _____
75 ☐ Linens _____
76 ☐ Kitchen Cabinets: Base _____ lin. ft. _____
76 ☐ Kitchen Cabinets: Upper _____ lin. ft. _____
76 ☐ Kitchen Cabinets: Full-Length _____ lin. ft. _____
76 ☐ Kitchen Cabinets: _____
76 ☐ _____
76 ☐ Custom Made _____ Modular _____
76 ☐ Door Style: 3/8 Lip   Flat _____ Raised _____
76 ☐ Door Style: _____
76 ☐ Type of Wood Veneer _____
76 ☐ Natural Finish Stained Finish Unfinished _____
76 ☐ _____
77 ☐ Backs: Upper ___ Lower ___ Full _____
77 ☐ Soffit: Existing _____ New _____
78 ☐ Wardrobes: _____ lin. ft. _____
78 ☐ _____
☐ _____

FINISHING
79 ☐ CERAMIC TILE _____
79 ☐ Kitchen _____ Bathroom _____
79 ☐ Counter Tops: _____ lin. ft. _____
79 ☐ Full-Splash or _____ Inch Splash _____
79 ☐ Side-Splash _____ Right _____ Left _____
79 ☐ Tub-Splash _____ ft. above tub _____
79 ☐ Shower Walls: _____ ft. above floor _____
79 ☐ Shower Floor: _____ Shower Jambs _____
79 ☐ Other: _____
80 ☐ PLASTIC LAMINATE — FORMICA STYLE _____
80 ☐ Kitchen _____ Bathroom _____
80 ☐ Counter Tops: _____ lin. ft. _____
80 ☐ Full-Splash: _____ Inch Splash _____
80 ☐ Cove Back _____ Butt Back _____
81 ☐ Marlite Tub-Splash: _____ ft. over tub _____
81 ☐ Marlite Walls: _____
81 ☐ Marlite Other: _____
82 ☐ MIRRORS: SIZE _____
82 ☐   Regular Plate _____ Antique Plate _____
83 ☐ Fencing: _____ lin. ft. _____ ft. ht. _____

83 ☐ Chain-Link, – Wood, – _____
83 ☐ Gates # _____ Size: _____
83 ☐ **FINISH FLOORING** _____
84 ☐ Flooring Area: _____
84 ☐ By Owner _____ By Contractor _____
84 ☐ Remove Existing: _____
84 ☐ Install Underlayment _____
84 ☐ Repair Only: _____
84 ☐ Floor Material: See Allowances #12 _____
84 ☐ Coving: _____
84 ☐ Hardwood Floors: Area _____
84 ☐ Parquet – Other: _____
84 ☐ Refinish Existing Hardwood Floors _____
84 ☐ Terrazzo _____
84 ☐ Diatto _____
84 ☐ Steps: # _____ Landings: # _____
85 ☐ Breakfast Nook: _____
86 ☐ Ornamental Iron: See Allowances #16 _____
86 ☐ Railings – Standard: _____ lin. ft. _____
86 ☐ Columns – Standard ____ # _____
86 ☐ . Gates: _____
87 ☐ Sheet Metal Vents: # _____ Relocate - New _____
87 ☐ Vent Bath Fan _____ Vent Dryer _____
87 ☐ Vent Oven _____ Vent Hood _____
87 ☐ Vent HWT _____ Vent Metal Fireplace _____
87 ☐ _____
87 ☐ Metal Fireplace: See Allowances #16 _____
87 ☐ Gutters on: Old _____ New _____ ft. _____
87 ☐ Downspout: # _____ lin. ft. _____
88 ☐ Weatherstripping _____
88 ☐ Doors # _____ Windows # _____
89 ☐ Cleanup: By Contractor _____ By Owner _____
89 ☐ Cultured Marble: Area _____
89 ☐ Window Cleaning _____
90 ☐ Other: _____
91 ☐ Describe: _____
91 ☐ House Numbers _____
91 ☐ Doggie Door _____
91 ☐ Drapes _____
91 ☐ Shades _____
91 ☐ Blinds _____
☐ . _____

DECORATING AND PAINTING
92 ☐ Sandblast: _____ Exhaust _____
☐ _____

MISCELLANEOUS
93 ☐ Patching – Floating _____
94 ☐ Pacificote _____
95 ☐ Trim Paint _____
96 ☐ Decorator Materials _____
97 ☐ Supervision _____
98 ☐ Sales Design _____
99 ☐ Overhead Items _____
☐ . _____

NOTES:

Index

OTHER PRACTICAL REFERENCES

Painter's Handbook
Loaded with "how-to" information you'll use every day to get professional results on any job: The best way to prepare a surface for painting or repainting. Selecting and using the right materials and tools (including airless spray). Tips for repainting kitchens, bathrooms, cabinets, eaves and porches. How to match and blend colors. Why coatings fail and what to do about it. Thirty profitable specialties that could be your gravy train in the painting business. Every professional painter needs this practical handbook. **320 pages, 8½ x 11, $21.25**

Remodeler's Handbook
The complete manual of home improvement contracting: Planning the job, estimating costs, doing the work, running your company and making profits. Pages of sample forms, contracts, documents, clear illustrations and examples. Chapters on evaluating the work, rehabilitation, kitchens, bathrooms, adding living area, re-flooring, re-siding, re-roofing, replacing windows and doors, installing new wall and ceiling cover, repainting, upgrading insulation, combating moisture damage, estimating, selling your services, and bookkeeping for remodelers. **416 pages, 8½ x 11, $18.50**

Wood-Frame House Construction
From the layout of the outer walls, excavation and formwork, to finish carpentry, and painting, every step of construction is covered in detail with clear illustrations and explanations. Everything the builder needs to know about framing, roofing, siding, insulation and vapor barrier, interior finishing, floor coverings, and stairs. . . complete step by step "how to" information on what goes into building a frame house. **240 pages, 8½ x 11, $14.25. Revised edition**

Rough Carpentry
All rough carpentry is covered in detail: sills, girders, columns, joists, sheathing, ceiling, roof and wall framing, roof trusses, dormers, bay windows, furring and grounds, stairs and insulation. Many of the 24 chapters explain practical code approved methods for saving lumber and time without sacrificing quality. Chapters on columns, headers, rafters, joists and girders show how to use simple engineering principles to select the right lumber dimension for whatever species and grade you are using. **288 pages, 8½ x 11, $16.00**

Building Cost Manual
Square foot costs for residential, commercial, industrial, and farm buildings. In a few minutes you work up a reliable budget estimate based on the actual materials and design features, area, shape, wall height, number of floors and support requirements. Most important, you include all the important variables that can make any building unique from a cost standpoint. **240 pages, 8½ x 11, $14.00. Revised annually**

Building Layout
Shows how to use a transit to locate the building on the lot correctly, plan proper grades with minimum excavation, find utility lines and easements, establish correct elevations, lay out accurate foundations and set correct floor heights. Explains planning sewer connections, leveling a foundation out of level, using a story pole and batterboards, working on steep sites, and minimizing excavation costs. **240 pages, 5½ x 8½, $11.75**

National Construction Estimator
Current building costs in dollars and cents for residential, commercial and industrial construction. Prices for every commonly used building material, and the proper labor cost associated with installation of the material. Everything figured out to give you the "in place" cost in seconds. Many time-saving rules of thumb, waste and coverage factors and estimating tables are included. **544 pages, 8½ x 11, $19.50. Revised annually.**

Manual of Professional Remodeling
This is the practical manual of professional remodeling written by an experienced and successful remodeling contractor. Shows how to evaluate a job and avoid 30-minute jobs that take all day, what to fix and what to leave alone, and what to watch for in dealing with subcontractors. Includes chapters on calculating space requirements, repairing structural defects, remodeling kitchens, baths, walls and ceilings, doors and windows, floors, roofs, installing fireplaces and chimneys (including built-ins), skylights, and exterior siding. Includes blank forms, checklists, sample contracts, and proposals you can copy and use. **400 pages, 8½ x 11, $18.75**

Contractor's Guide to the Building Code
Explains in plain English exactly what the Uniform Building Code requires and shows how to design and construct residential and light commercial buildings that will pass inspection the first time. Suggests how to work with the inspector to minimize construction costs, what common building short cuts are likely to be cited, and where exceptions are granted. **312 pages, 5½ x 8½, $16.25**

How to Sell Remodeling
Proven, effective sales methods for repair and remodeling contractors: finding qualified leads, making the sales call, identifying what your prospects really need, pricing the job, arranging financing, and closing the sale. Explains how to organize and staff a sales team, how to bring in the work to keep your crews busy and your business growing, and much more. Includes blank forms, tables, and charts. **240 pages, 8½ x 11, $17.50**

Residential Electrical Design
Explains what every builder needs to know about designing electrical systems for residential construction. Shows how to draw up an electrical plan from the blueprints, including the service entrance, grounding, lighting requirements for kitchen, bedroom and bath and how to lay them out. Explains how to plan electrical heating systems and what equipment you'll need, how to plan outdoor lighting, and much more. If you are a builder who ever has to plan an electrical system, you should have this book. **194 pages, 8½ x 11, $11.50**

Basic Plumbing with Illustrations
The journeyman's and apprentice's guide to installing plumbing, piping and fixtures in residential and light commercial buildings: how to select the right materials, lay out the job and do professional quality plumbing work. Explains the use of essential tools and materials, how to make repairs, maintain plumbing systems, install fixtures and add to existing systems. **320 pages, 8½ x 11, $17.50**

Spec Builder's Guide
Explains how to plan and build a home, control your construction costs, and then sell the house at a price that earns a decent return on the time and money you've invested. Includes professional tips to ensure success as a spec builder: how government statistics help you judge the housing market, cutting costs at every opportunity without sacrificing quality, and taking advantage of construction cycles. Every chapter includes checklists, diagrams, charts, figures, and estimating tables. **448 pages, 8½ x 11, $24.00**

Paint Contractor's Manual
How to start and run a profitable paint contracting company: getting set up and organized to handle volume work, avoiding the mistakes most painters make, getting top production from your crews and the most value from your advertising dollar. Shows how to estimate all prep and painting. Loaded with manhour estimates, sample forms, contracts, charts, tables and examples you can use. **224 pages, 8½ x 11, $19.25**

Stair Builders Handbook

If you know the floor to floor rise, this handbook will give you everything else: the number and dimension of treads and risers, the total run, the correct well hole opening, the angle of incline, the quantity of materials and settings for your framing square for over 3,500 code approved rise and run combinations—several for every 1/8 inch interval from a 3 foot to a 12 foot floor to floor rise. **416 pages, 8½ x 5½, $13.75**

Carpentry for Residential Construction

How to do professional quality carpentry work in homes and apartments. Illustrated instructions show you everything from setting batter boards to framing floors and walls, installing floor, wall and roof sheathing, and applying roofing. Covers finish carpentry, also: How to install each type of cornice, frieze, lookout, ledger, fascia and soffit; how to hang windows and doors; how to install siding, drywall and trim. Each job description includes the tools and materials needed, the estimated manhours required, and a step-by-step guide to each part of the task. **400 pages, 5½ x 8½, $19.75**

Carpentry in Commercial Construction

Covers forming, framing, exteriors, interior finish and cabinet installation in commercial buildings: designing and building concrete forms, selecting lumber dimensions, grades and species for the design load, what you should know when installing materials selected for their fire rating or sound transmission characteristics, and how to plan and organize the job to improve production. Loaded with illustrations, tables, charts and diagrams. **272 pages, 5½ x 8½, $19.00**

Roof Framing

Frame any type of roof in common use today, even if you've never framed a roof before. Shows how to use a pocket calculator to figure any common, hip, valley, and jack rafter length in seconds. Over 400 illustrations take you through every measurement and every cut on each type of roof: gable, hip, Dutch, Tudor, gambrel, shed, gazebo and more. **480 pages, 5½ x 8½, $22.00**

Video: Roof Framing 1

A complete step-by step training video on the basics of roof cutting by Marshall Gross, the author of the book **Roof Framing**. Shows and explains calculating rise, run, and pitch, and laying out and cutting common rafters. **90 minutes, VHS, $80.00**

Video: Roof Framing 2

A complete training video on the more advanced techniques of roof framing by Marshall Gross, the author of **Roof Framing**, shows and explains layout and framing an irregular roof, and making tie-ins to an existing roof. **90 minutes, VHS, $80.00**

Builder's Office Manual, Revised

Explains how to create routine ways of doing all the things that must be done in every construction office — in the minimum time, at the lowest cost, and with the least supervision possible: Organizing the office space, establishing effective procedures and forms, setting priorities and goals, finding and keeping an effective staff, getting the most from your record-keeping system (whether manual or computerized). Loaded with practical tips, charts and sample forms for your use. **192 pages, 8½ x 11, $15.50**

Craftsman Book Company
6058 Corte del Cedro
P.O. Box 6500
Carlsbad, CA 92008
FAX No. (619) 438-0398

In a hurry?
We accept phone orders charged to your MasterCard, Visa or American Express Call (619) 438-7828

Name _____

Company _____

Address _____

City _____ State _____ Zip _____

Send check or money order
Total Enclosed _____ (In California add 6% tax)
If you prefer, use your ☐ Visa, ☐ MasterCard or ☐ American Express
Card # _____
Expiration date _____ Initials _____

10 Day Money Back GUARANTEE

- ☐ 17.50 Basic Plumbing with Illustrations
- ☐ 15.50 Builder's Office Manual Revised
- ☐ 14.00 Building Cost Manual
- ☐ 11.75 Building Layout
- ☐ 19.75 Carpentry for Residential Construction
- ☐ 19.00 Carpentry in Commercial Construction
- ☐ 16.25 Contractor's Guide to the Building Code
- ☐ 17.50 How to Sell Remodeling
- ☐ 18.75 Manual of Professional Remodeling
- ☐ 19.50 National Construction Estimator
- ☐ 19.25 Paint Contractor's Manual
- ☐ 21.25 Painter's Handbook
- ☐ 18.50 Remodeler's Handbook
- ☐ 11.50 Residential Electrical Design
- ☐ 22.00 Roof Framing
- ☐ 16.00 Rough Carpentry
- ☐ 24.00 Spec Builder's Guide
- ☐ 13.75 Stair Builder's Handbook
- ☐ 80.00 Video: Roof Framing 1
- ☐ 80.00 Video: Roof Framing 2
- ☐ 14.25 Wood-Frame House Construction
- ☐ 21.00 Running Your Remodeling Business

Mail Orders

We pay shipping when your check covers your order in full.

BUSINESS REPLY MAIL
FIRST CLASS   PERMIT NO. 271   CARLSBAD, CA

POSTAGE WILL BE PAID BY ADDRESSEE

Craftsman Book Company
6058 Corte Del Cedro
P. O. Box 6500
Carlsbad, CA 92008-0992

BUSINESS REPLY MAIL
FIRST CLASS   PERMIT NO. 271   CARLSBAD, CA

POSTAGE WILL BE PAID BY ADDRESSEE

Craftsman Book Company
6058 Corte Del Cedro
P. O. Box 6500
Carlsbad, CA 92008-0992

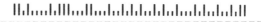

BUSINESS REPLY MAIL
FIRST CLASS   PERMIT NO. 271   CARLSBAD, CA

POSTAGE WILL BE PAID BY ADDRESSEE

Craftsman Book Company
6058 Corte Del Cedro
P. O. Box 6500
Carlsbad, CA 92008-0992